INTERVIEWS WITH MONSTER GIRLS

Volume 1

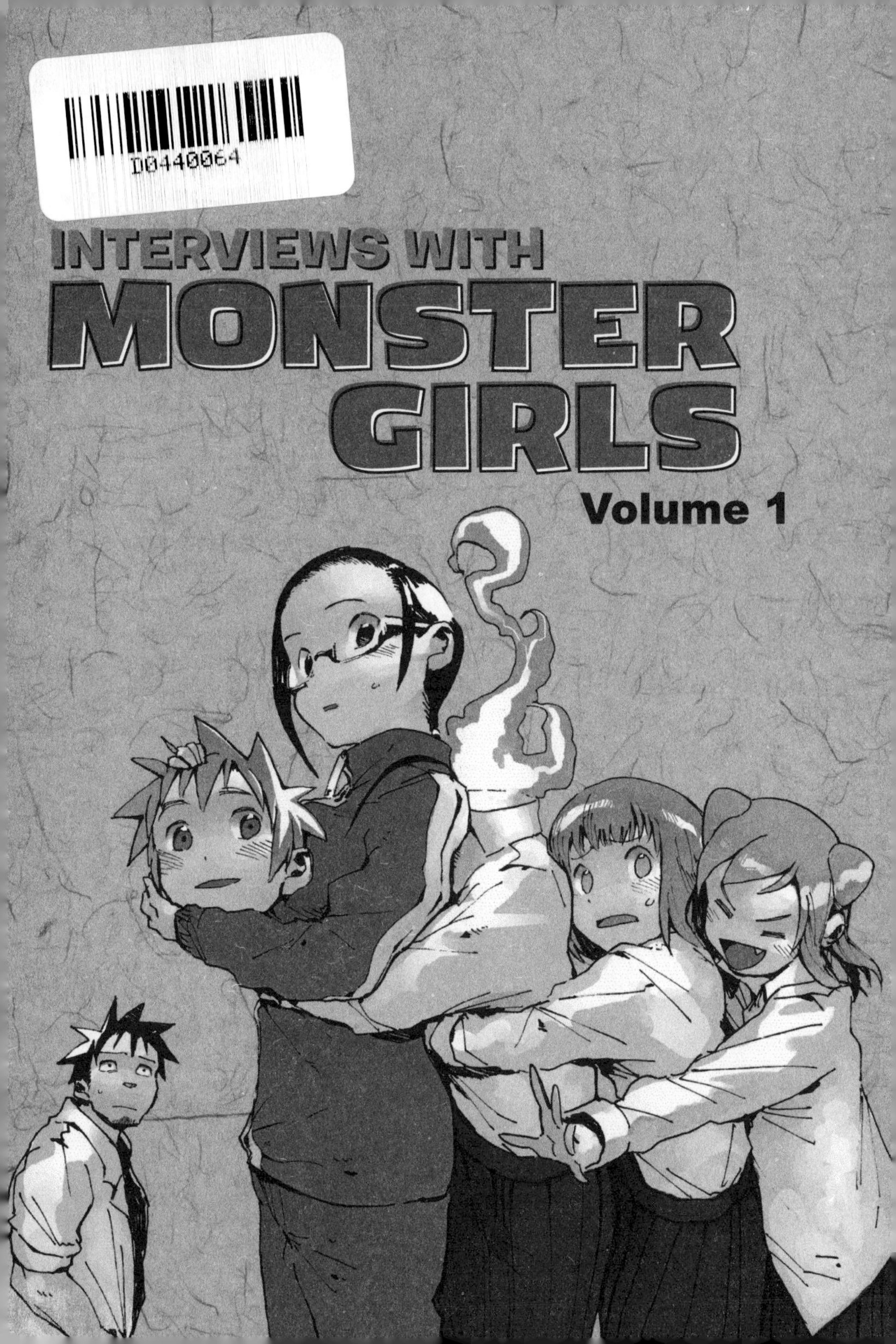

INTERVIEWS WITH MONSTER GIRLS

CONTENTS

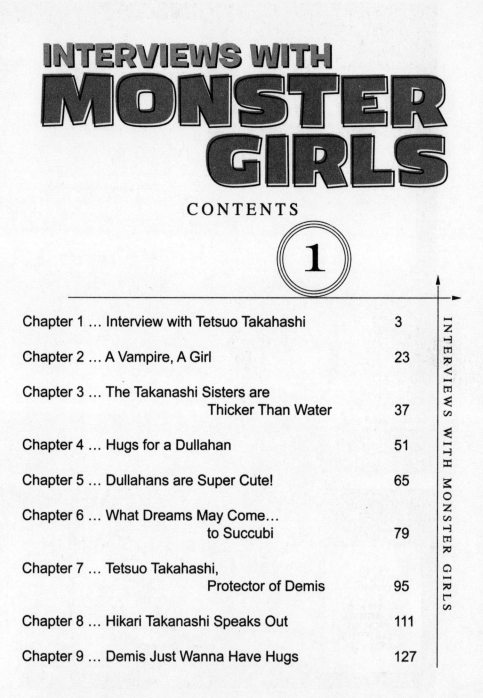

1

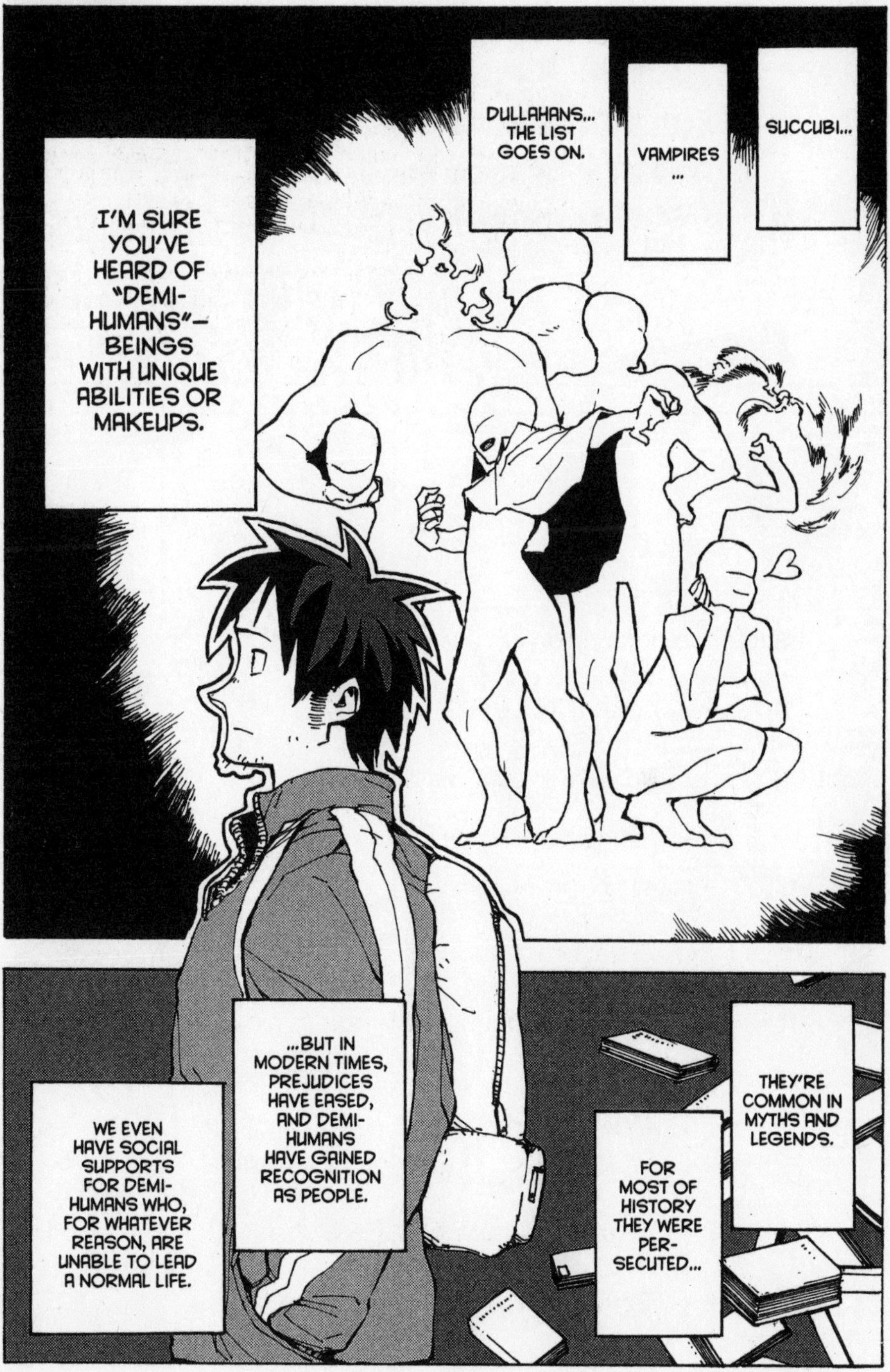
SUCCUBI...
VAMPIRES ...
DULLAHANS... THE LIST GOES ON.
I'M SURE YOU'VE HEARD OF "DEMI-HUMANS"—BEINGS WITH UNIQUE ABILITIES OR MAKEUPS.
THEY'RE COMMON IN MYTHS AND LEGENDS.
FOR MOST OF HISTORY THEY WERE PER-SECUTED...
...BUT IN MODERN TIMES, PREJUDICES HAVE EASED, AND DEMI-HUMANS HAVE GAINED RECOGNITION AS PEOPLE.
WE EVEN HAVE SOCIAL SUPPORTS FOR DEMI-HUMANS WHO, FOR WHATEVER REASON, ARE UNABLE TO LEAD A NORMAL LIFE.

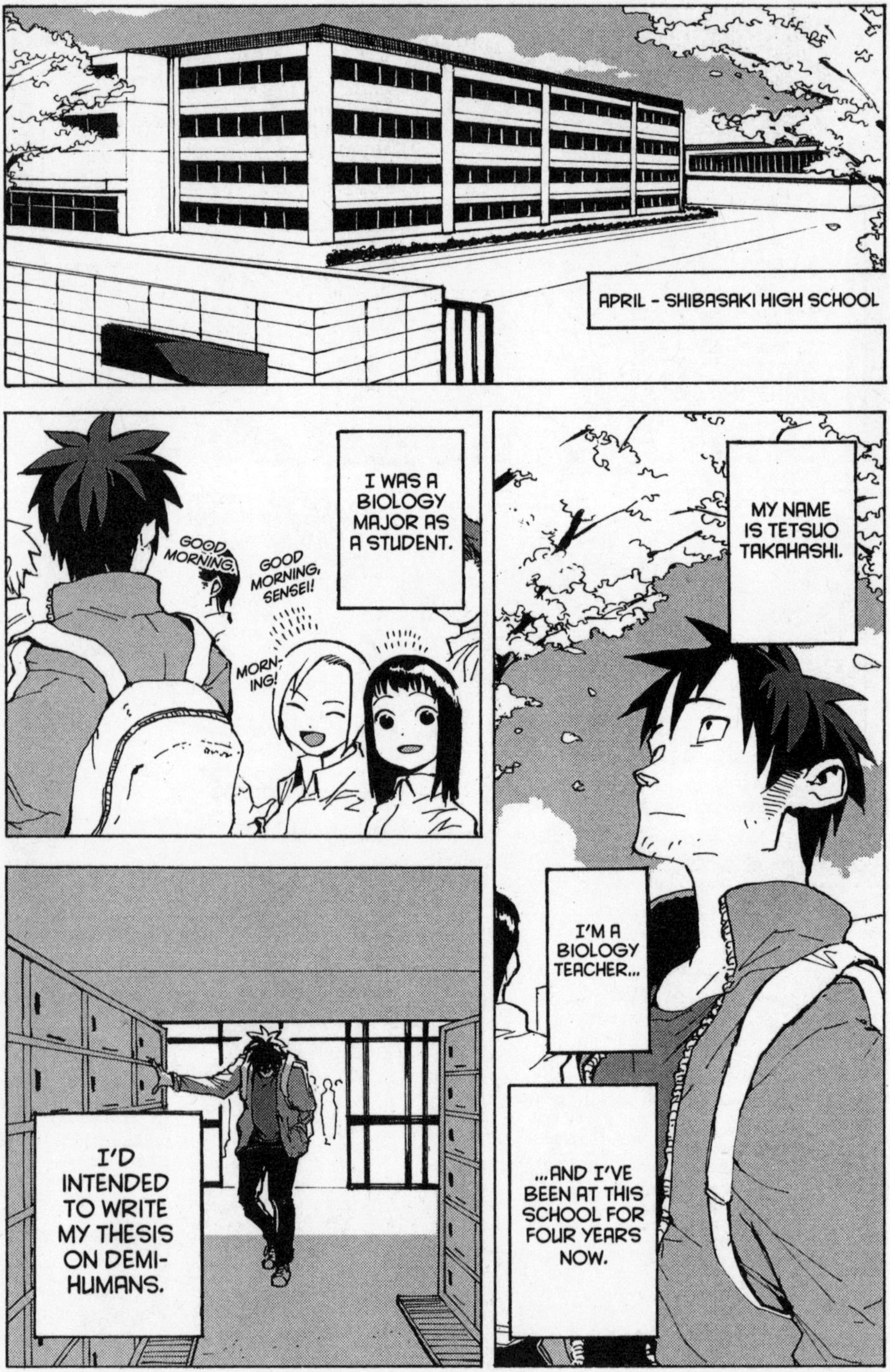
APRIL - SHIBASAKI HIGH SCHOOL
MY NAME IS TETSUO TAKAHASHI.
I'M A BIOLOGY TEACHER...
...AND I'VE BEEN AT THIS SCHOOL FOR FOUR YEARS NOW.
I WAS A BIOLOGY MAJOR AS A STUDENT.
GOOD MORNING, SENSEI!
GOOD MORNING.
MORN-ING!
I'D INTENDED TO WRITE MY THESIS ON DEMI-HUMANS.

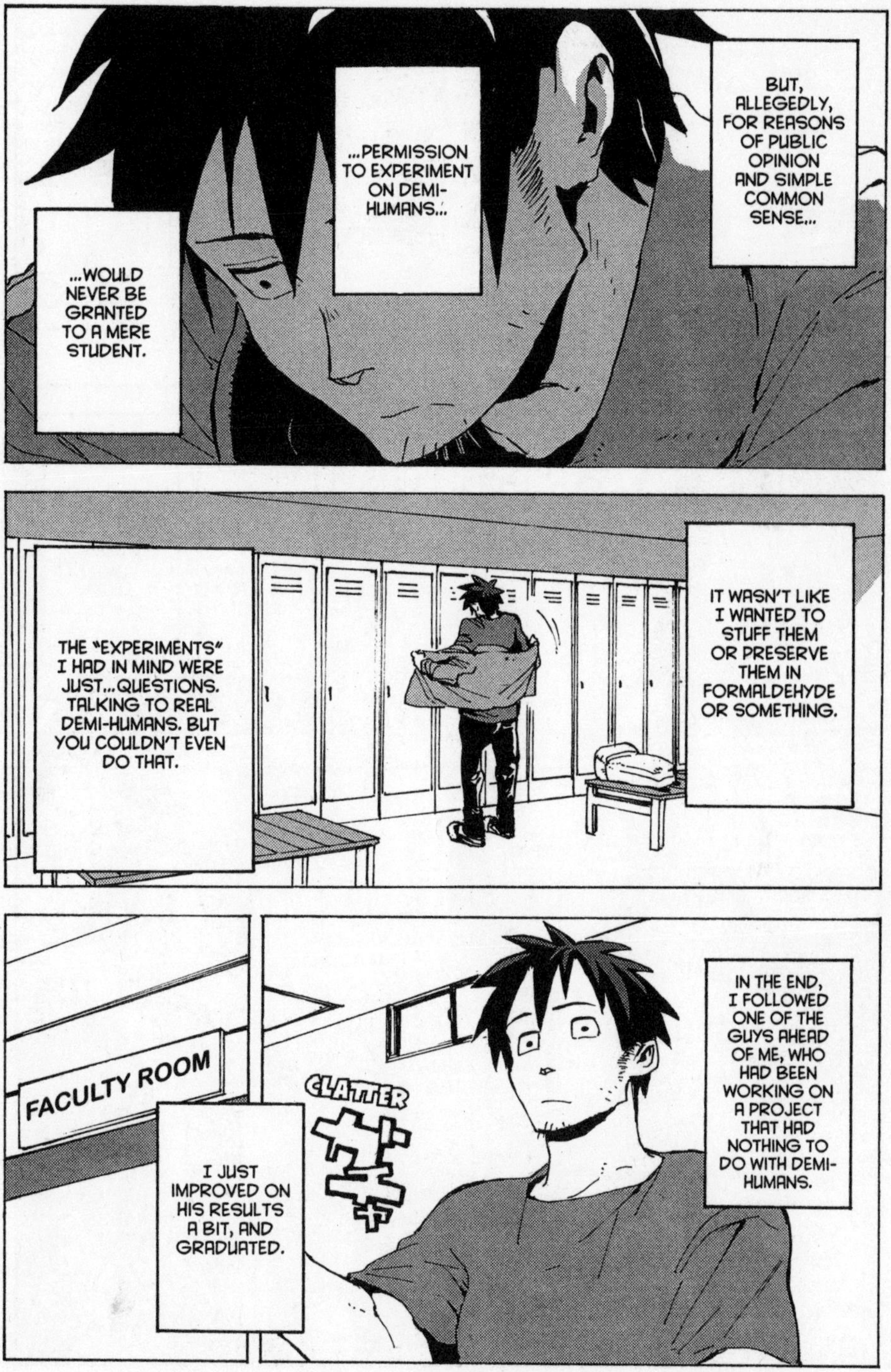
BUT, ALLEGEDLY, FOR REASONS OF PUBLIC OPINION AND SIMPLE COMMON SENSE...
...PERMISSION TO EXPERIMENT ON DEMI-HUMANS...
...WOULD NEVER BE GRANTED TO A MERE STUDENT.
IT WASN'T LIKE I WANTED TO STUFF THEM OR PRESERVE THEM IN FORMALDEHYDE OR SOMETHING.
THE "EXPERIMENTS" I HAD IN MIND WERE JUST...QUESTIONS. TALKING TO REAL DEMI-HUMANS. BUT YOU COULDN'T EVEN DO THAT.
IN THE END, I FOLLOWED ONE OF THE GUYS AHEAD OF ME, WHO HAD BEEN WORKING ON A PROJECT THAT HAD NOTHING TO DO WITH DEMI-HUMANS.
CLATTER
I JUST IMPROVED ON HIS RESULTS A BIT, AND GRADUATED.
FACULTY ROOM

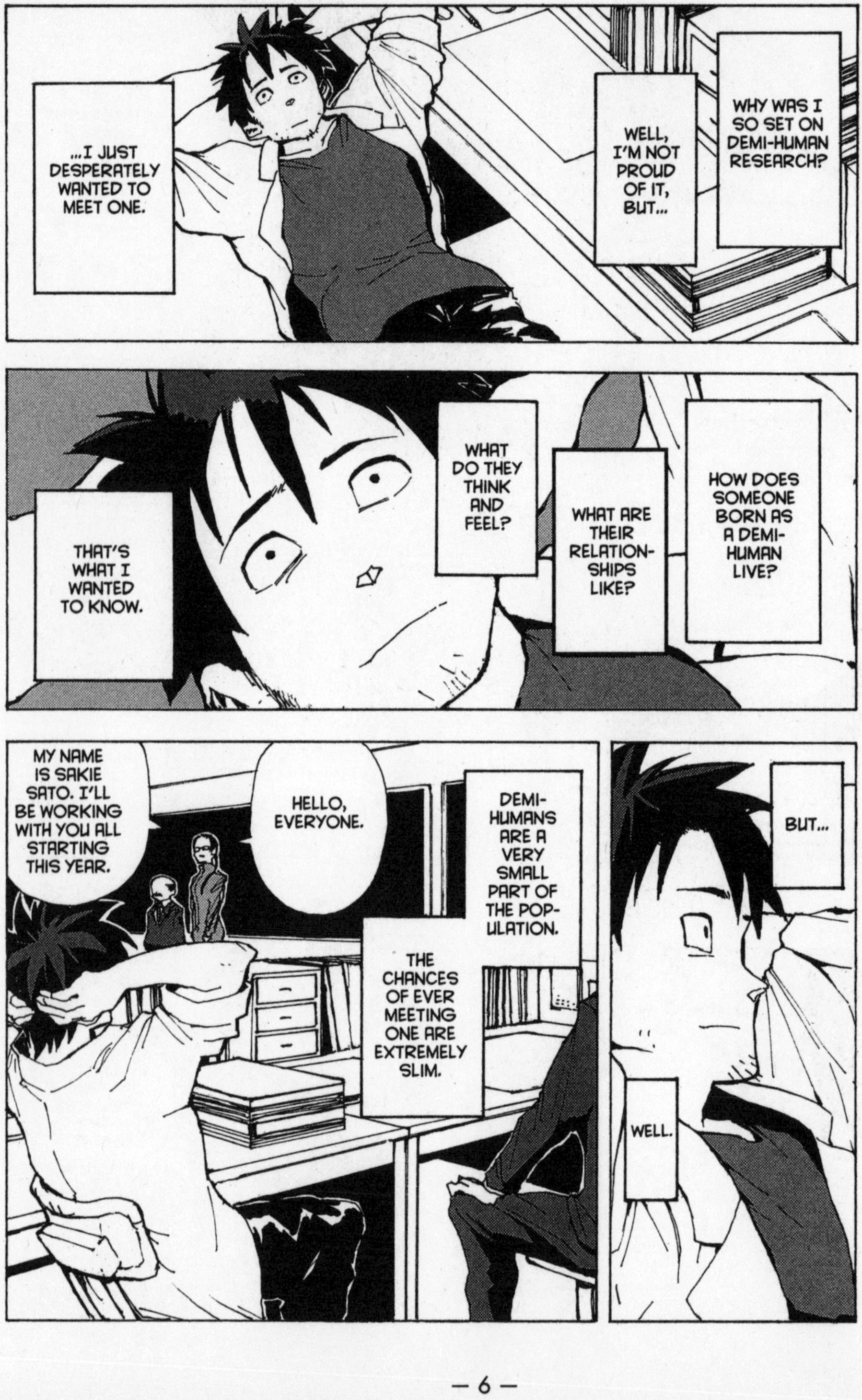
WHY WAS I SO SET ON DEMI-HUMAN RESEARCH?
WELL, I'M NOT PROUD OF IT, BUT...
...I JUST DESPERATELY WANTED TO MEET ONE.
HOW DOES SOMEONE BORN AS A DEMI-HUMAN LIVE?
WHAT ARE THEIR RELATIONSHIPS LIKE?
WHAT DO THEY THINK AND FEEL?
THAT'S WHAT I WANTED TO KNOW.
BUT...
WELL.
DEMI-HUMANS ARE A VERY SMALL PART OF THE POPULATION.
HELLO, EVERYONE.
MY NAME IS SAKIE SATO. I'LL BE WORKING WITH YOU ALL STARTING THIS YEAR.
THE CHANCES OF EVER MEETING ONE ARE EXTREMELY SLIM.

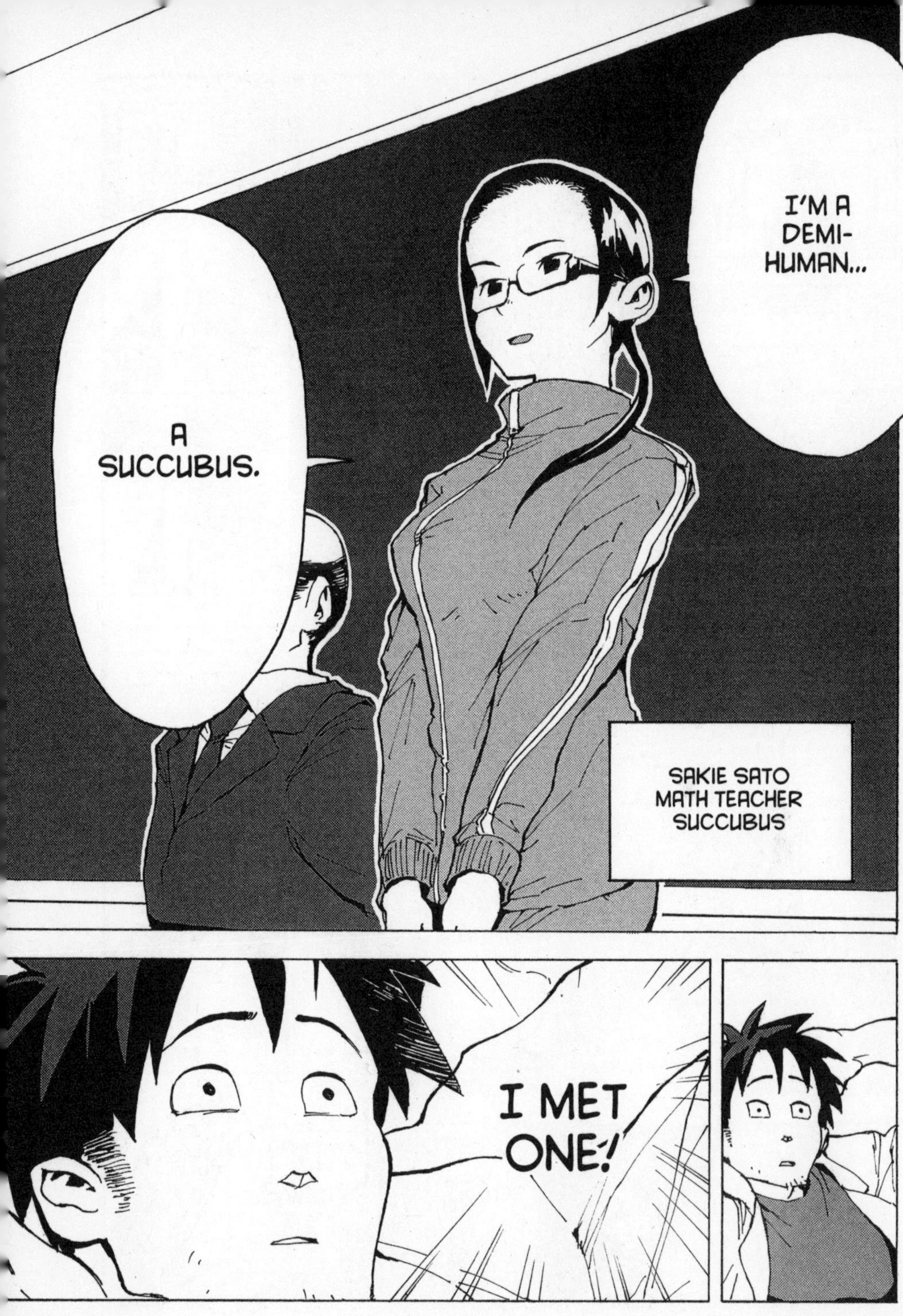
I'M A DEMI-HUMAN...
A SUCCUBUS.
SAKIE SATO
MATH TEACHER
SUCCUBUS
I MET ONE!

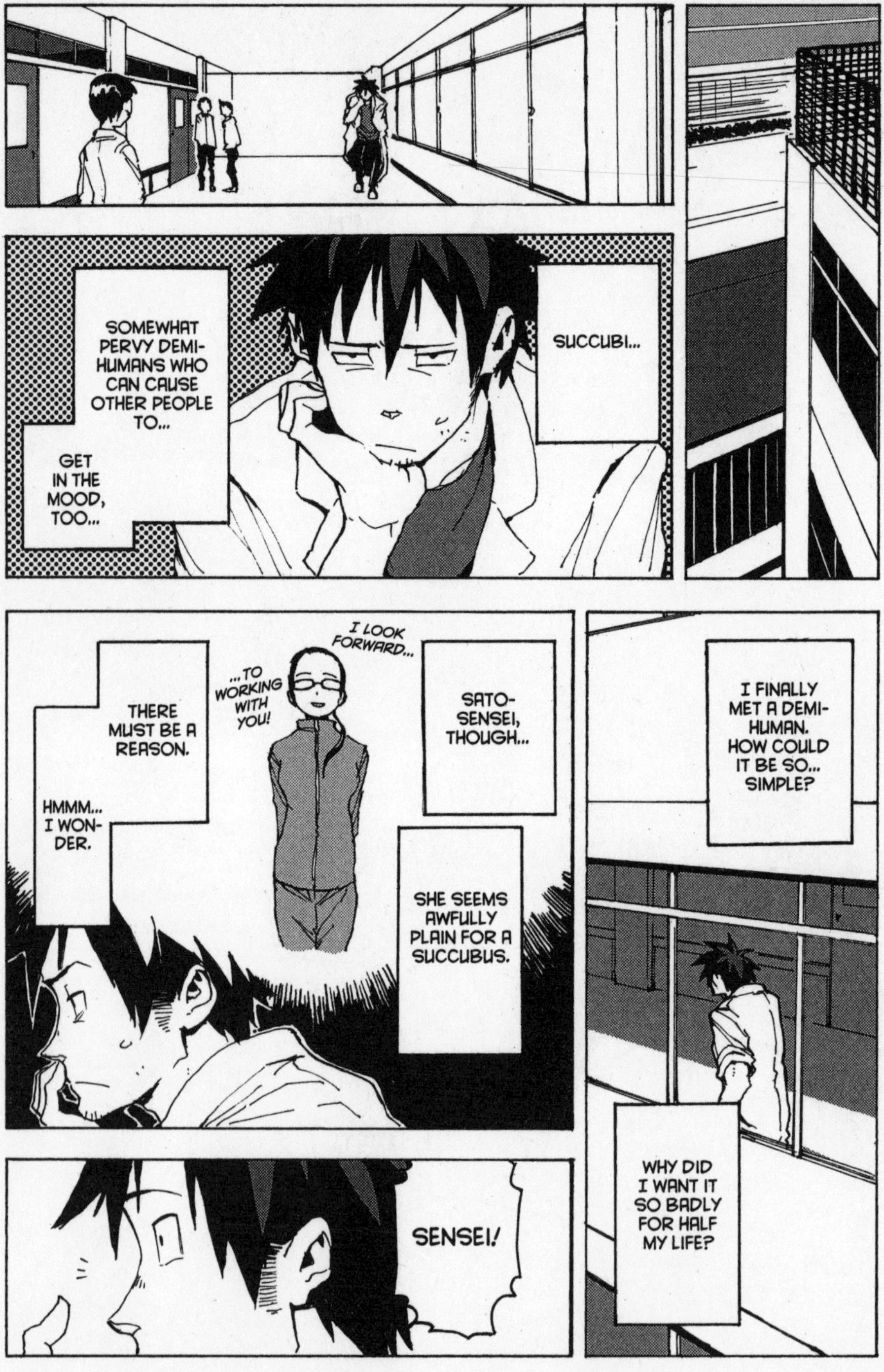

SUCCUBI...
SOMEWHAT PERVY DEMI-HUMANS WHO CAN CAUSE OTHER PEOPLE TO...
GET IN THE MOOD, TOO...
I FINALLY MET A DEMI-HUMAN. HOW COULD IT BE SO... SIMPLE?
WHY DID I WANT IT SO BADLY FOR HALF MY LIFE?
SATO-SENSEI, THOUGH...
SHE SEEMS AWFULLY PLAIN FOR A SUCCUBUS.
I LOOK FORWARD...
...TO WORKING WITH YOU!
THERE MUST BE A REASON.
HMMM... I WONDER.
SENSEI!

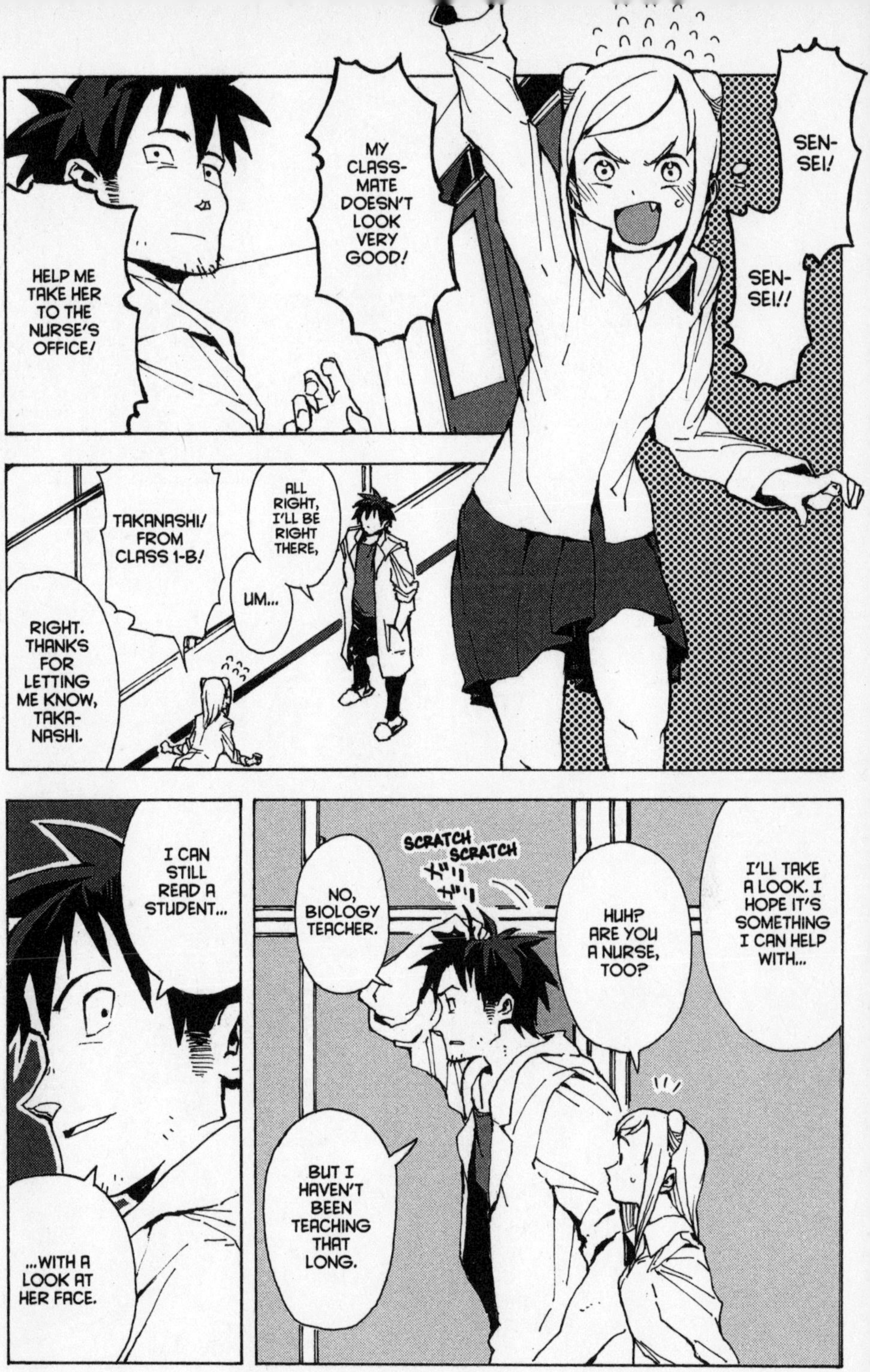
SEN-SEI!
SEN-SEI!!
MY CLASS-MATE DOESN'T LOOK VERY GOOD!
HELP ME TAKE HER TO THE NURSE'S OFFICE!
ALL RIGHT, I'LL BE RIGHT THERE,
UM...
TAKANASHI! FROM CLASS 1-B!
RIGHT. THANKS FOR LETTING ME KNOW, TAKA-NASHI.
I'LL TAKE A LOOK. I HOPE IT'S SOMETHING I CAN HELP WITH...
HUH? ARE YOU A NURSE, TOO?
SCRATCH SCRATCH
NO, BIOLOGY TEACHER.
BUT I HAVEN'T BEEN TEACHING THAT LONG.
I CAN STILL READ A STUDENT...
...WITH A LOOK AT HER FACE.

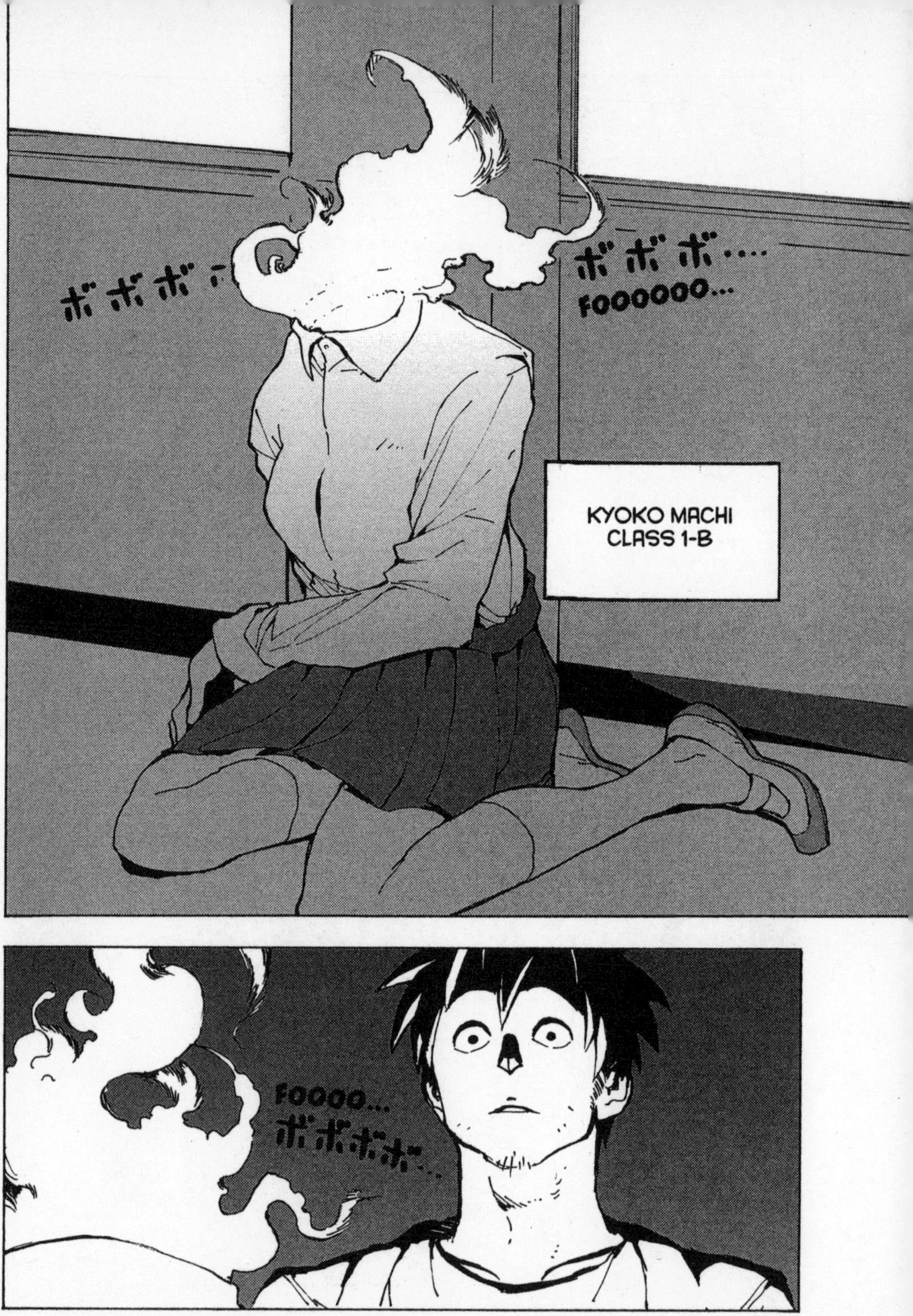
ボボボ....
FOOOOOO...
ボボボ
KYOKO MACHI
CLASS 1-B
FOOOO...
ボボボボ...

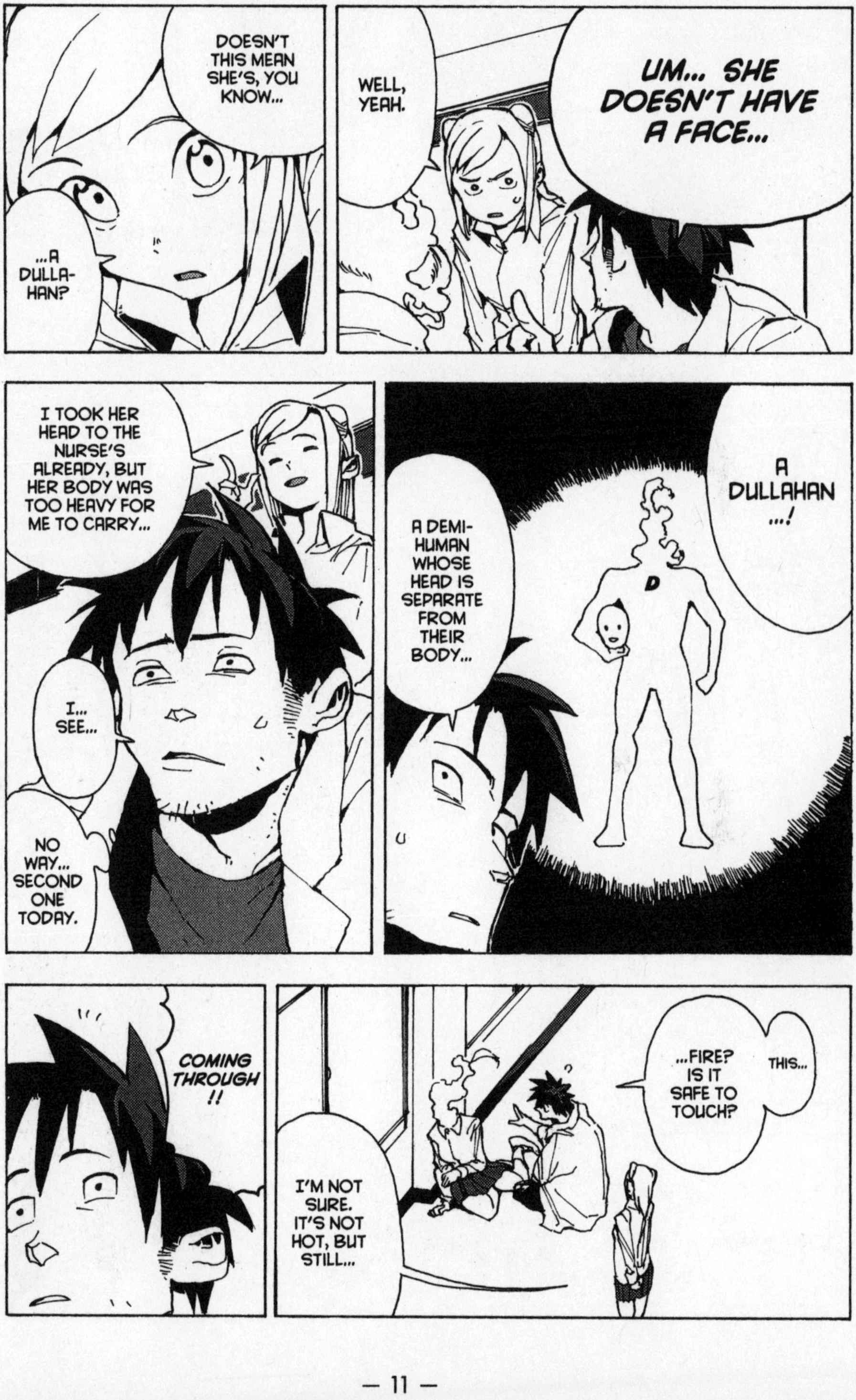
UM... SHE DOESN'T HAVE A FACE...
WELL, YEAH.
DOESN'T THIS MEAN SHE'S, YOU KNOW...
...A DULLAHAN?
A DULLAHAN ...!
A DEMI-HUMAN WHOSE HEAD IS SEPARATE FROM THEIR BODY...
D
I TOOK HER HEAD TO THE NURSE'S ALREADY, BUT HER BODY WAS TOO HEAVY FOR ME TO CARRY...
I... SEE...
NO WAY... SECOND ONE TODAY.
THIS...
...FIRE? IS IT SAFE TO TOUCH?
I'M NOT SURE. IT'S NOT HOT, BUT STILL...
COMING THROUGH !!

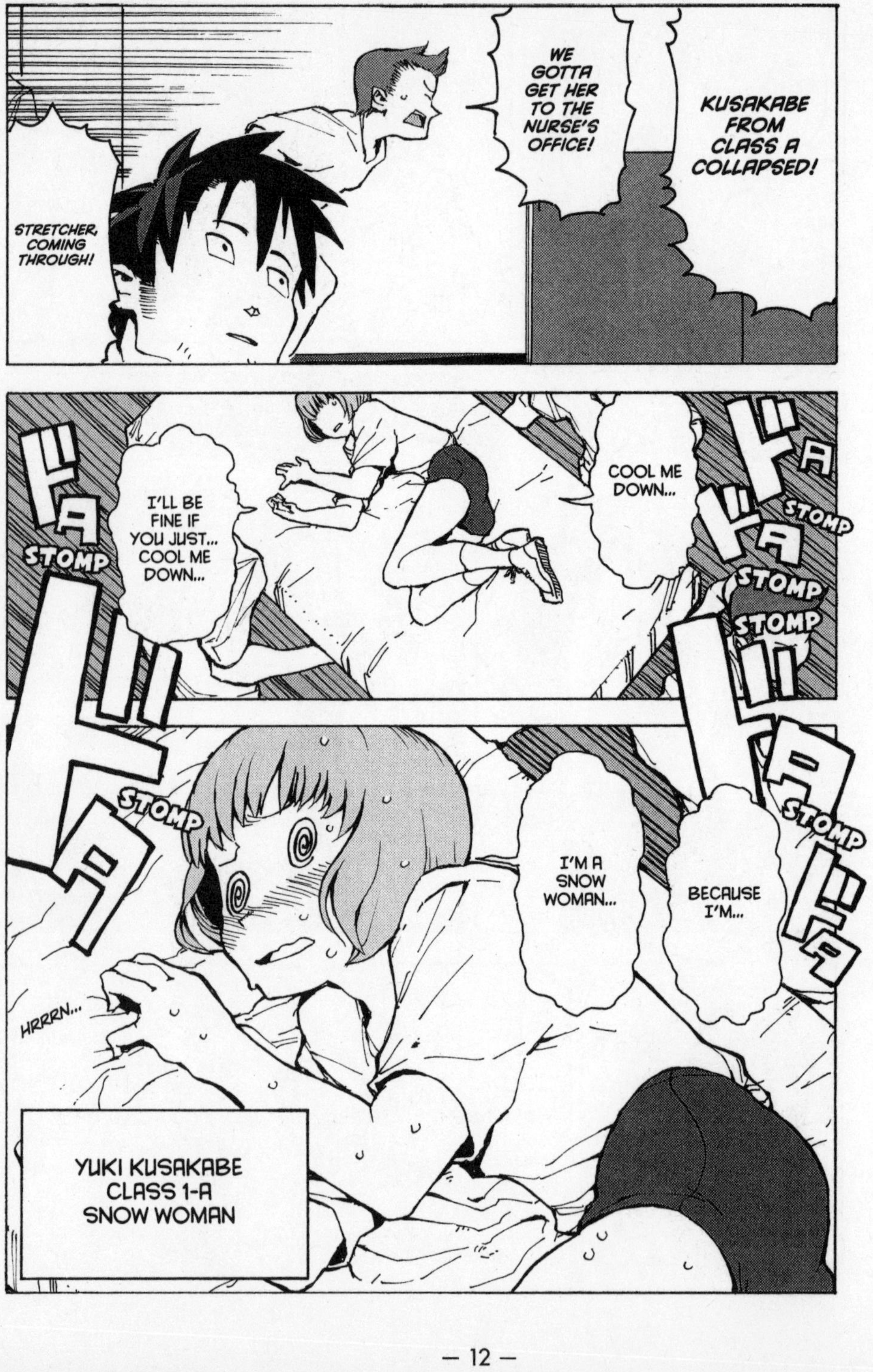
KUSAKABE FROM CLASS A COLLAPSED!
WE GOTTA GET HER TO THE NURSE'S OFFICE!
STRETCHER, COMING THROUGH!
STOMP
STOMP
STOMP
COOL ME DOWN...
I'LL BE FINE IF YOU JUST... COOL ME DOWN...
STOMP
STOMP
BECAUSE I'M...
I'M A SNOW WOMAN...
STOMP
HRRRN...
YUKI KUSAKABE
CLASS 1-A
SNOW WOMAN

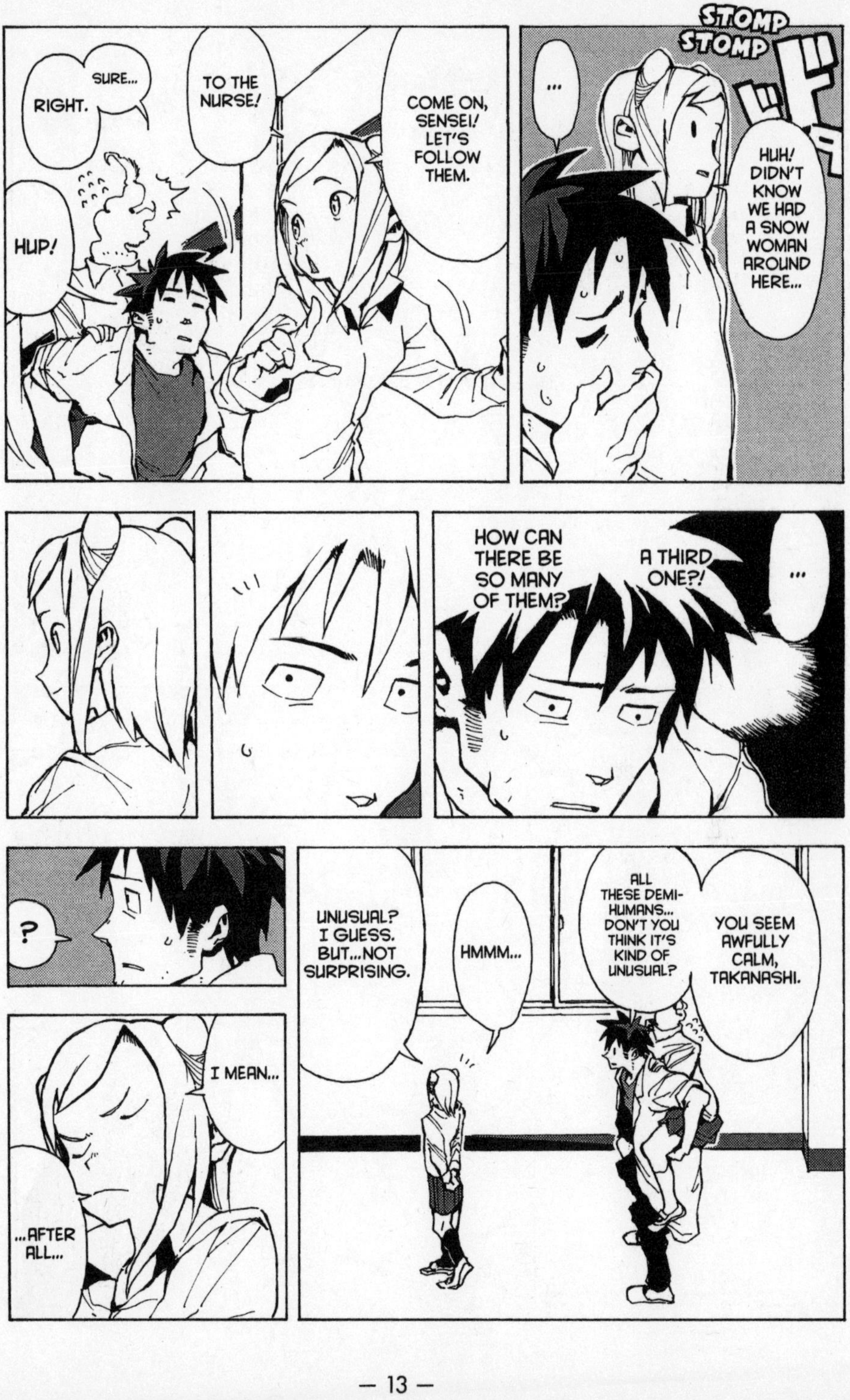

STOMP STOMP
...
HUH! DIDN'T KNOW WE HAD A SNOW WOMAN AROUND HERE...
COME ON, SENSEI! LET'S FOLLOW THEM.
TO THE NURSE!
SURE... RIGHT.
HUP!
...
A THIRD ONE?!
HOW CAN THERE BE SO MANY OF THEM?
YOU SEEM AWFULLY CALM, TAKANASHI.
ALL THESE DEMI-HUMANS... DON'T YOU THINK IT'S KIND OF UNUSUAL?
HMMM...
UNUSUAL? I GUESS. BUT...NOT SURPRISING.
?
I MEAN...
...AFTER ALL...

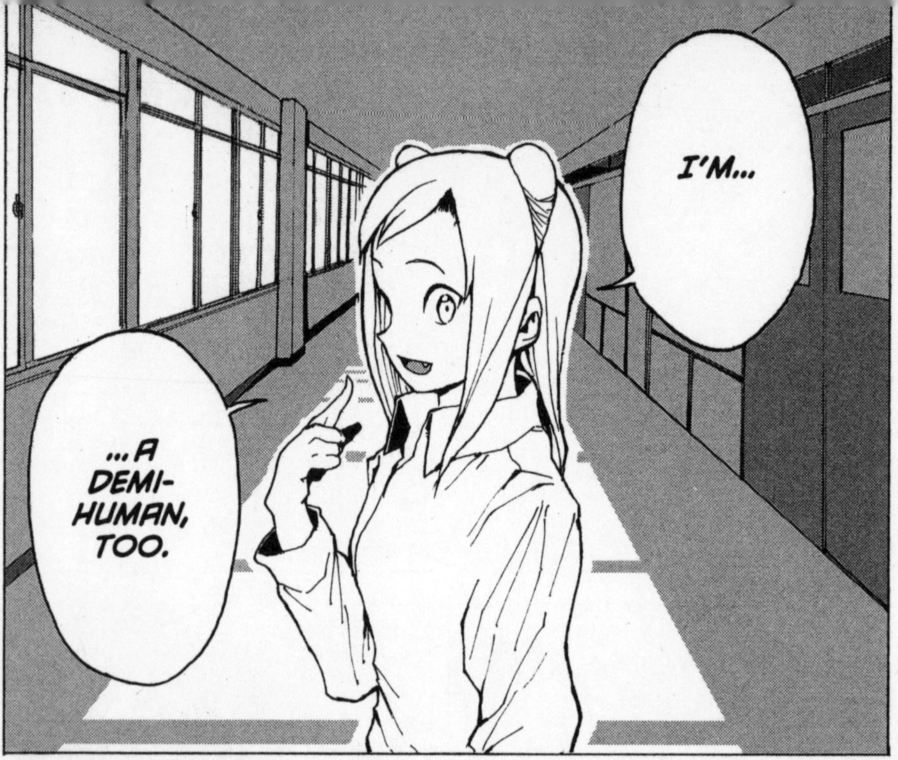
I'M...
...A DEMI-HUMAN, TOO.

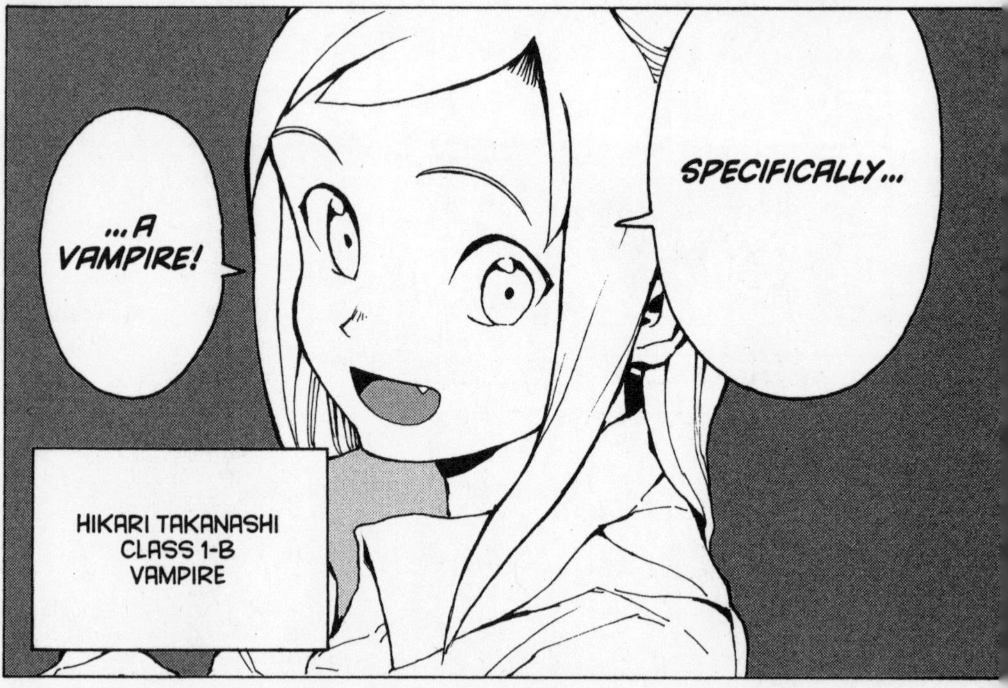
SPECIFICALLY...
...A VAMPIRE!
HIKARI TAKANASHI CLASS 1-B VAMPIRE

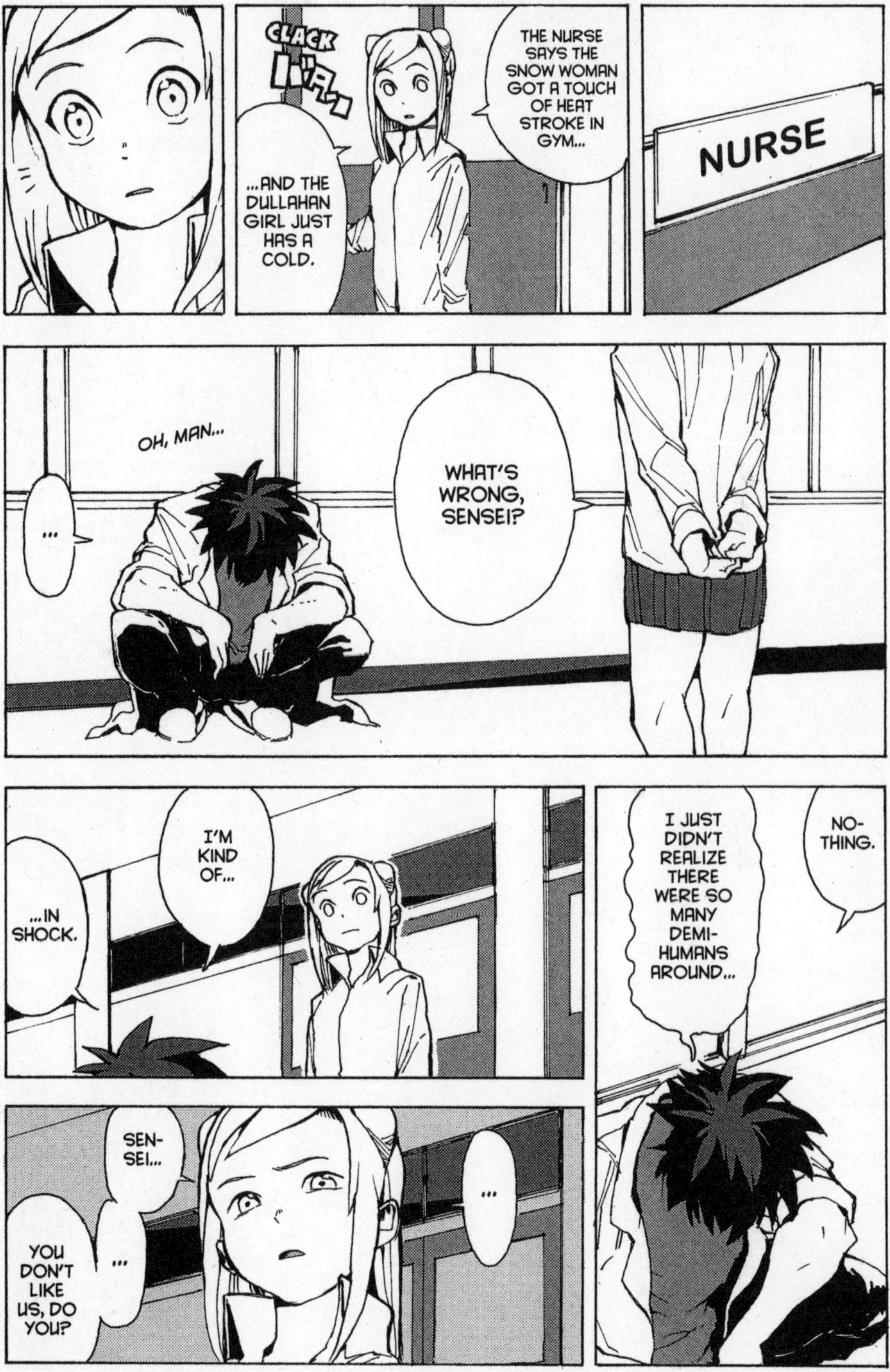
NURSE
THE NURSE SAYS THE SNOW WOMAN GOT A TOUCH OF HEAT STROKE IN GYM...
CLACK
...AND THE DULLAHAN GIRL JUST HAS A COLD.
WHAT'S WRONG, SENSEI?
OH, MAN...
...
NO-THING.
I JUST DIDN'T REALIZE THERE WERE SO MANY DEMI-HUMANS AROUND...
I'M KIND OF...
...IN SHOCK.
...
SEN-SEI...
...
YOU DON'T LIKE US, DO YOU?

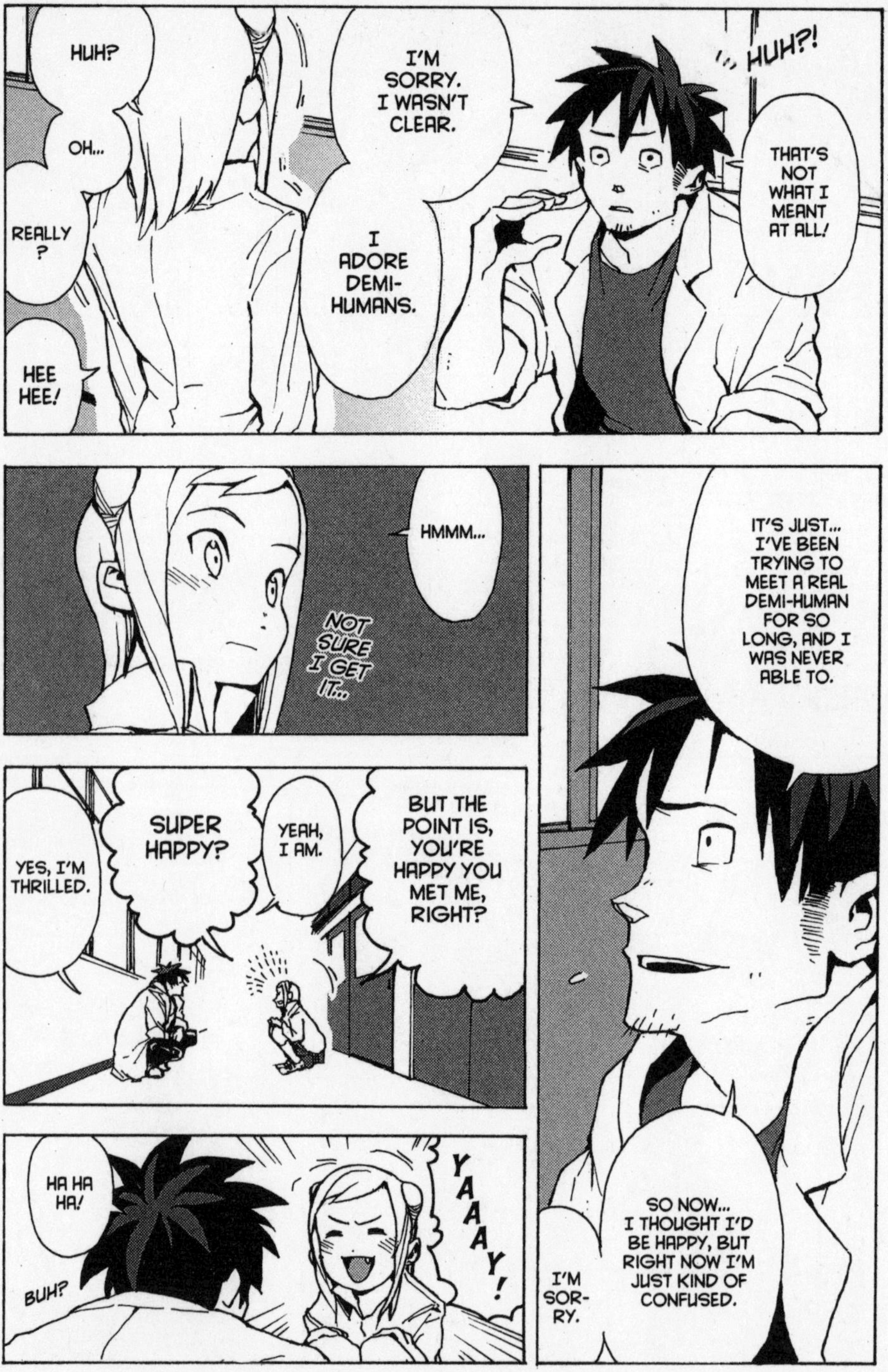
HUH?!
THAT'S NOT WHAT I MEANT AT ALL!
I'M SORRY. I WASN'T CLEAR.
I ADORE DEMI-HUMANS.
HUH?
OH...
REALLY?
HEE HEE!
IT'S JUST... I'VE BEEN TRYING TO MEET A REAL DEMI-HUMAN FOR SO LONG, AND I WAS NEVER ABLE TO.
SO NOW... I THOUGHT I'D BE HAPPY, BUT RIGHT NOW I'M JUST KIND OF CONFUSED.
I'M SOR-RY.
HMMM...
NOT SURE I GET IT...
BUT THE POINT IS, YOU'RE HAPPY YOU MET ME, RIGHT?
YEAH, I AM.
SUPER HAPPY?
YES, I'M THRILLED.
YAAAY!
HA HA HA!
BUH?

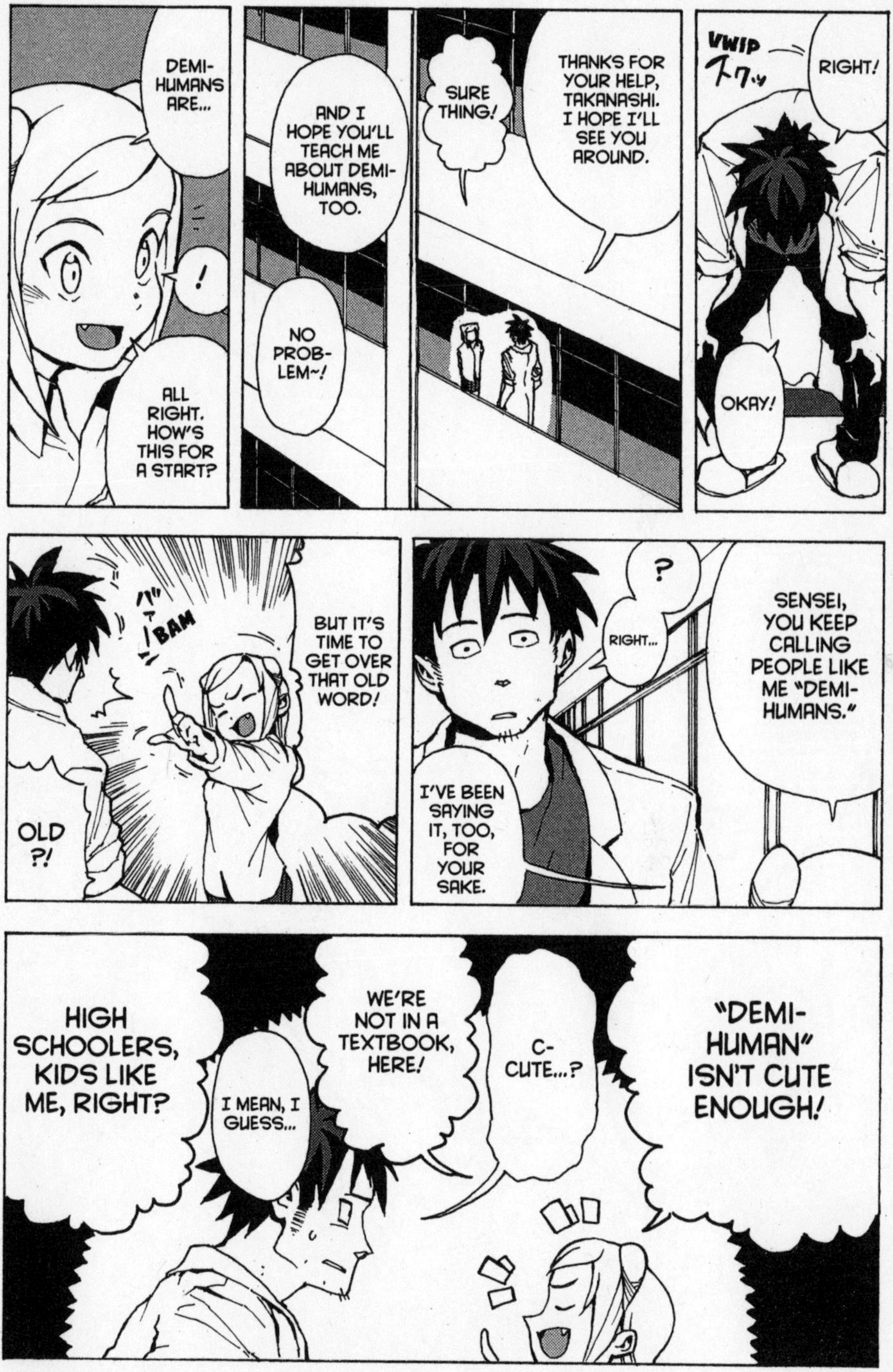
RIGHT!
VWIP
スクッ
OKAY!
THANKS FOR YOUR HELP, TAKANASHI. I HOPE I'LL SEE YOU AROUND.
SURE THING!
AND I HOPE YOU'LL TEACH ME ABOUT DEMI-HUMANS, TOO.
NO PROBLEM~!
DEMI-HUMANS ARE...
!
ALL RIGHT. HOW'S THIS FOR A START?
SENSEI, YOU KEEP CALLING PEOPLE LIKE ME "DEMI-HUMANS."
?
RIGHT...
I'VE BEEN SAYING IT, TOO, FOR YOUR SAKE.
BUT IT'S TIME TO GET OVER THAT OLD WORD!
BAM
OLD ?!
"DEMI-HUMAN" ISN'T CUTE ENOUGH!
C-CUTE...?
WE'RE NOT IN A TEXTBOOK, HERE!
I MEAN, I GUESS...
HIGH SCHOOLERS, KIDS LIKE ME, RIGHT?

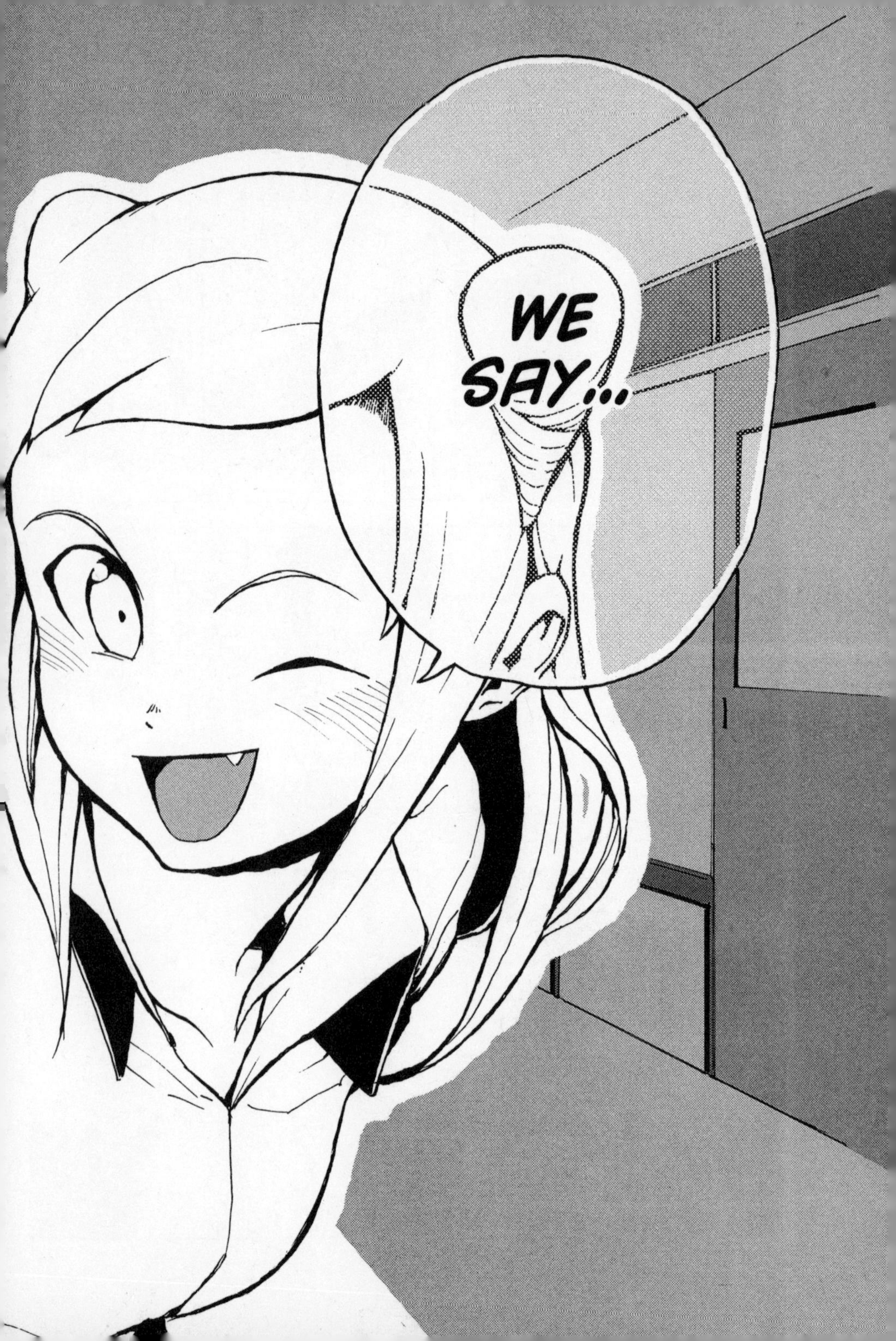
WE SAY...

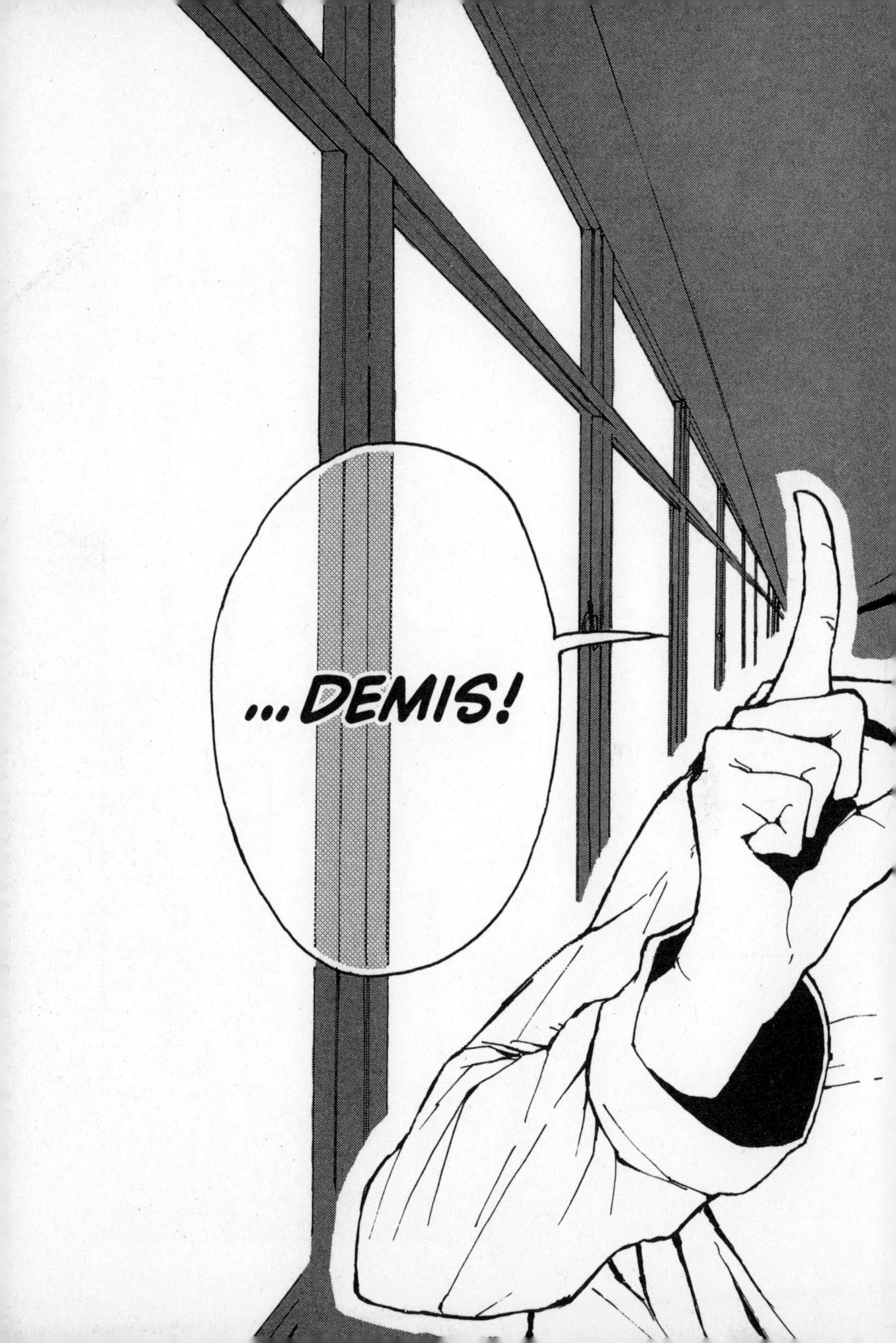
...DEMIS!

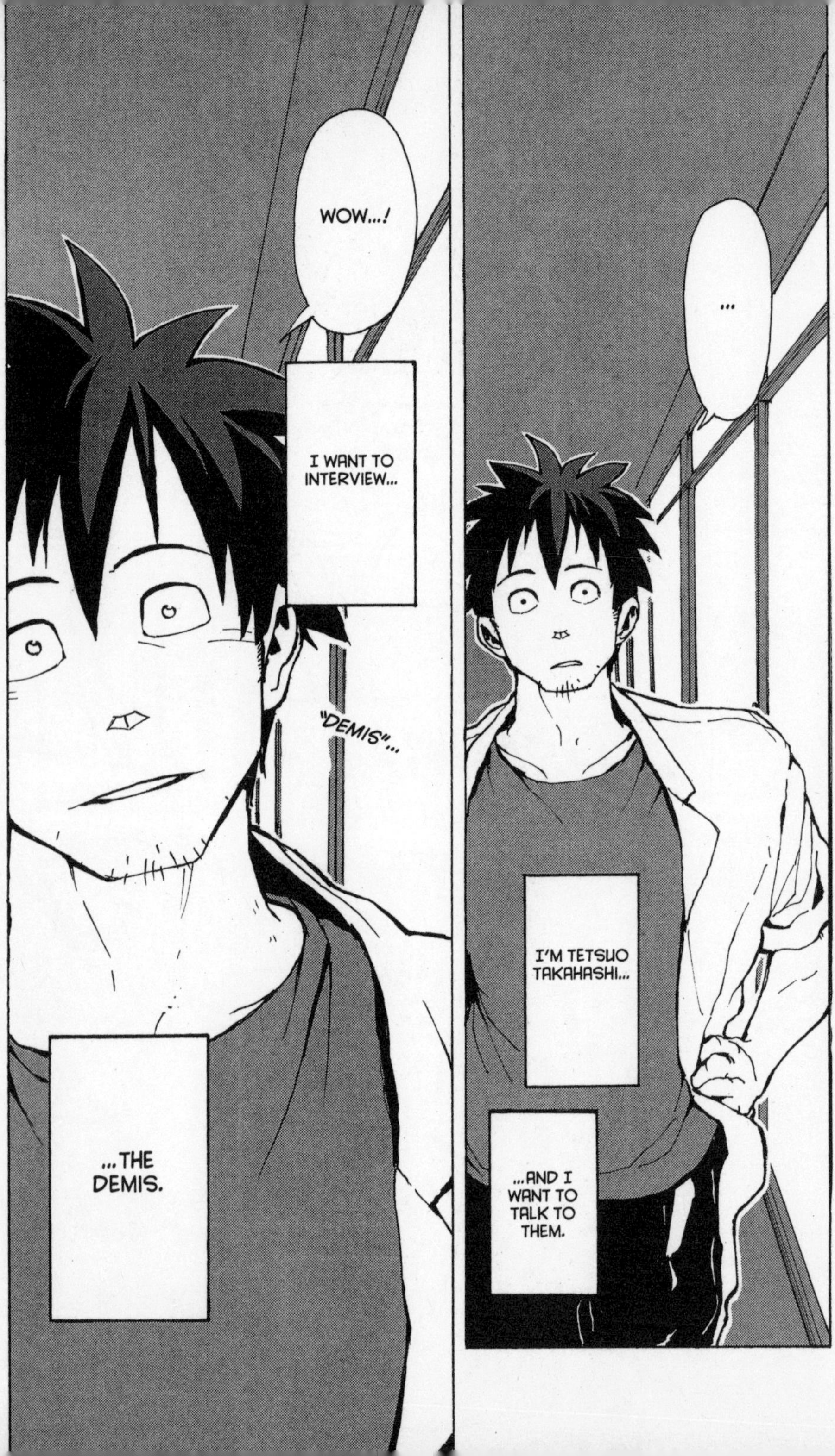
...
I'M TETSUO TAKAHASHI...
...AND I WANT TO TALK TO THEM.
WOW...!
I WANT TO INTERVIEW...
"DEMIS"...
...THE DEMIS.

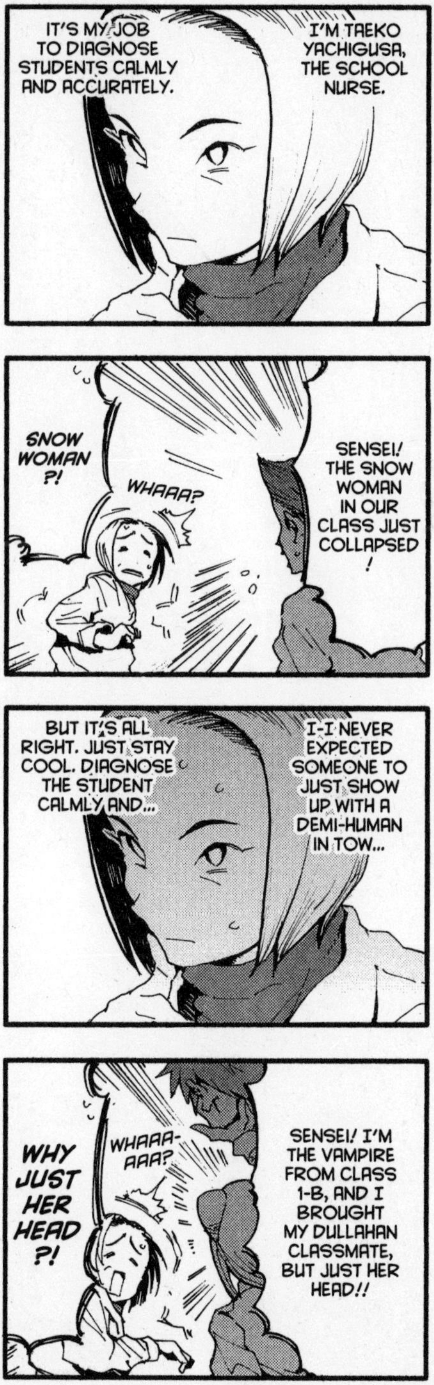
I'M TAEKO YACHIGUSA, THE SCHOOL NURSE.
IT'S MY JOB TO DIAGNOSE STUDENTS CALMLY AND ACCURATELY.
SENSEI! THE SNOW WOMAN IN OUR CLASS JUST COLLAPSED!
WHAAA?
SNOW WOMAN?!
I-I NEVER EXPECTED SOMEONE TO JUST SHOW UP WITH A DEMI-HUMAN IN TOW...
BUT IT'S ALL RIGHT. JUST STAY COOL. DIAGNOSE THE STUDENT CALMLY AND...
SENSEI! I'M THE VAMPIRE FROM CLASS 1-B, AND I BROUGHT MY DULLAHAN CLASSMATE, BUT JUST HER HEAD!!
WHAAA-AAA?
WHY JUST HER HEAD?!

INTERVIEWS WITH MONSTER GIRLS

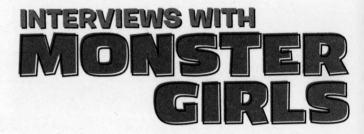

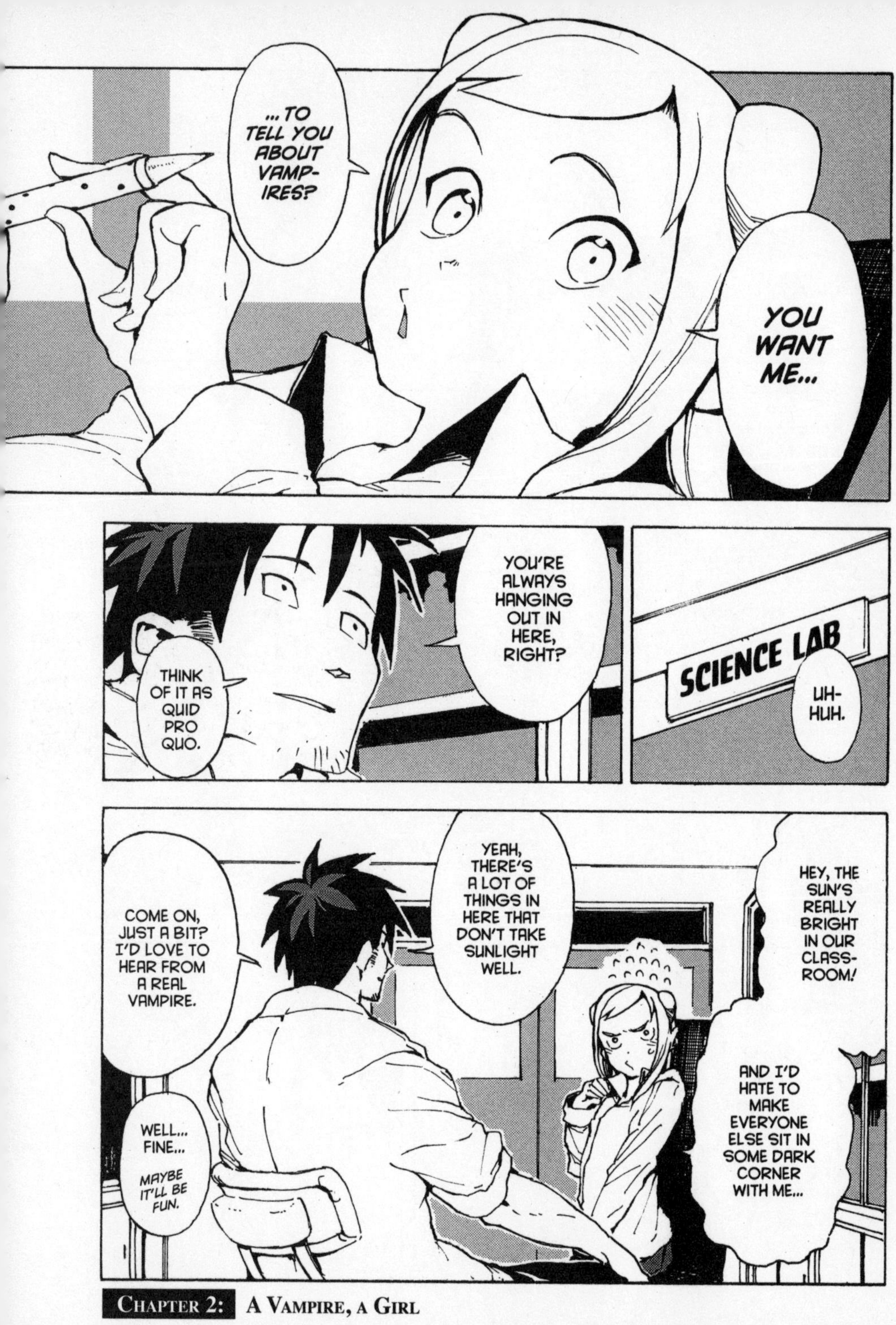
YOU WANT ME...
...TO TELL YOU ABOUT VAMPIRES?
SCIENCE LAB
UH-HUH.
YOU'RE ALWAYS HANGING OUT IN HERE, RIGHT?
THINK OF IT AS QUID PRO QUO.
HEY, THE SUN'S REALLY BRIGHT IN OUR CLASSROOM!
AND I'D HATE TO MAKE EVERYONE ELSE SIT IN SOME DARK CORNER WITH ME...
YEAH, THERE'S A LOT OF THINGS IN HERE THAT DON'T TAKE SUNLIGHT WELL.
COME ON, JUST A BIT? I'D LOVE TO HEAR FROM A REAL VAMPIRE.
WELL... FINE...
MAYBE IT'LL BE FUN.

CHAPTER 2: A VAMPIRE, A GIRL

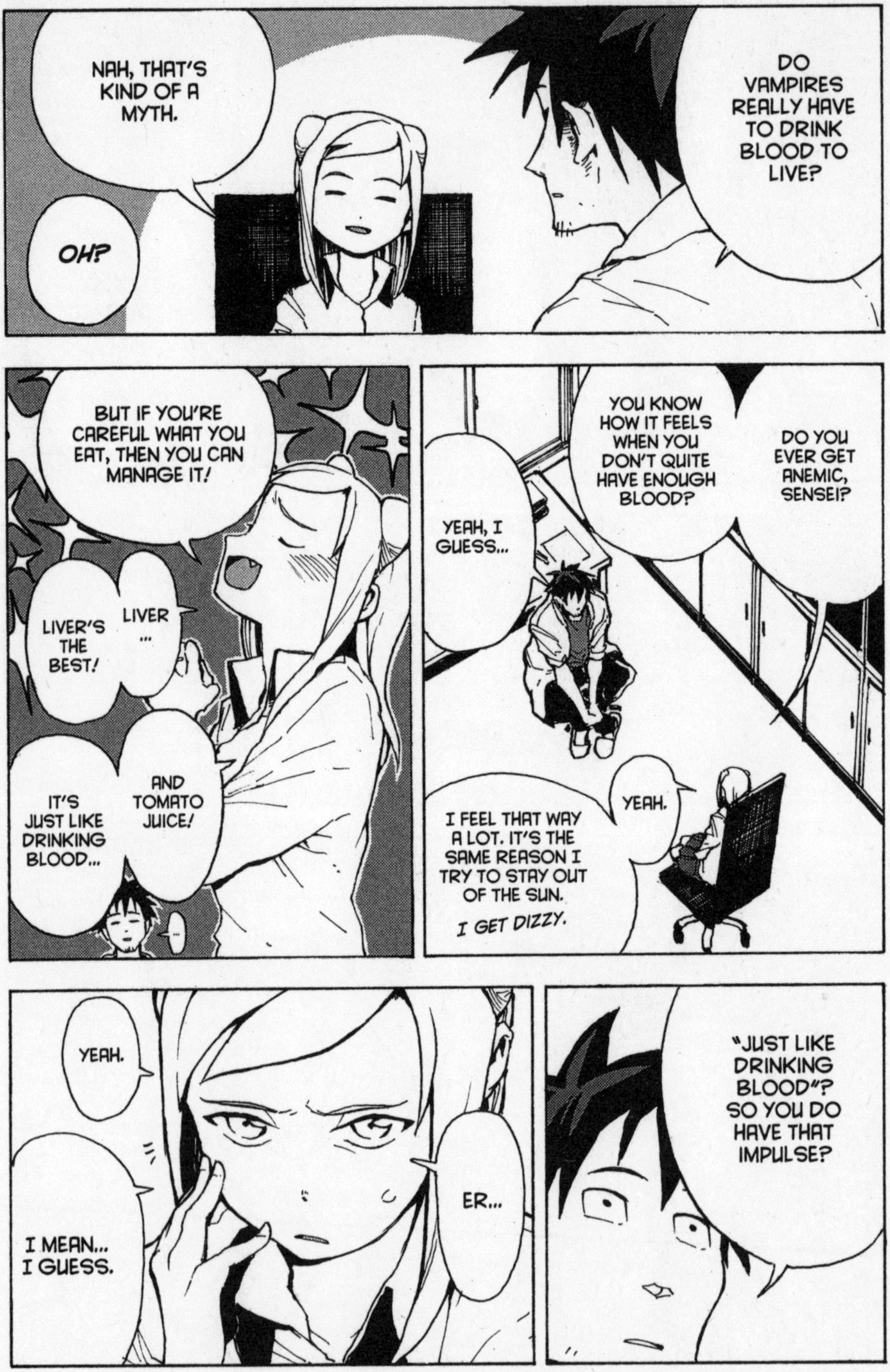
DO VAMPIRES REALLY HAVE TO DRINK BLOOD TO LIVE?
NAH, THAT'S KIND OF A MYTH.
OH?
DO YOU EVER GET ANEMIC, SENSEI?
YOU KNOW HOW IT FEELS WHEN YOU DON'T QUITE HAVE ENOUGH BLOOD?
YEAH, I GUESS...
YEAH.
I FEEL THAT WAY A LOT. IT'S THE SAME REASON I TRY TO STAY OUT OF THE SUN.
I GET DIZZY.
BUT IF YOU'RE CAREFUL WHAT YOU EAT, THEN YOU CAN MANAGE IT!
LIVER ...
LIVER'S THE BEST!
AND TOMATO JUICE!
IT'S JUST LIKE DRINKING BLOOD...
...
"JUST LIKE DRINKING BLOOD"? SO YOU DO HAVE THAT IMPULSE?
ER...
YEAH.
I MEAN... I GUESS.

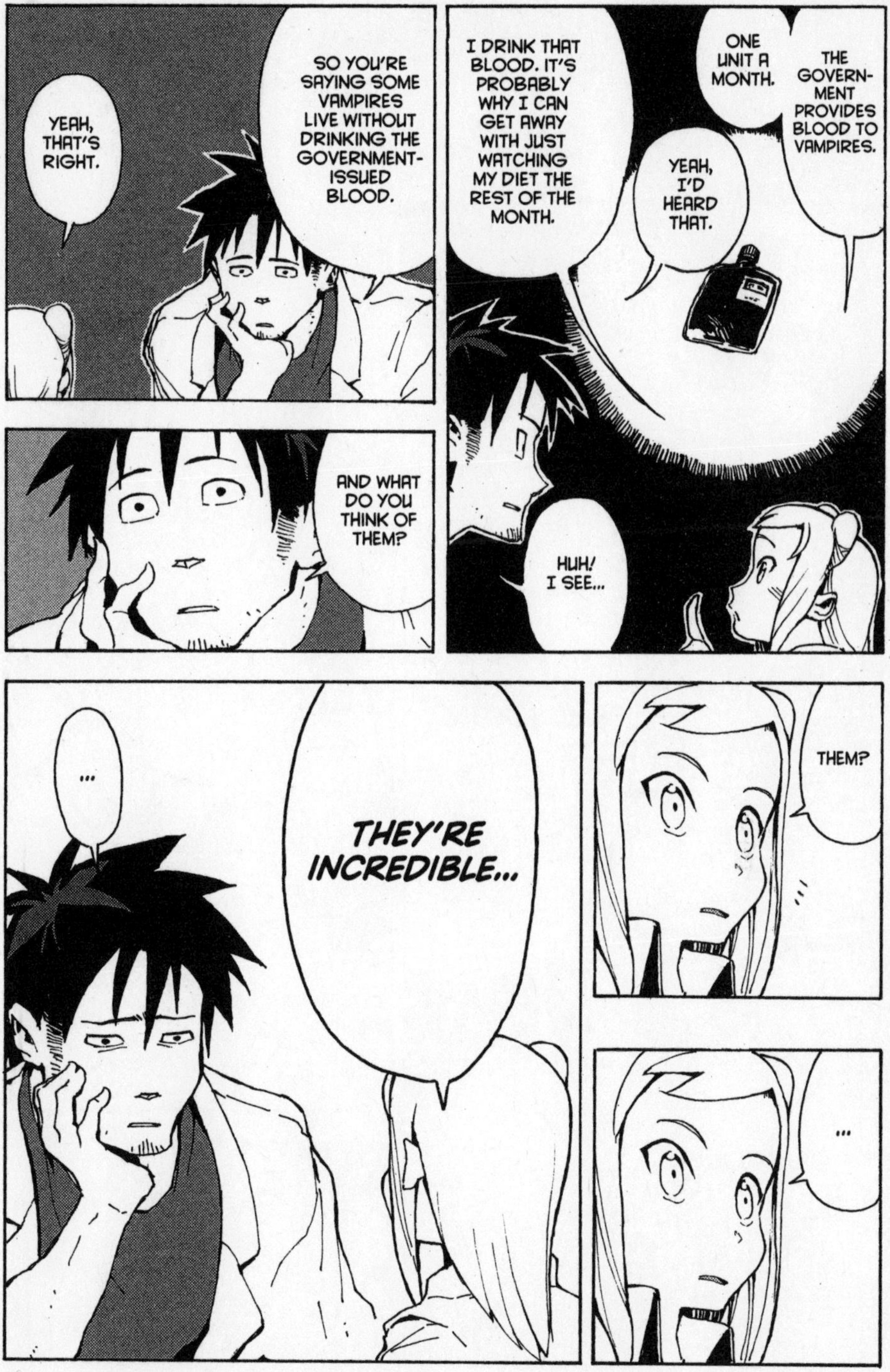
THE GOVERNMENT PROVIDES BLOOD TO VAMPIRES.
ONE UNIT A MONTH.
YEAH, I'D HEARD THAT.
I DRINK THAT BLOOD. IT'S PROBABLY WHY I CAN GET AWAY WITH JUST WATCHING MY DIET THE REST OF THE MONTH.
HUH! I SEE...
SO YOU'RE SAYING SOME VAMPIRES LIVE WITHOUT DRINKING THE GOVERNMENT-ISSUED BLOOD.
YEAH, THAT'S RIGHT.
AND WHAT DO YOU THINK OF THEM?
THEM?
...
THEY'RE INCREDIBLE...
...

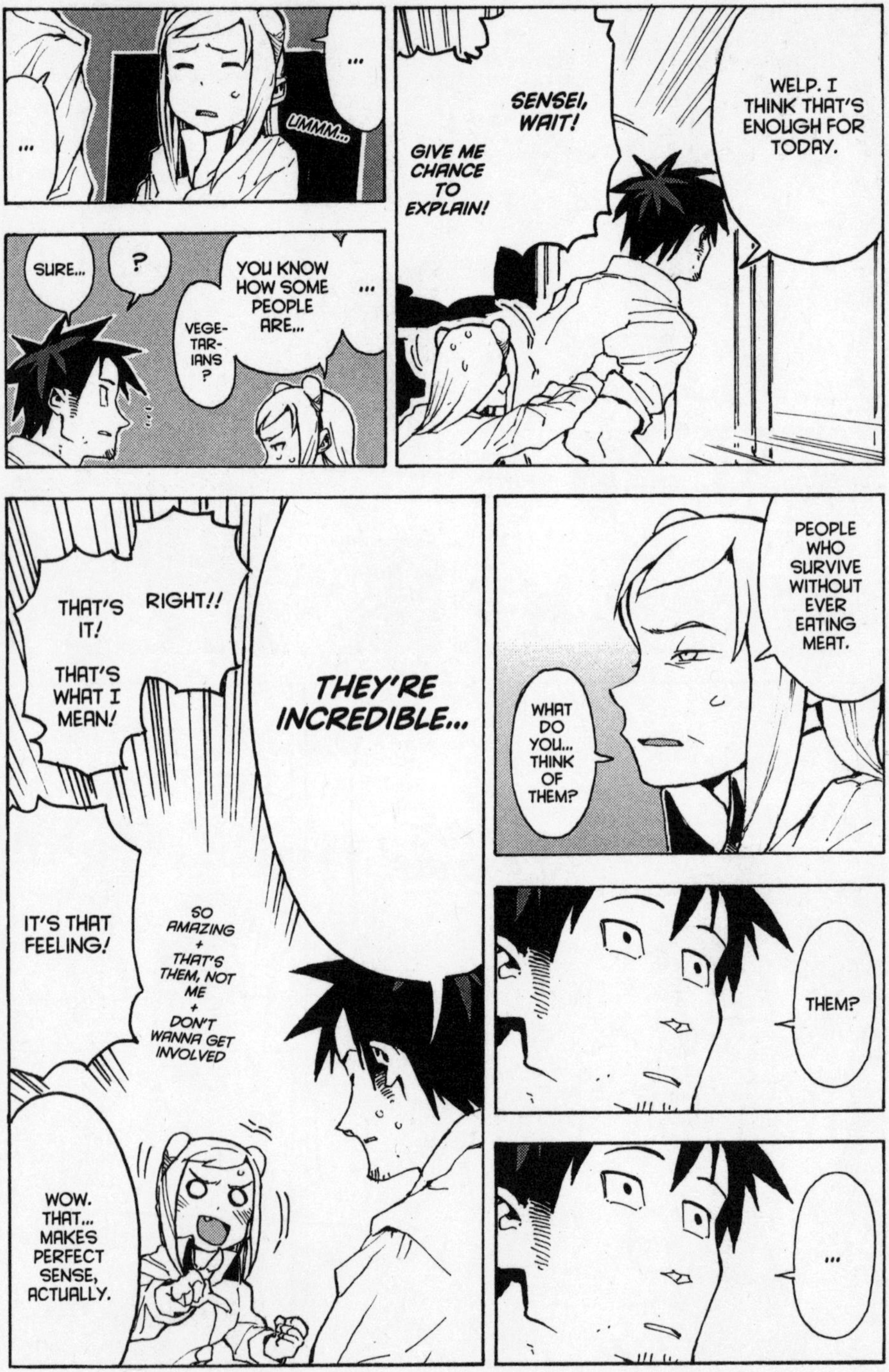
WELP. I THINK THAT'S ENOUGH FOR TODAY.
SENSEI, WAIT!
GIVE ME CHANCE TO EXPLAIN!
...
UMMM...
...
...
YOU KNOW HOW SOME PEOPLE ARE...
?
VEGE-TAR-IANS?
SURE...
PEOPLE WHO SURVIVE WITHOUT EVER EATING MEAT.
WHAT DO YOU... THINK OF THEM?
THEM?
...
THEY'RE INCREDIBLE...
RIGHT!!
THAT'S IT!
THAT'S WHAT I MEAN!
SO AMAZING + THAT'S THEM, NOT ME + DON'T WANNA GET INVOLVED
IT'S THAT FEELING!
WOW. THAT... MAKES PERFECT SENSE, ACTUALLY.

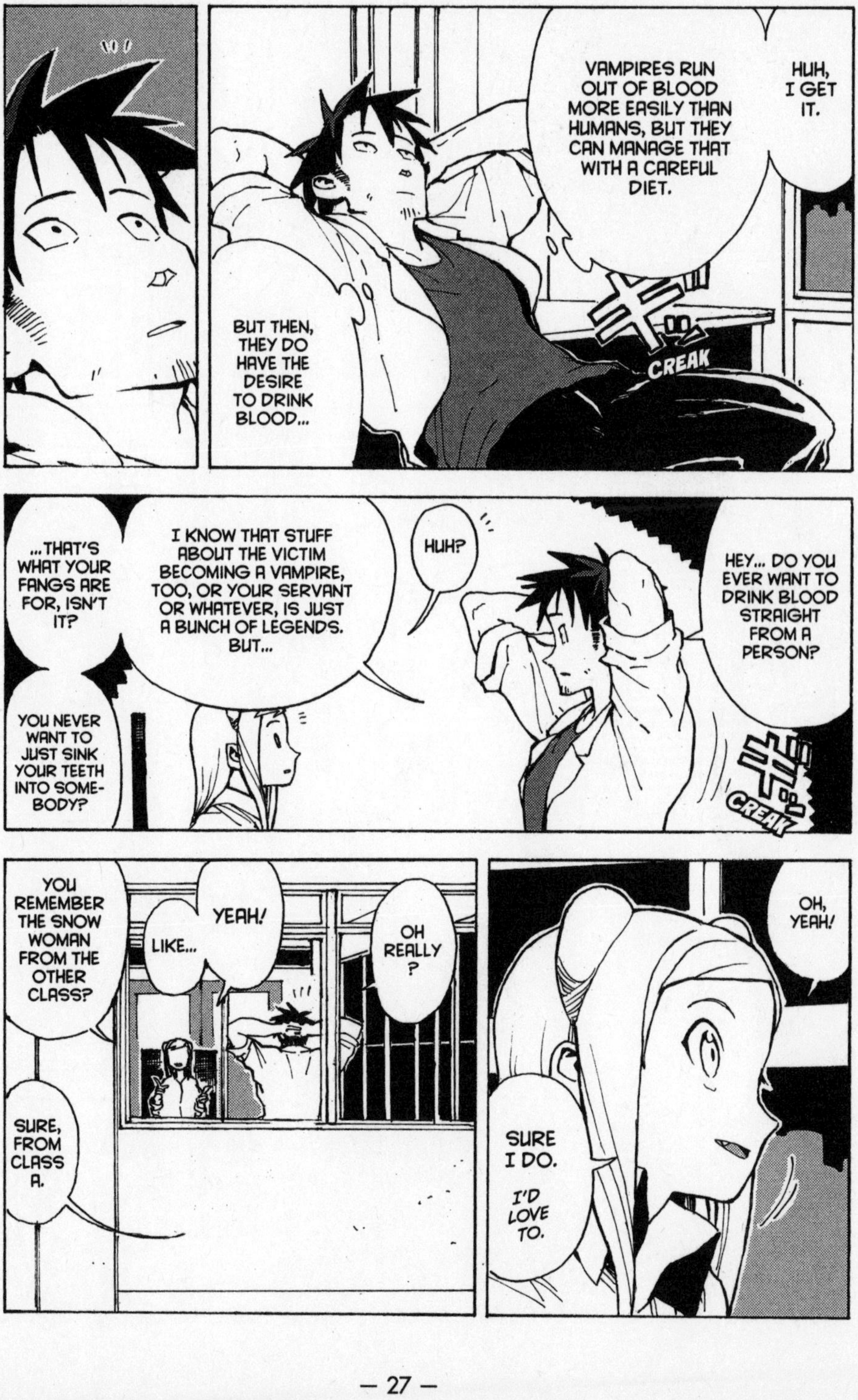
HUH, I GET IT.
VAMPIRES RUN OUT OF BLOOD MORE EASILY THAN HUMANS, BUT THEY CAN MANAGE THAT WITH A CAREFUL DIET.
CREAK
BUT THEN, THEY DO HAVE THE DESIRE TO DRINK BLOOD...
HEY... DO YOU EVER WANT TO DRINK BLOOD STRAIGHT FROM A PERSON?
HUH?
CREAK
I KNOW THAT STUFF ABOUT THE VICTIM BECOMING A VAMPIRE, TOO, OR YOUR SERVANT OR WHATEVER, IS JUST A BUNCH OF LEGENDS. BUT...
...THAT'S WHAT YOUR FANGS ARE FOR, ISN'T IT?
YOU NEVER WANT TO JUST SINK YOUR TEETH INTO SOME-BODY?
OH, YEAH!
SURE I DO.
I'D LOVE TO.
OH REALLY ?
YEAH!
LIKE...
YOU REMEMBER THE SNOW WOMAN FROM THE OTHER CLASS?
SURE, FROM CLASS A.

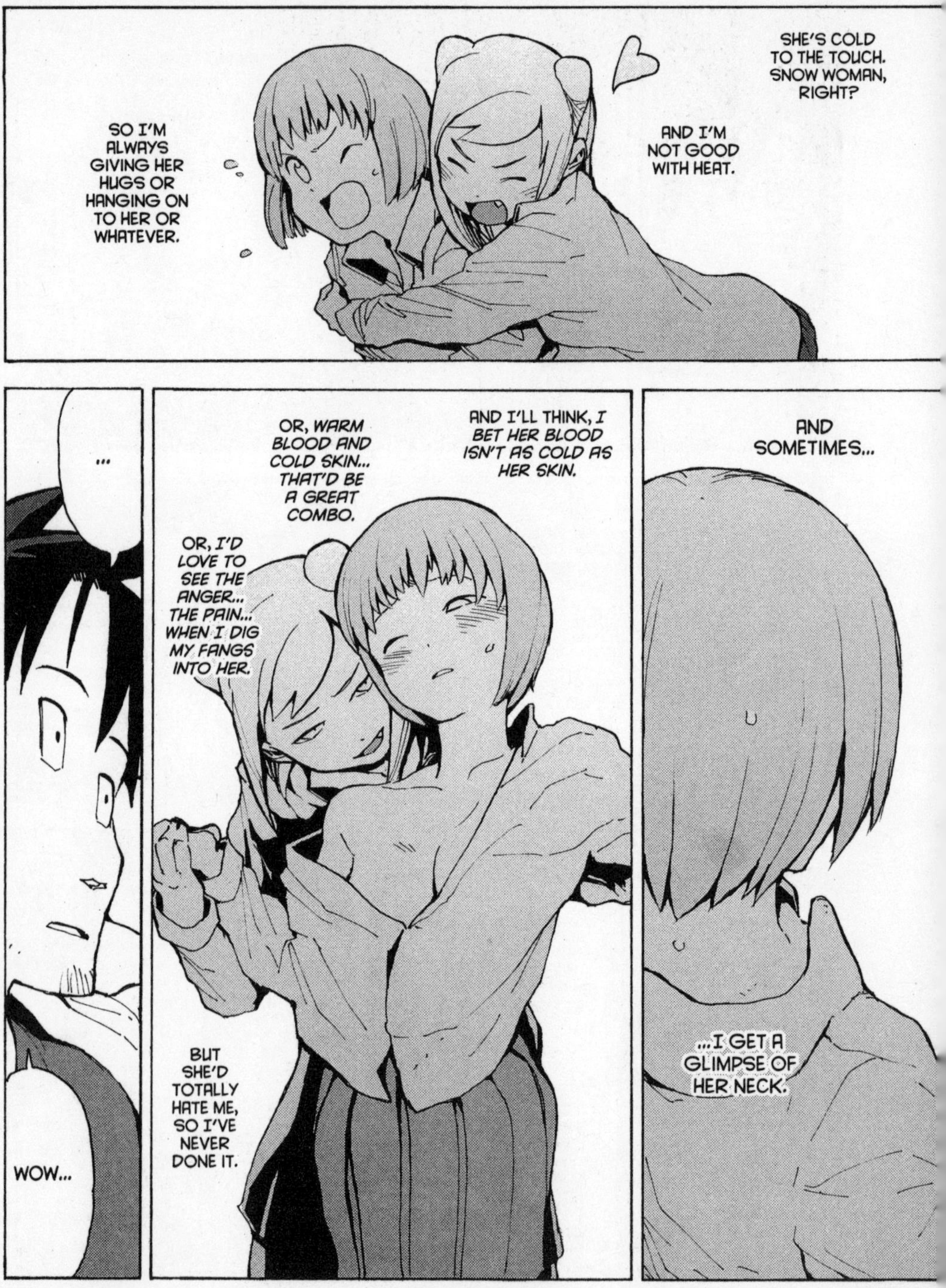
SHE'S COLD TO THE TOUCH. SNOW WOMAN, RIGHT?
AND I'M NOT GOOD WITH HEAT.
SO I'M ALWAYS GIVING HER HUGS OR HANGING ON TO HER OR WHATEVER.
AND SOMETIMES...
...I GET A GLIMPSE OF HER NECK.
AND I'LL THINK, I BET HER BLOOD ISN'T AS COLD AS HER SKIN.
OR, WARM BLOOD AND COLD SKIN... THAT'D BE A GREAT COMBO.
OR, I'D LOVE TO SEE THE ANGER... THE PAIN... WHEN I DIG MY FANGS INTO HER.
BUT SHE'D TOTALLY HATE ME, SO I'VE NEVER DONE IT.
...
WOW...

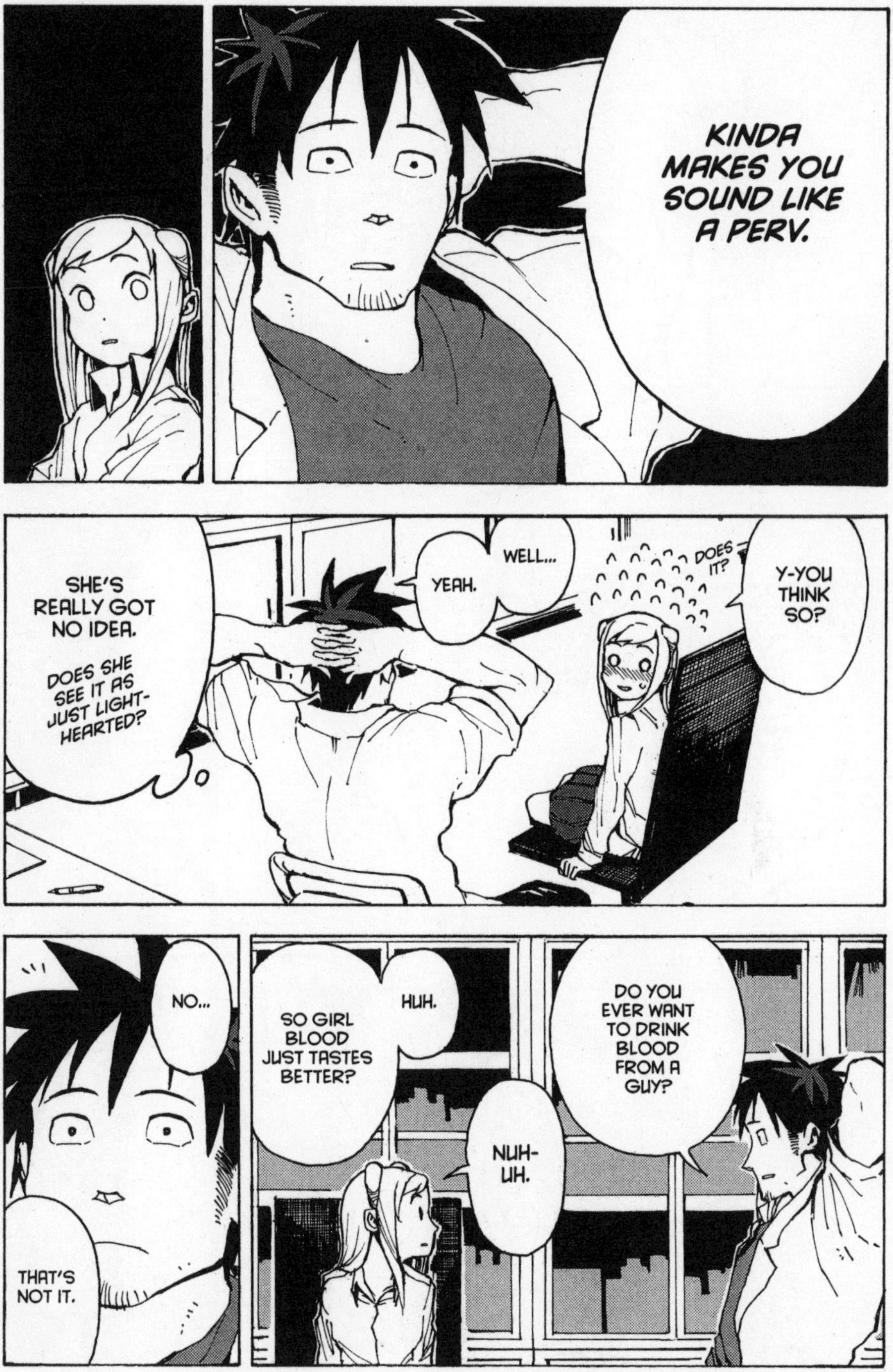
KINDA MAKES YOU SOUND LIKE A PERV.
Y-YOU THINK SO?
DOES IT?
WELL...
YEAH.
SHE'S REALLY GOT NO IDEA.
DOES SHE SEE IT AS JUST LIGHT-HEARTED?
DO YOU EVER WANT TO DRINK BLOOD FROM A GUY?
NUH-UH.
HUH.
SO GIRL BLOOD JUST TASTES BETTER?
NO...
THAT'S NOT IT.

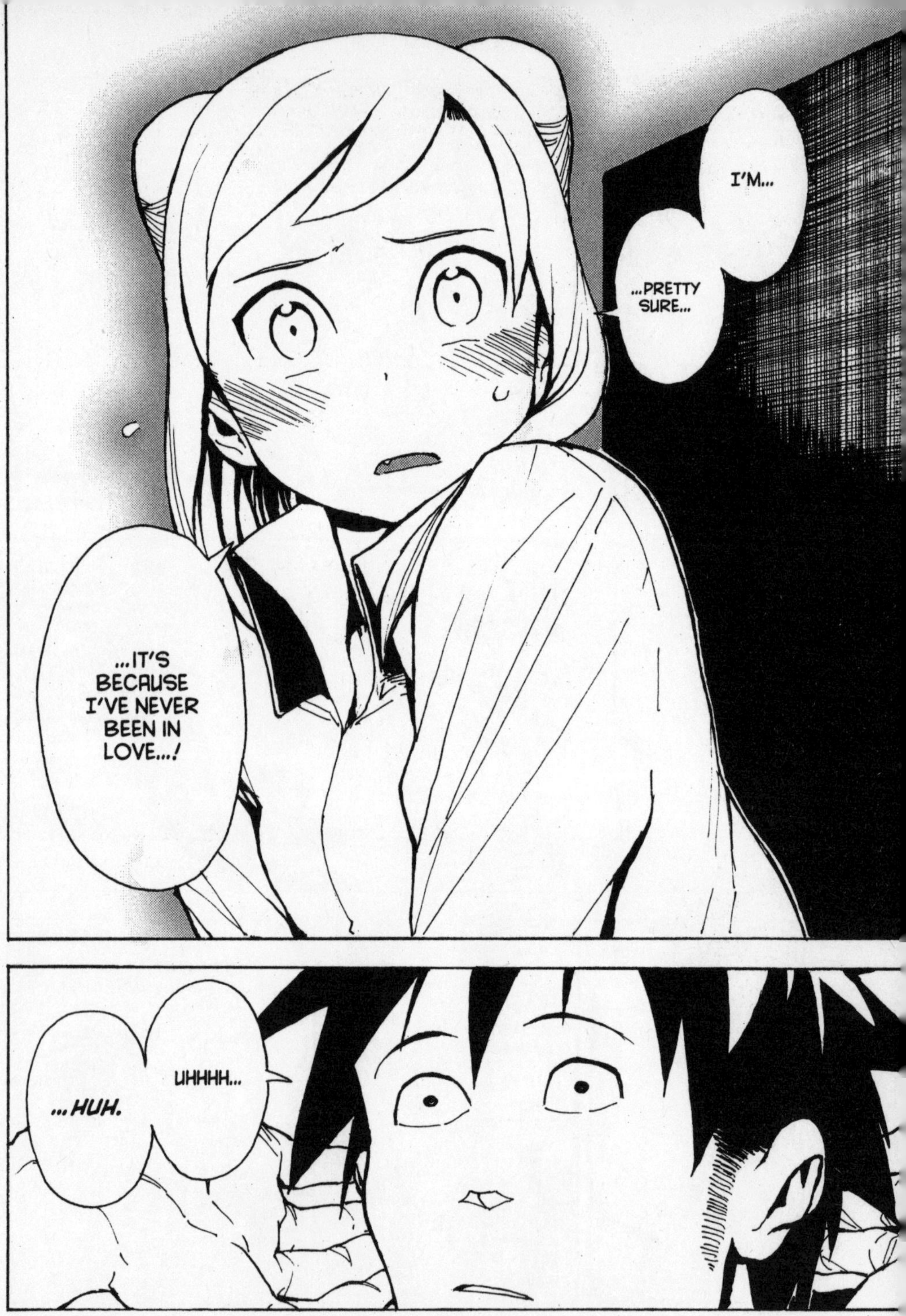
I'M...
...PRETTY SURE...
...IT'S BECAUSE I'VE NEVER BEEN IN LOVE...!
UHHHH...
...HUH.

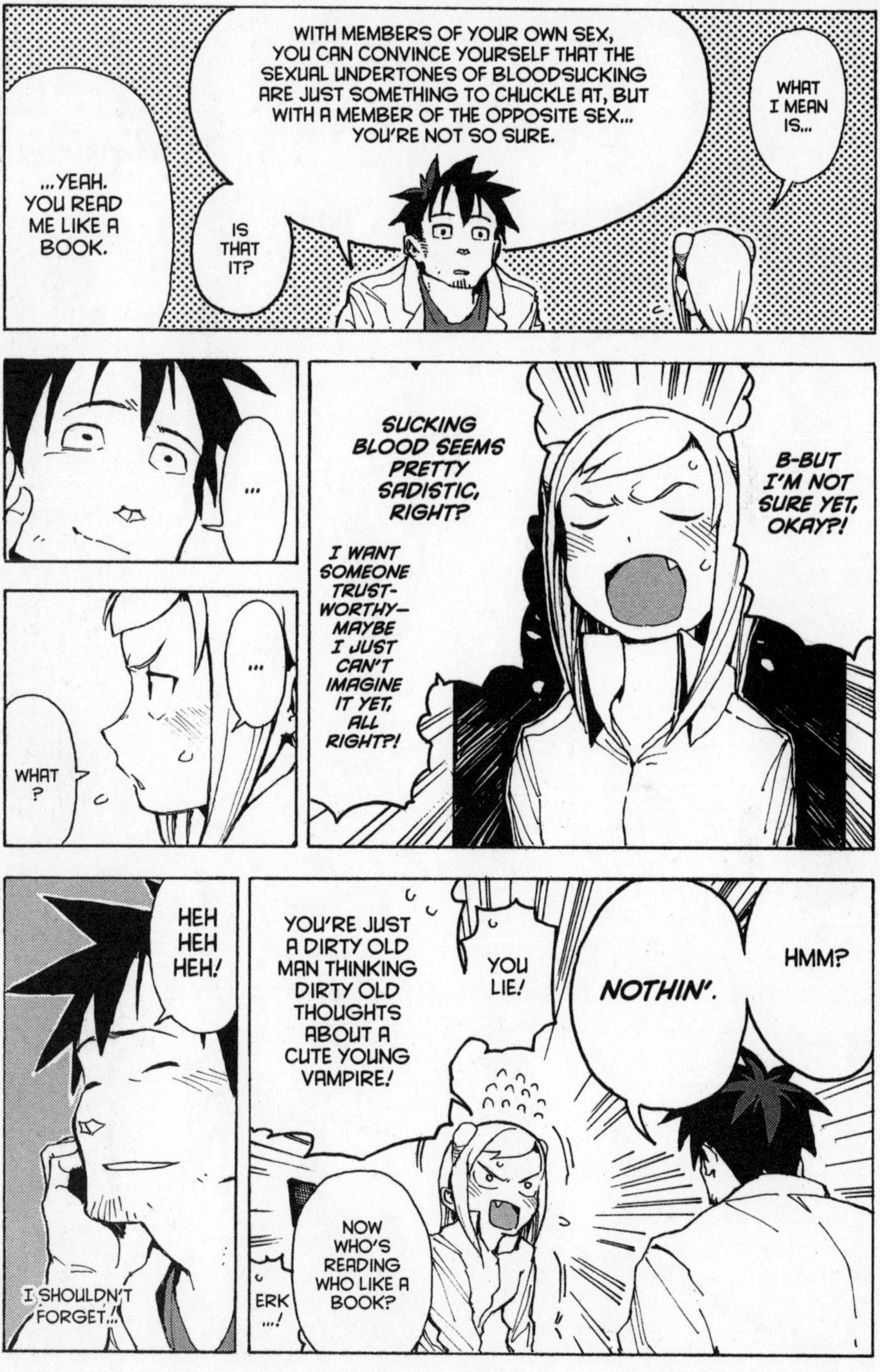
WHAT I MEAN IS...
WITH MEMBERS OF YOUR OWN SEX, YOU CAN CONVINCE YOURSELF THAT THE SEXUAL UNDERTONES OF BLOODSUCKING ARE JUST SOMETHING TO CHUCKLE AT, BUT WITH A MEMBER OF THE OPPOSITE SEX... YOU'RE NOT SO SURE.
IS THAT IT?
...YEAH. YOU READ ME LIKE A BOOK.
B-BUT I'M NOT SURE YET, OKAY?!
SUCKING BLOOD SEEMS PRETTY SADISTIC, RIGHT?
I WANT SOMEONE TRUST-WORTHY—MAYBE I JUST CAN'T IMAGINE IT YET, ALL RIGHT?!
...
...
WHAT?
HMM?
NOTHIN'.
YOU LIE!
YOU'RE JUST A DIRTY OLD MAN THINKING DIRTY OLD THOUGHTS ABOUT A CUTE YOUNG VAMPIRE!
NOW WHO'S READING WHO LIKE A BOOK?
ERK ...!
HEH HEH HEH!
I SHOULDN'T FORGET...!

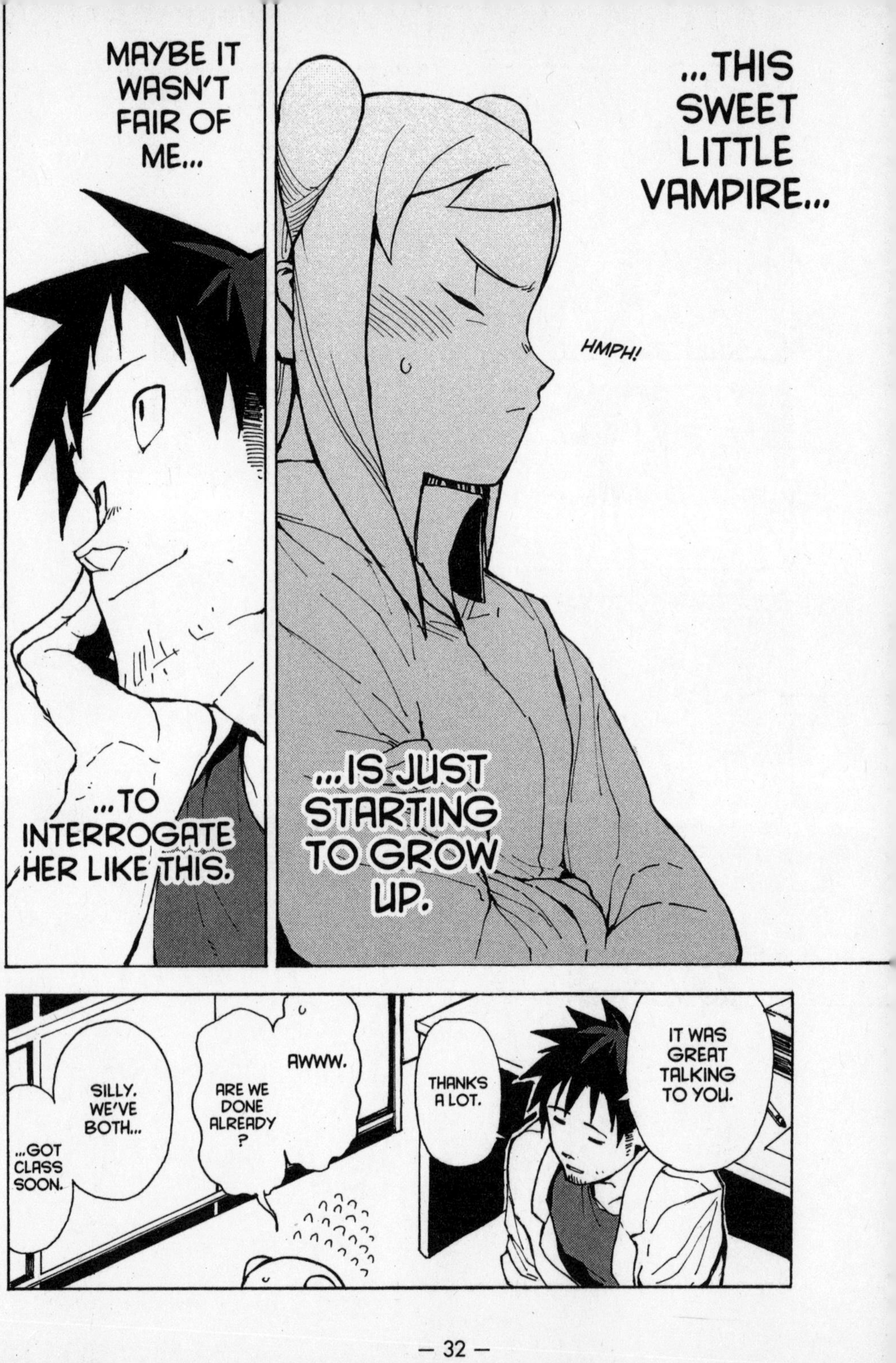
...THIS SWEET LITTLE VAMPIRE...
HMPH!
...IS JUST STARTING TO GROW UP.
MAYBE IT WASN'T FAIR OF ME...
...TO INTERROGATE HER LIKE THIS.
IT WAS GREAT TALKING TO YOU.
THANKS A LOT.
AWWW.
ARE WE DONE ALREADY?
SILLY. WE'VE BOTH...
...GOT CLASS SOON.

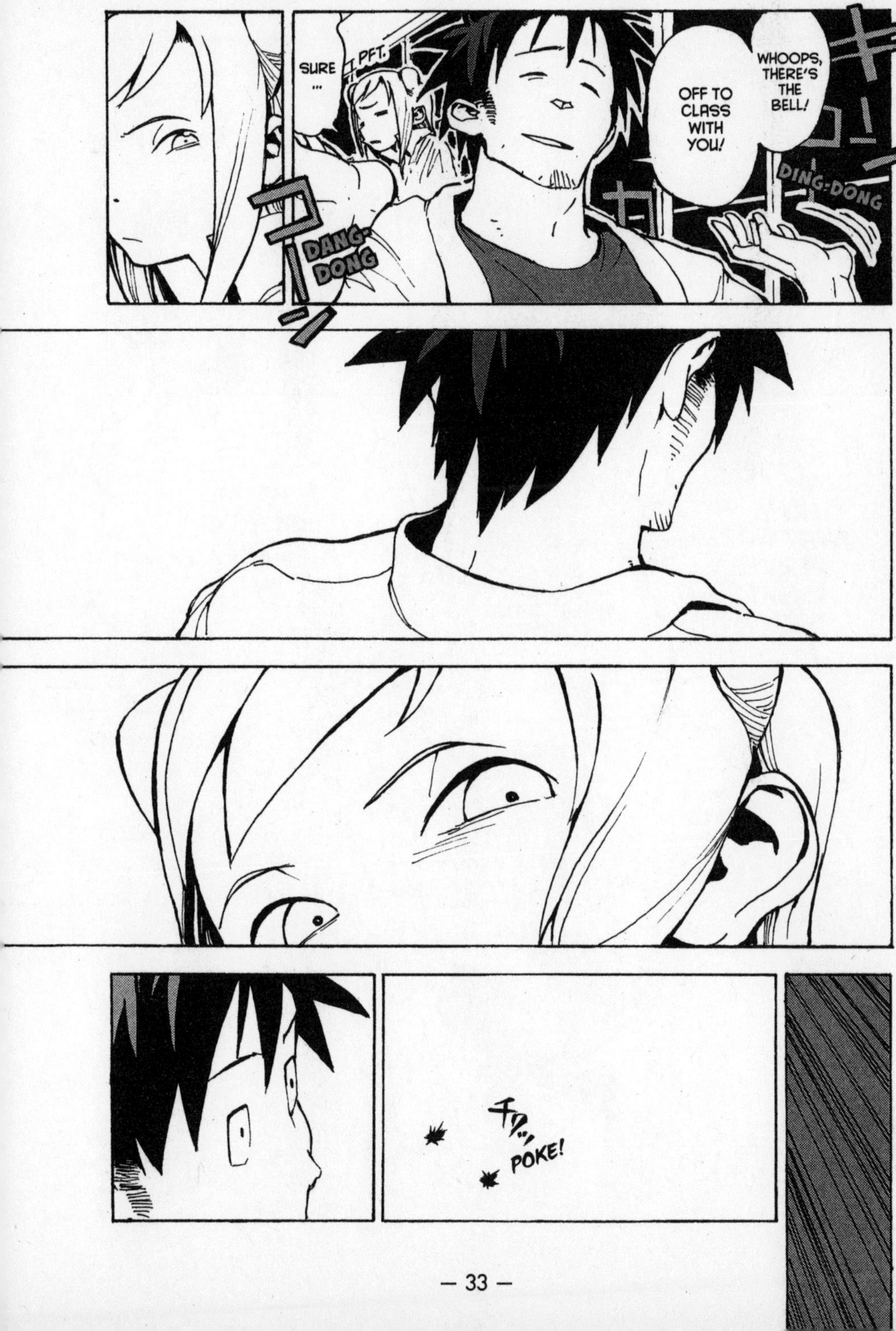
WHOOPS, THERE'S THE BELL!
OFF TO CLASS WITH YOU!
DING-DONG
PFT.
SURE ...
DANG-DONG
POKE!

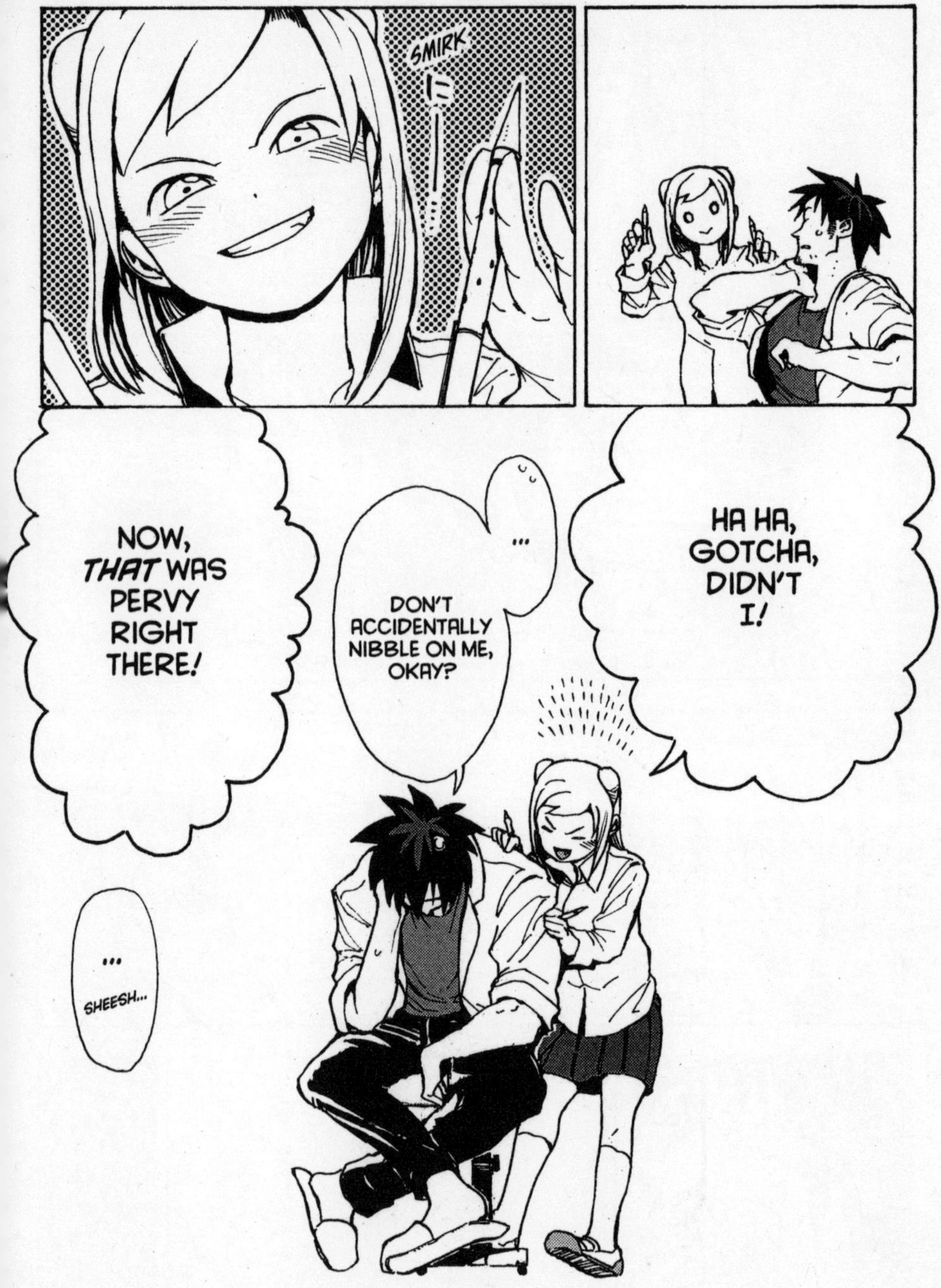
SMIRK
に
HA HA, GOTCHA, DIDN'T I!
...
DON'T ACCIDENTALLY NIBBLE ON ME, OKAY?
NOW, *THAT* WAS PERVY RIGHT THERE!
...
SHEESH...

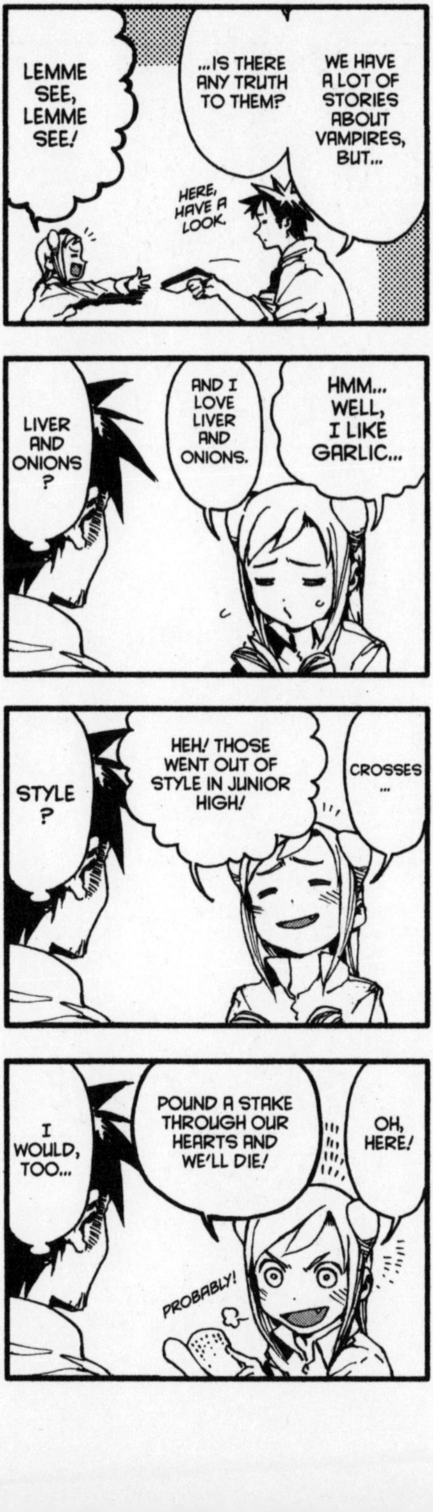
WE HAVE A LOT OF STORIES ABOUT VAMPIRES, BUT...
...IS THERE ANY TRUTH TO THEM?
HERE, HAVE A LOOK.
LEMME SEE, LEMME SEE!
HMM... WELL, I LIKE GARLIC...
AND I LOVE LIVER AND ONIONS.
LIVER AND ONIONS?
CROSSES...
HEH! THOSE WENT OUT OF STYLE IN JUNIOR HIGH!
STYLE?
OH, HERE!
POUND A STAKE THROUGH OUR HEARTS AND WE'LL DIE!
I WOULD, TOO...
PROBABLY!

INTERVIEWS WITH MONSTER GIRLS

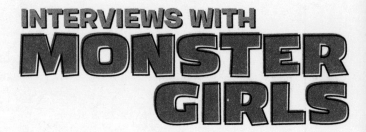

Chapter 3: The Takanashi Sisters are Thicker Than Water

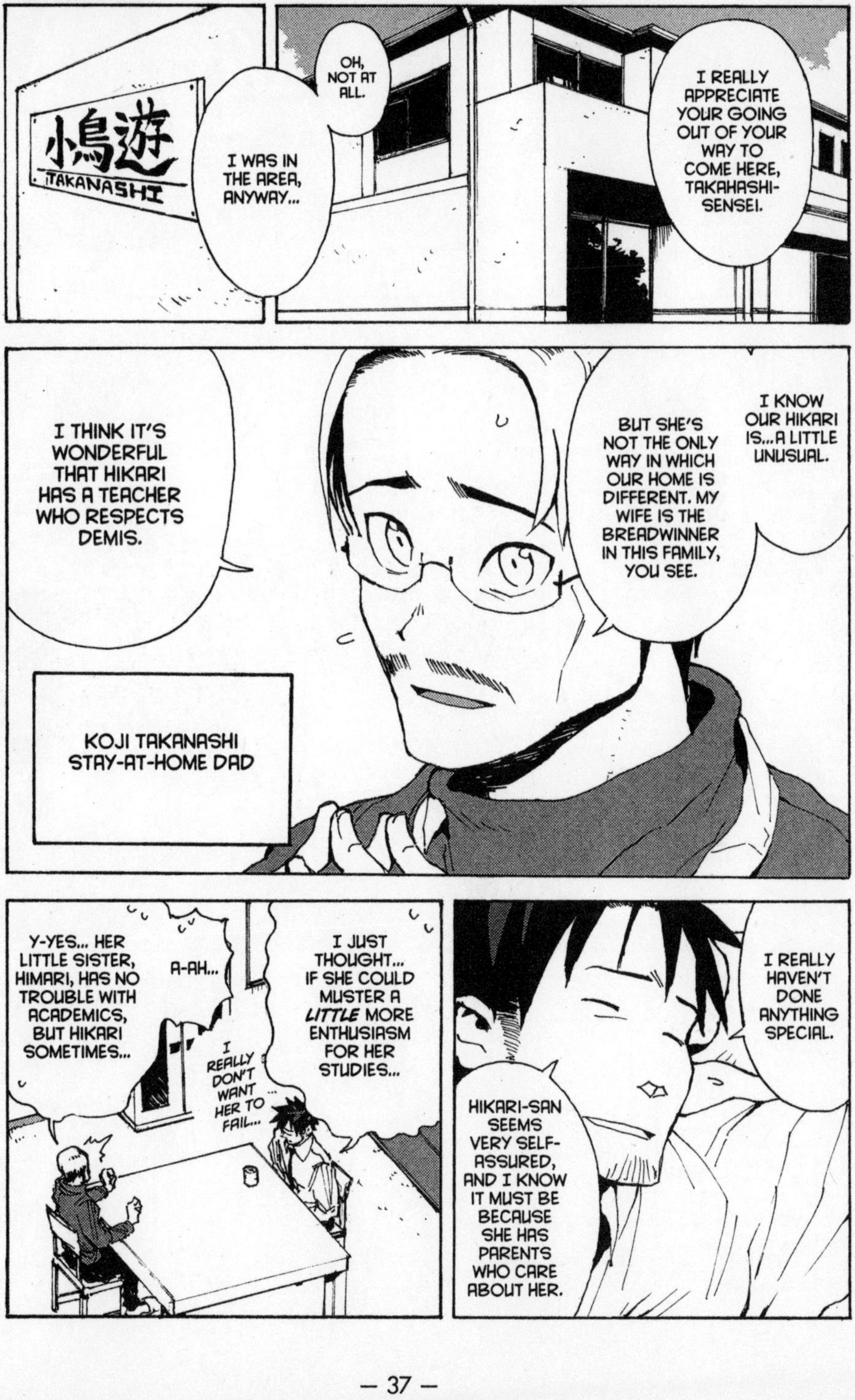
I REALLY APPRECIATE YOUR GOING OUT OF YOUR WAY TO COME HERE, TAKAHASHI-SENSEI.
OH, NOT AT ALL.
I WAS IN THE AREA, ANYWAY...
小鳥遊
TAKANASHI
I KNOW OUR HIKARI IS...A LITTLE UNUSUAL.
BUT SHE'S NOT THE ONLY WAY IN WHICH OUR HOME IS DIFFERENT. MY WIFE IS THE BREADWINNER IN THIS FAMILY, YOU SEE.
I THINK IT'S WONDERFUL THAT HIKARI HAS A TEACHER WHO RESPECTS DEMIS.
KOJI TAKANASHI
STAY-AT-HOME DAD
I REALLY HAVEN'T DONE ANYTHING SPECIAL.
HIKARI-SAN SEEMS VERY SELF-ASSURED, AND I KNOW IT MUST BE BECAUSE SHE HAS PARENTS WHO CARE ABOUT HER.
I JUST THOUGHT... IF SHE COULD MUSTER A *LITTLE* MORE ENTHUSIASM FOR HER STUDIES...
A-AH...
Y-YES... HER LITTLE SISTER, HIMARI, HAS NO TROUBLE WITH ACADEMICS, BUT HIKARI SOMETIMES...
I REALLY DON'T WANT HER TO FAIL...

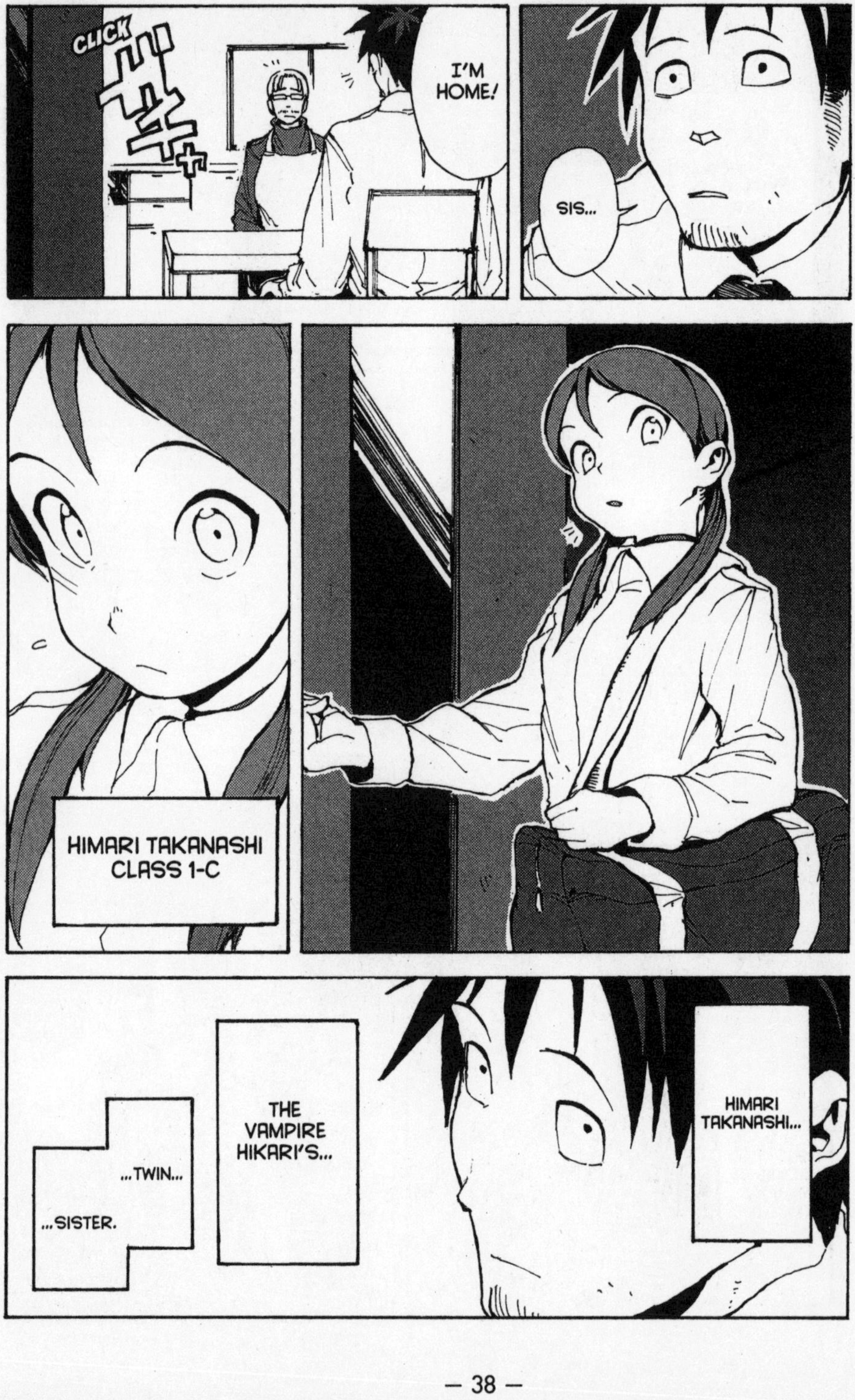
SIS...
I'M HOME!
CLICK
HIMARI TAKANASHI CLASS 1-C
HIMARI TAKANASHI...
THE VAMPIRE HIKARI'S...
...TWIN...
...SISTER.

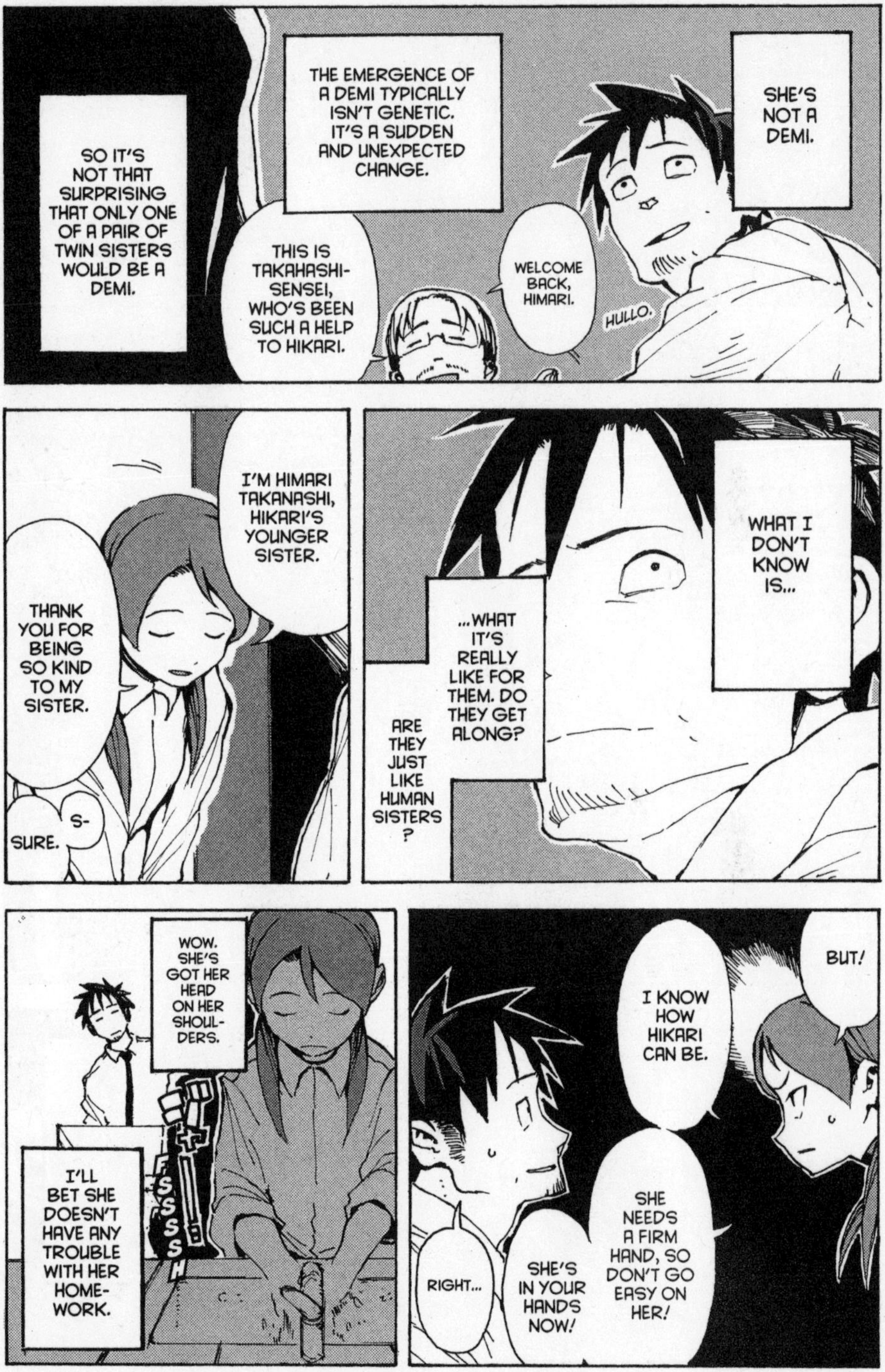
SHE'S NOT A DEMI.
THE EMERGENCE OF A DEMI TYPICALLY ISN'T GENETIC. IT'S A SUDDEN AND UNEXPECTED CHANGE.
SO IT'S NOT THAT SURPRISING THAT ONLY ONE OF A PAIR OF TWIN SISTERS WOULD BE A DEMI.
WELCOME BACK, HIMARI.
HULLO.
THIS IS TAKAHASHI-SENSEI, WHO'S BEEN SUCH A HELP TO HIKARI.
WHAT I DON'T KNOW IS...
...WHAT IT'S REALLY LIKE FOR THEM. DO THEY GET ALONG?
ARE THEY JUST LIKE HUMAN SISTERS?
I'M HIMARI TAKANASHI, HIKARI'S YOUNGER SISTER.
THANK YOU FOR BEING SO KIND TO MY SISTER.
S-SURE.
BUT!
I KNOW HOW HIKARI CAN BE.
SHE NEEDS A FIRM HAND, SO DON'T GO EASY ON HER!
SHE'S IN YOUR HANDS NOW!
RIGHT...
WOW. SHE'S GOT HER HEAD ON HER SHOULDERS.
FSSSSH
I'LL BET SHE DOESN'T HAVE ANY TROUBLE WITH HER HOMEWORK.

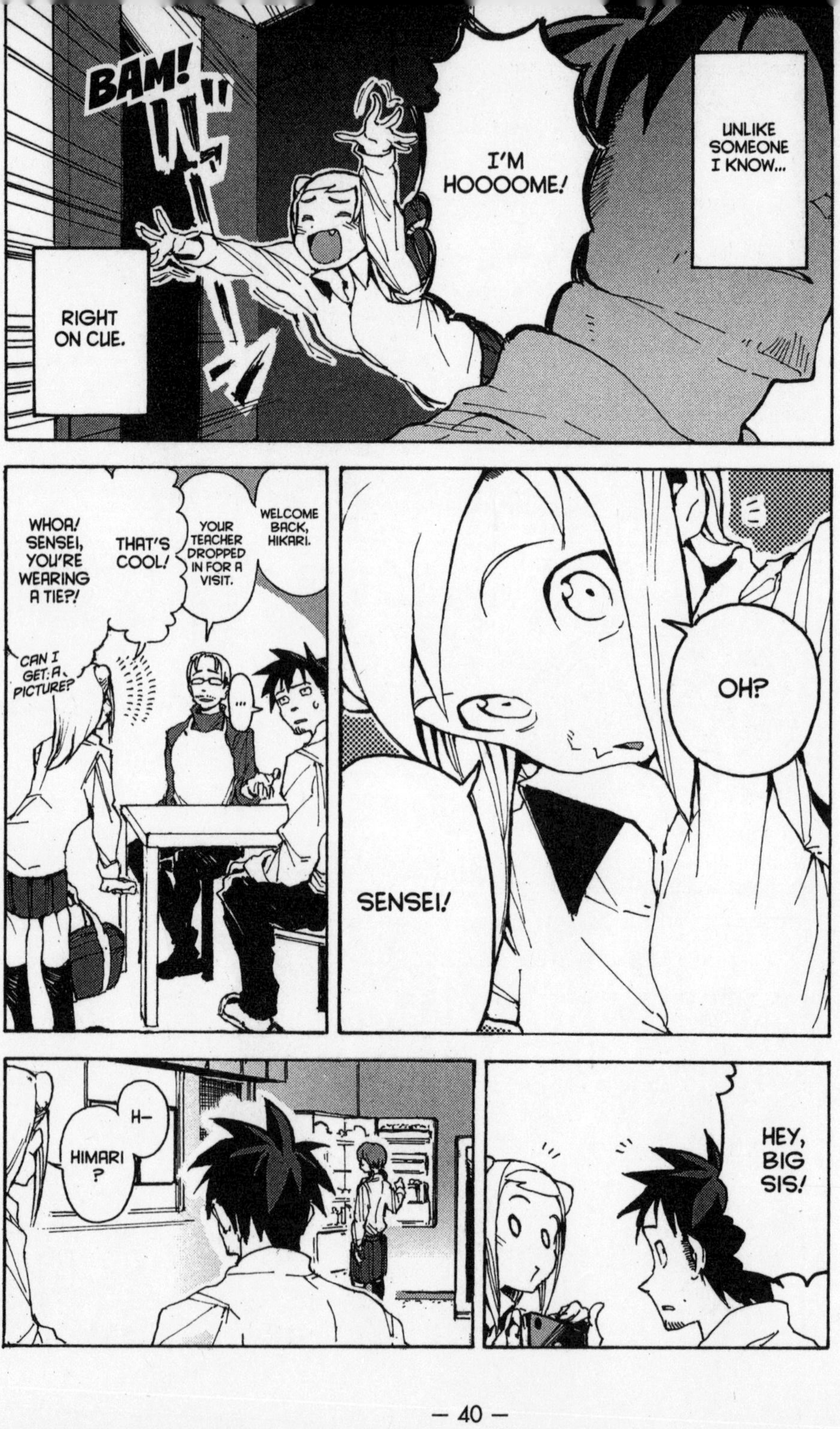
UNLIKE SOMEONE I KNOW...
I'M HOOOOME!
BAM!
RIGHT ON CUE.
OH?
SENSEI!
WELCOME BACK, HIKARI.
YOUR TEACHER DROPPED IN FOR A VISIT.
THAT'S COOL!
WHOA! SENSEI, YOU'RE WEARING A TIE?!
...
CAN I GET A PICTURE?
HEY, BIG SIS!
H— HIMARI?

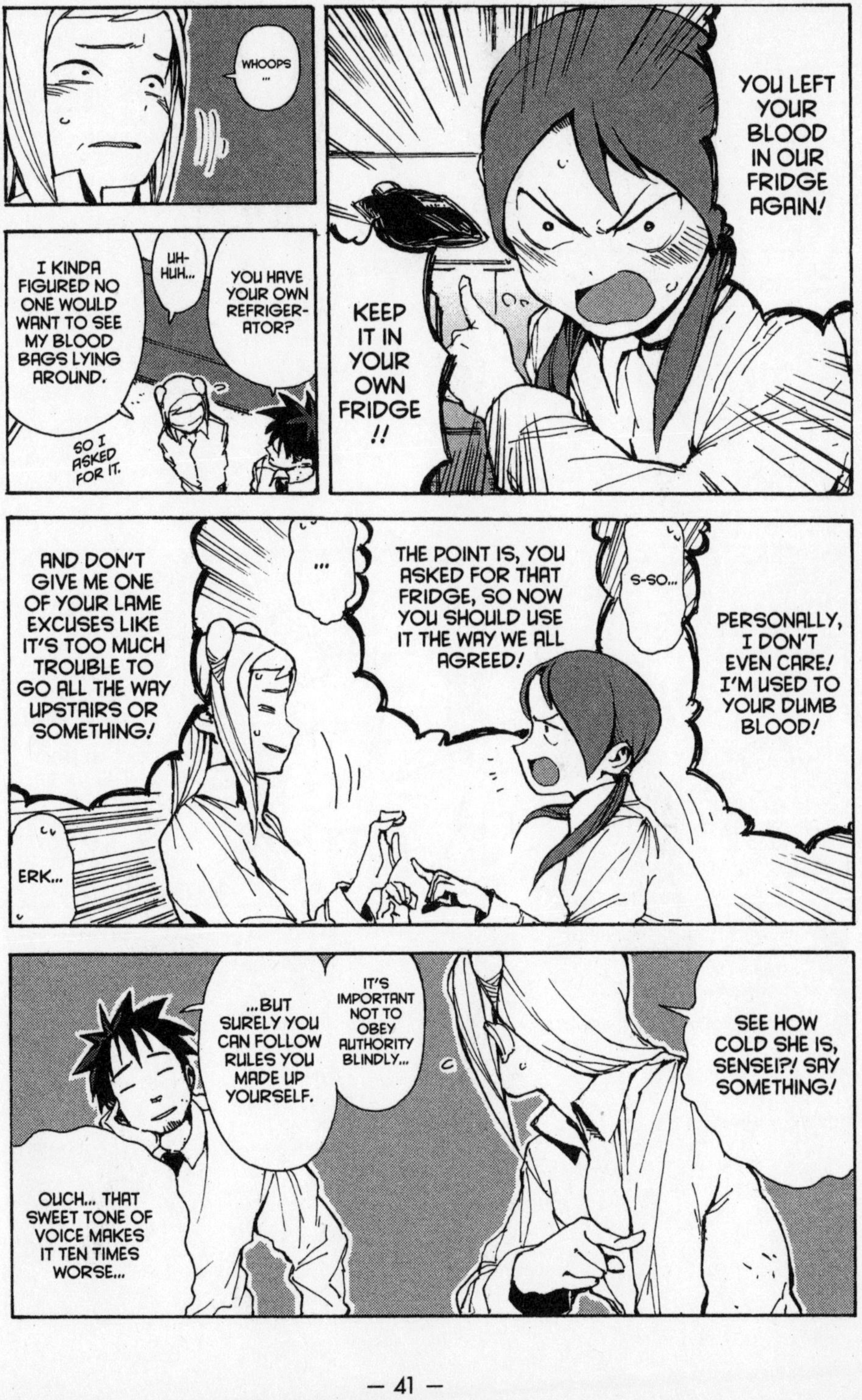
YOU LEFT YOUR BLOOD IN OUR FRIDGE AGAIN!
KEEP IT IN YOUR OWN FRIDGE !!
WHOOPS ...
YOU HAVE YOUR OWN REFRIGER-ATOR?
UH-HUH...
I KINDA FIGURED NO ONE WOULD WANT TO SEE MY BLOOD BAGS LYING AROUND.
SO I ASKED FOR IT.
PERSONALLY, I DON'T EVEN CARE! I'M USED TO YOUR DUMB BLOOD!
S-SO...
THE POINT IS, YOU ASKED FOR THAT FRIDGE, SO NOW YOU SHOULD USE IT THE WAY WE ALL AGREED!
...
AND DON'T GIVE ME ONE OF YOUR LAME EXCUSES LIKE IT'S TOO MUCH TROUBLE TO GO ALL THE WAY UPSTAIRS OR SOMETHING!
ERK...
SEE HOW COLD SHE IS, SENSEI?! SAY SOMETHING!
IT'S IMPORTANT NOT TO OBEY AUTHORITY BLINDLY...
...BUT SURELY YOU CAN FOLLOW RULES YOU MADE UP YOURSELF.
OUCH... THAT SWEET TONE OF VOICE MAKES IT TEN TIMES WORSE...

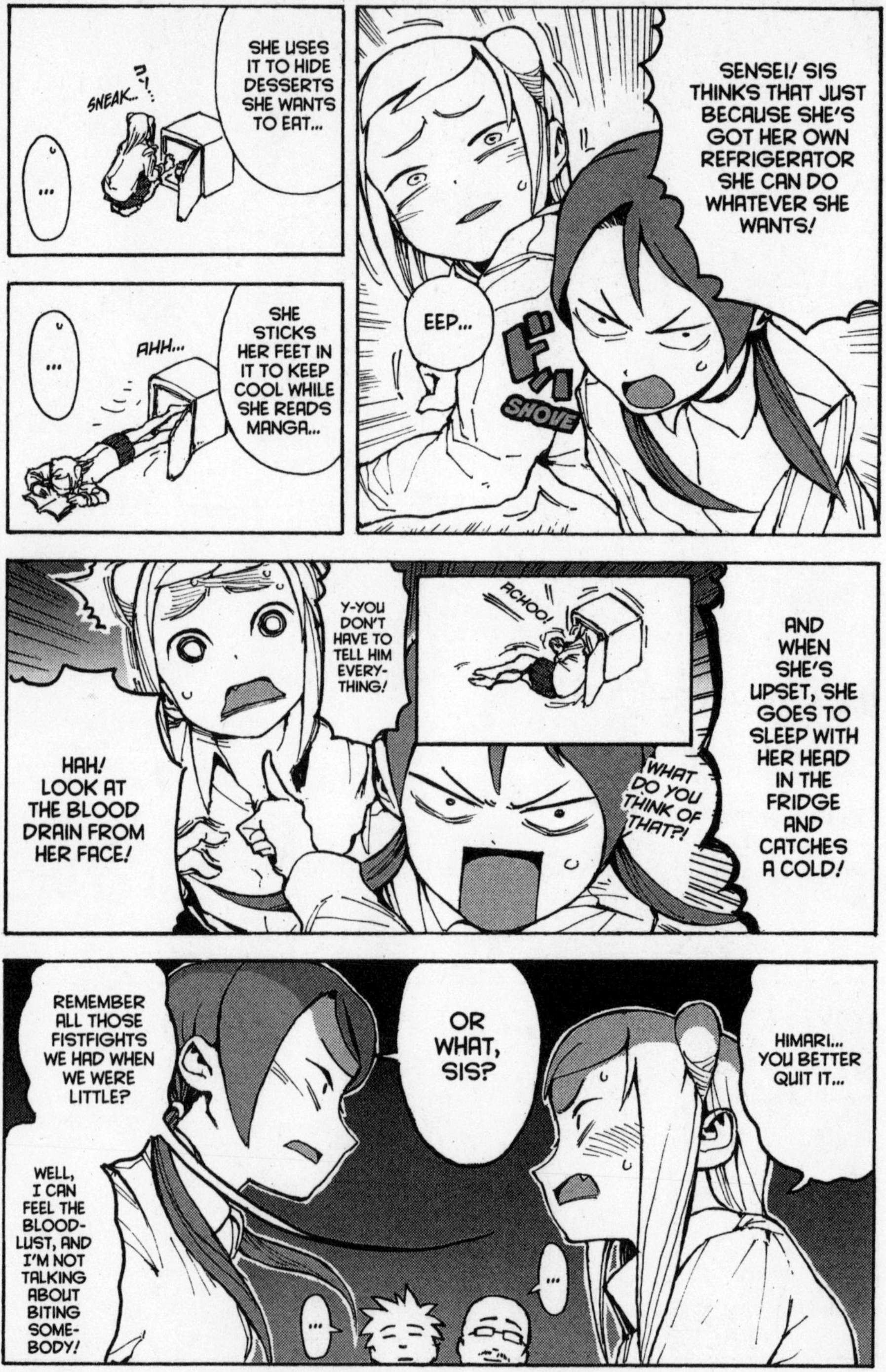
SENSEI! SIS THINKS THAT JUST BECAUSE SHE'S GOT HER OWN REFRIGERATOR SHE CAN DO WHATEVER SHE WANTS!
SHOVE
EEP...
SHE USES IT TO HIDE DESSERTS SHE WANTS TO EAT...
SNEAK...
...
SHE STICKS HER FEET IN IT TO KEEP COOL WHILE SHE READS MANGA...
AHH...
...
AND WHEN SHE'S UPSET, SHE GOES TO SLEEP WITH HER HEAD IN THE FRIDGE AND CATCHES A COLD!
WHAT DO YOU THINK OF THAT?!
ACHOO!
Y-YOU DON'T HAVE TO TELL HIM EVERYTHING!
HAH! LOOK AT THE BLOOD DRAIN FROM HER FACE!
HIMARI... YOU BETTER QUIT IT...
OR WHAT, SIS?
REMEMBER ALL THOSE FISTFIGHTS WE HAD WHEN WE WERE LITTLE?
WELL, I CAN FEEL THE BLOOD-LUST, AND I'M NOT TALKING ABOUT BITING SOME-BODY!
...
...

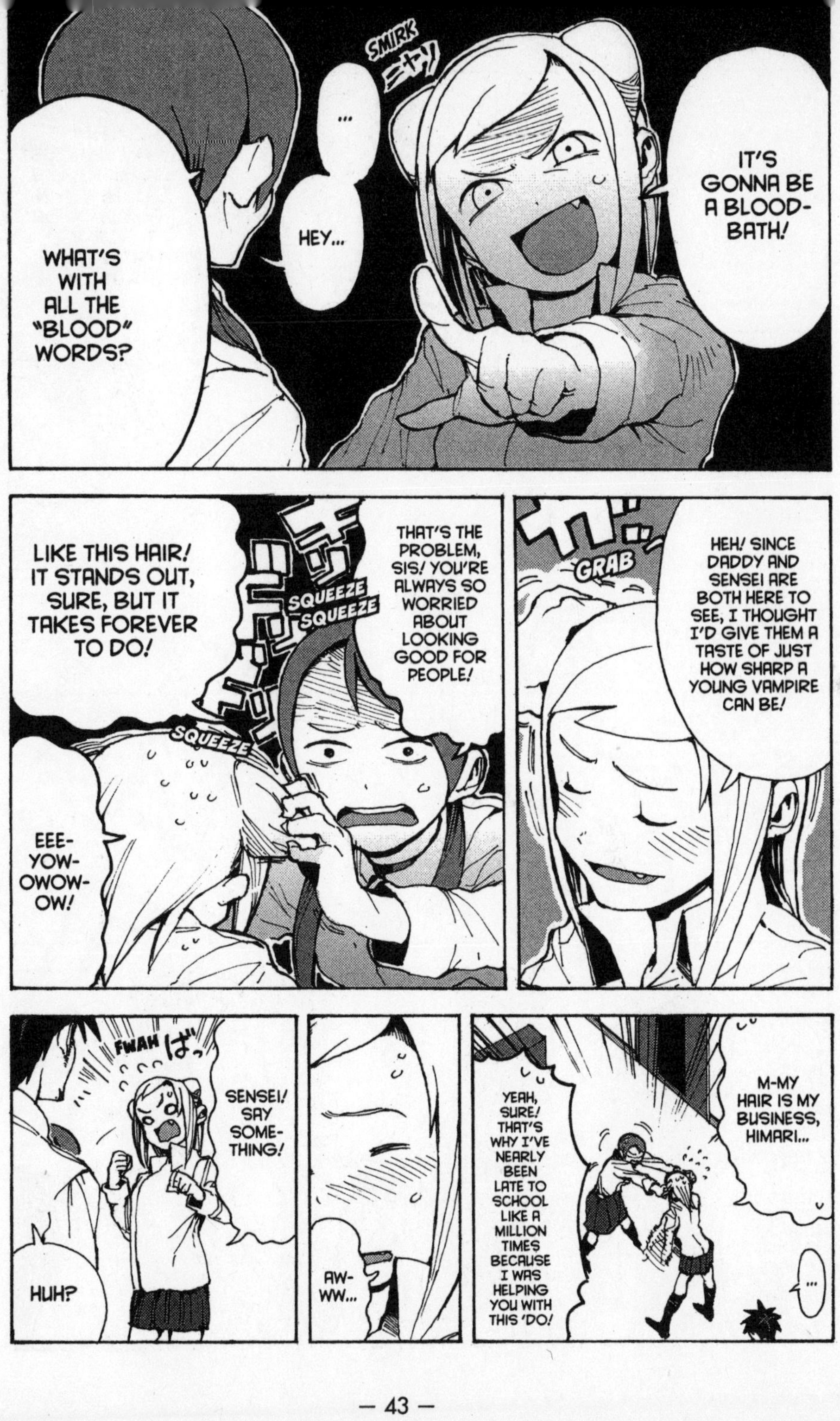
IT'S GONNA BE A BLOOD-BATH!
SMIRK
...
HEY...
WHAT'S WITH ALL THE "BLOOD" WORDS?
GRAB
HEH! SINCE DADDY AND SENSEI ARE BOTH HERE TO SEE, I THOUGHT I'D GIVE THEM A TASTE OF JUST HOW SHARP A YOUNG VAMPIRE CAN BE!
THAT'S THE PROBLEM, SIS! YOU'RE ALWAYS SO WORRIED ABOUT LOOKING GOOD FOR PEOPLE!
SQUEEZE SQUEEZE
LIKE THIS HAIR! IT STANDS OUT, SURE, BUT IT TAKES FOREVER TO DO!
SQUEEZE
EEE-YOW-OWOW-OW!
M-MY HAIR IS MY BUSINESS, HIMARI...
YEAH, SURE! THAT'S WHY I'VE NEARLY BEEN LATE TO SCHOOL LIKE A MILLION TIMES BECAUSE I WAS HELPING YOU WITH THIS 'DO!
...
AW-WW...
FWAH
SENSEI! SAY SOMETHING!
HUH?

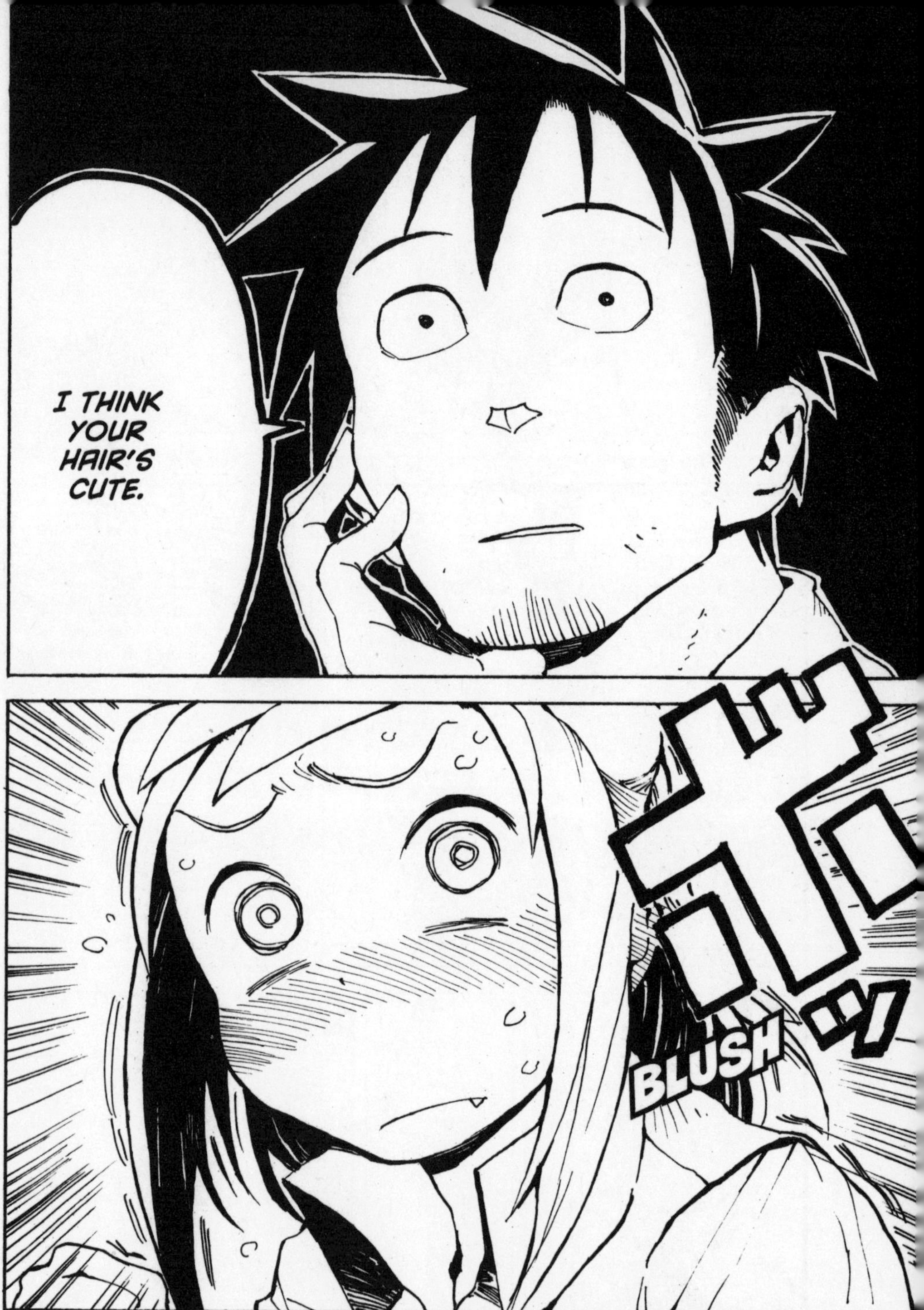
I THINK YOUR HAIR'S CUTE.
BLUSH

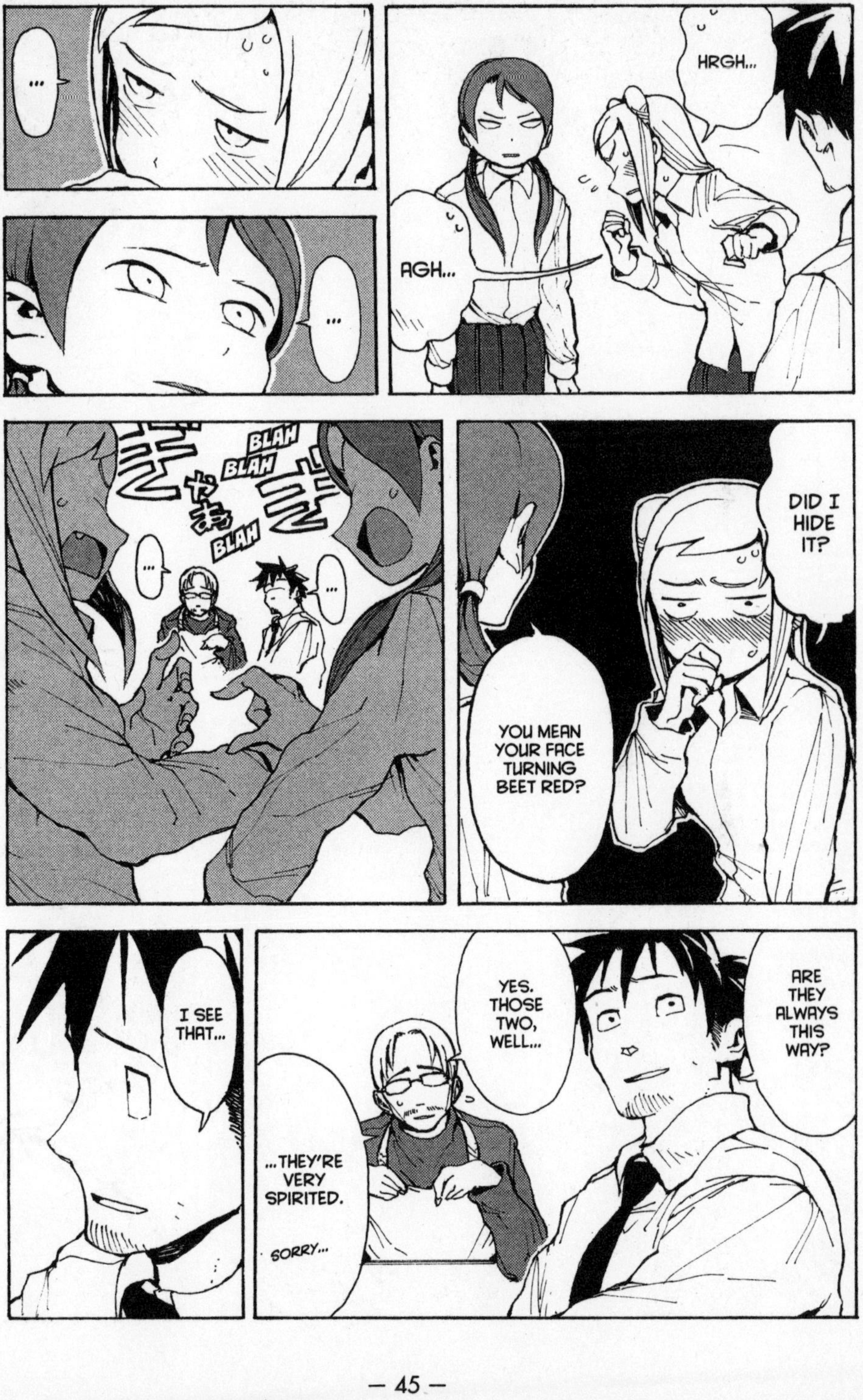
HRGH...
AGH...
...
...
DID I HIDE IT?
YOU MEAN YOUR FACE TURNING BEET RED?
BLAH BLAH BLAH
...
...
ARE THEY ALWAYS THIS WAY?
YES. THOSE TWO, WELL...
...THEY'RE VERY SPIRITED.
SORRY...
I SEE THAT...

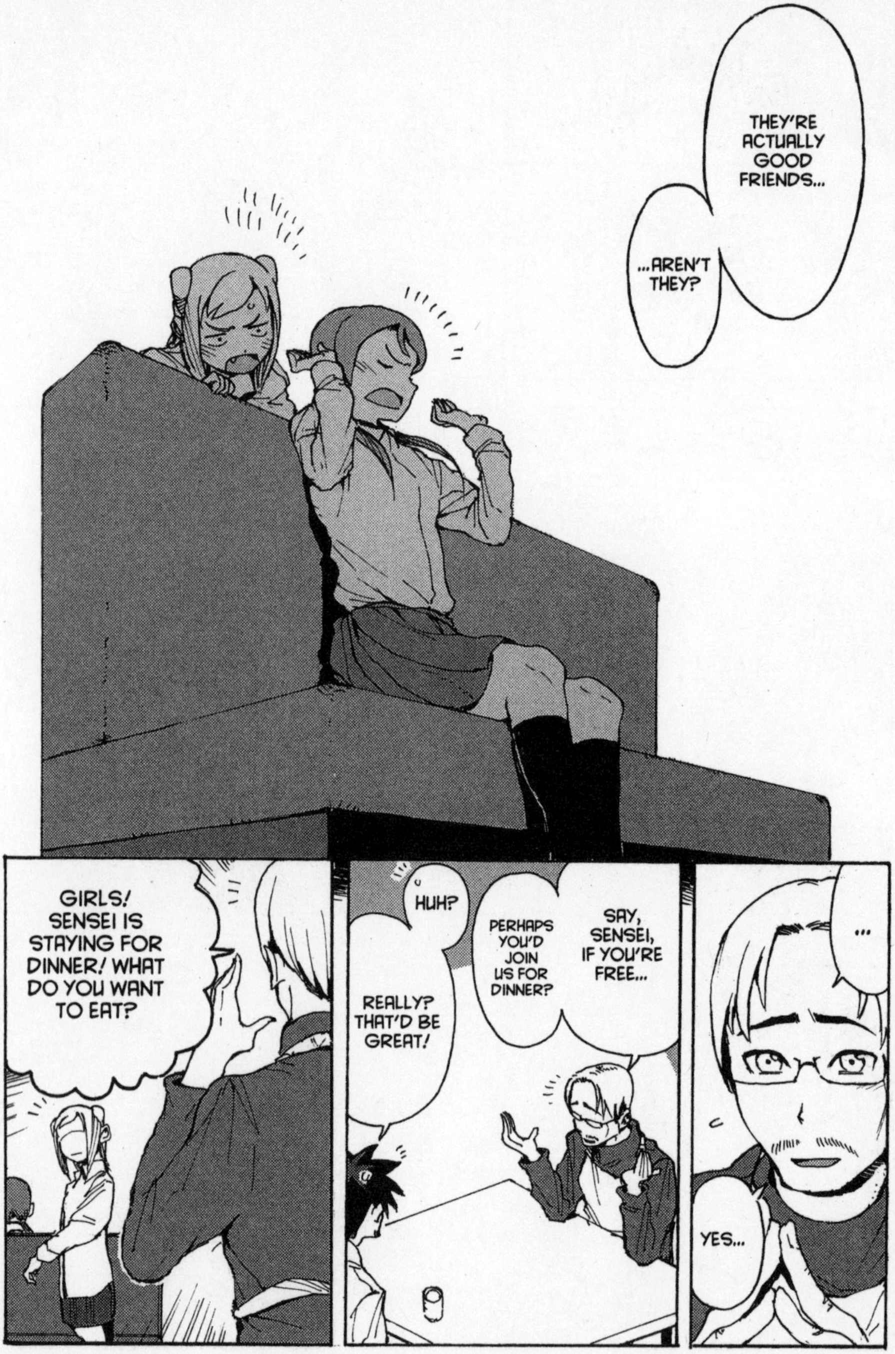
THEY'RE ACTUALLY GOOD FRIENDS...
...AREN'T THEY?
...
YES...
SAY, SENSEI, IF YOU'RE FREE...
PERHAPS YOU'D JOIN US FOR DINNER?
HUH?
REALLY? THAT'D BE GREAT!
GIRLS! SENSEI IS STAYING FOR DINNER! WHAT DO YOU WANT TO EAT?

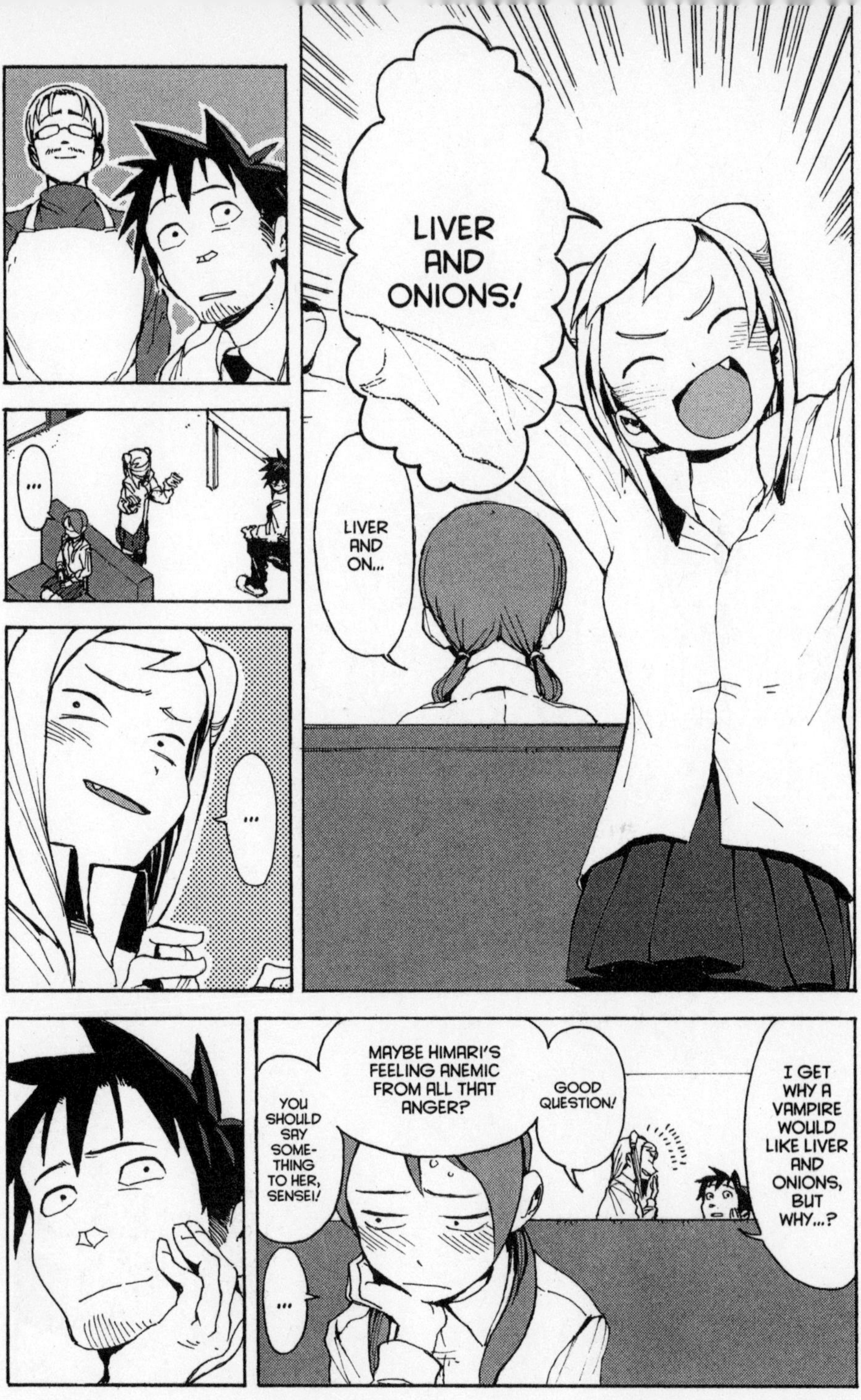
LIVER AND ONIONS!
LIVER AND ON...
...
...
I GET WHY A VAMPIRE WOULD LIKE LIVER AND ONIONS, BUT WHY...?
GOOD QUESTION!
MAYBE HIMARI'S FEELING ANEMIC FROM ALL THAT ANGER?
YOU SHOULD SAY SOME-THING TO HER, SENSEI!
...

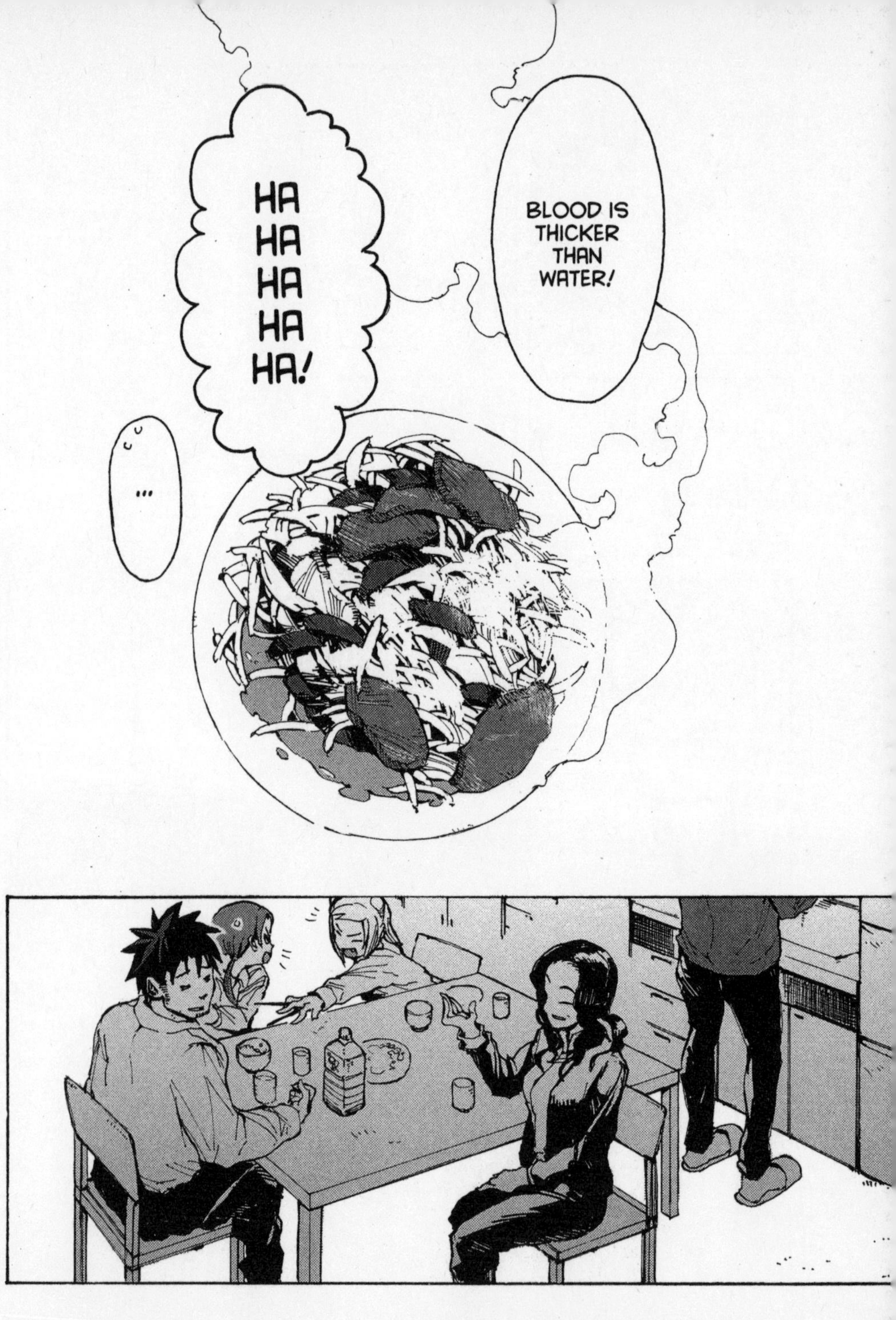
BLOOD IS THICKER THAN WATER!
HA HA HA HA HA!
...

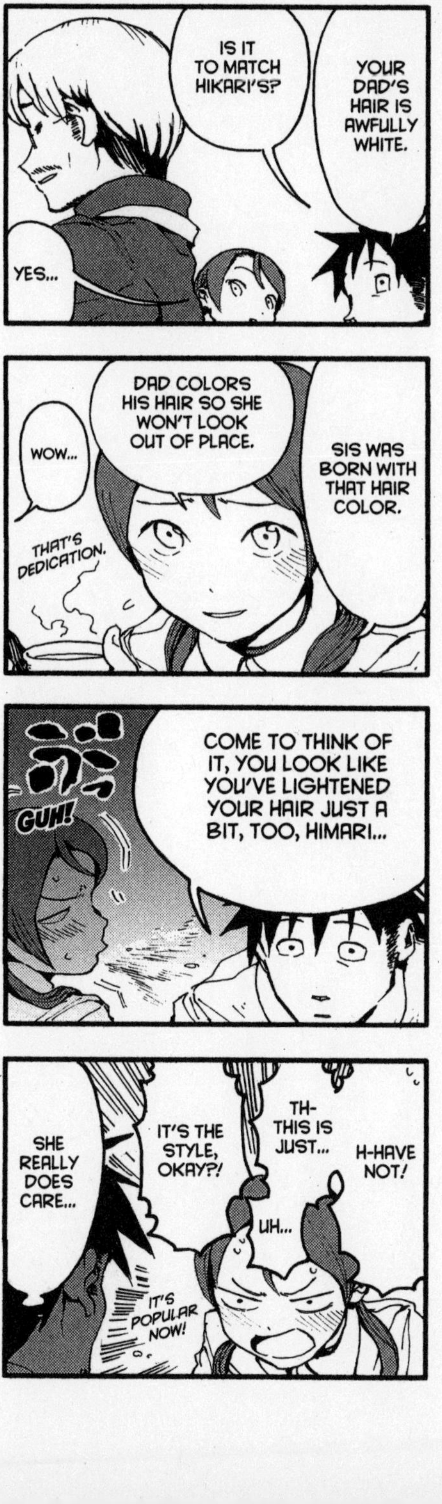
YOUR DAD'S HAIR IS AWFULLY WHITE.
IS IT TO MATCH HIKARI'S?
YES...
SIS WAS BORN WITH THAT HAIR COLOR.
DAD COLORS HIS HAIR SO SHE WON'T LOOK OUT OF PLACE.
WOW...
THAT'S DEDICATION.
COME TO THINK OF IT, YOU LOOK LIKE YOU'VE LIGHTENED YOUR HAIR JUST A BIT, TOO, HIMARI...
ぶっ
GUH!
H-HAVE NOT!
TH- THIS IS JUST...
IT'S THE STYLE, OKAY?!
UH...
SHE REALLY DOES CARE...
IT'S POPULAR NOW!

INTERVIEWS WITH MONSTER GIRLS

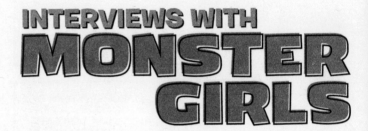

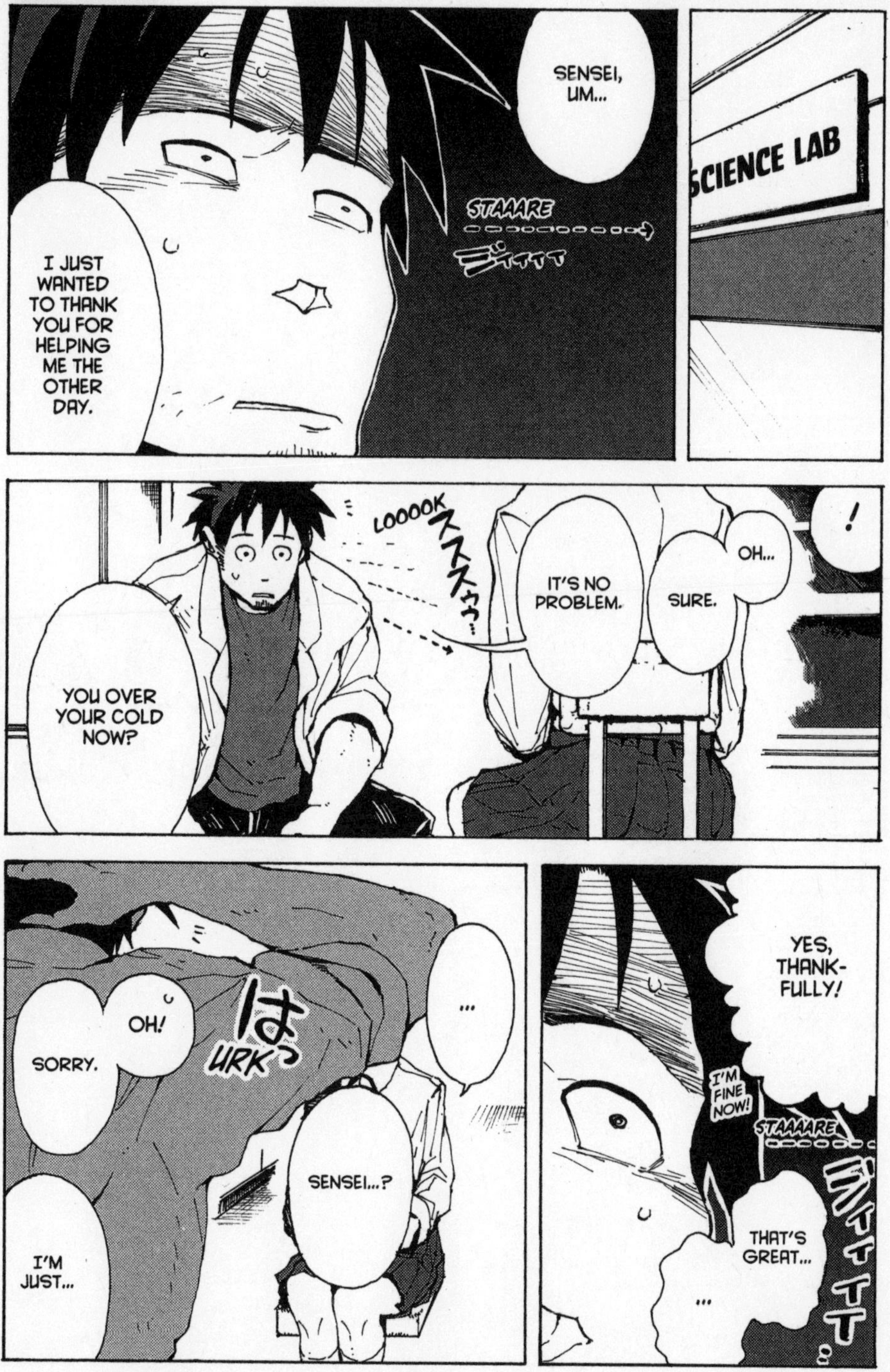
SCIENCE LAB
SENSEI, UM...
STAARE
I JUST WANTED TO THANK YOU FOR HELPING ME THE OTHER DAY.
!
OH... SURE.
IT'S NO PROBLEM.
LOOOOK
YOU OVER YOUR COLD NOW?
YES, THANKFULLY!
I'M FINE NOW!
STAAAARE
THAT'S GREAT...
...
...
URK
OH! SORRY.
SENSEI...?
I'M JUST...

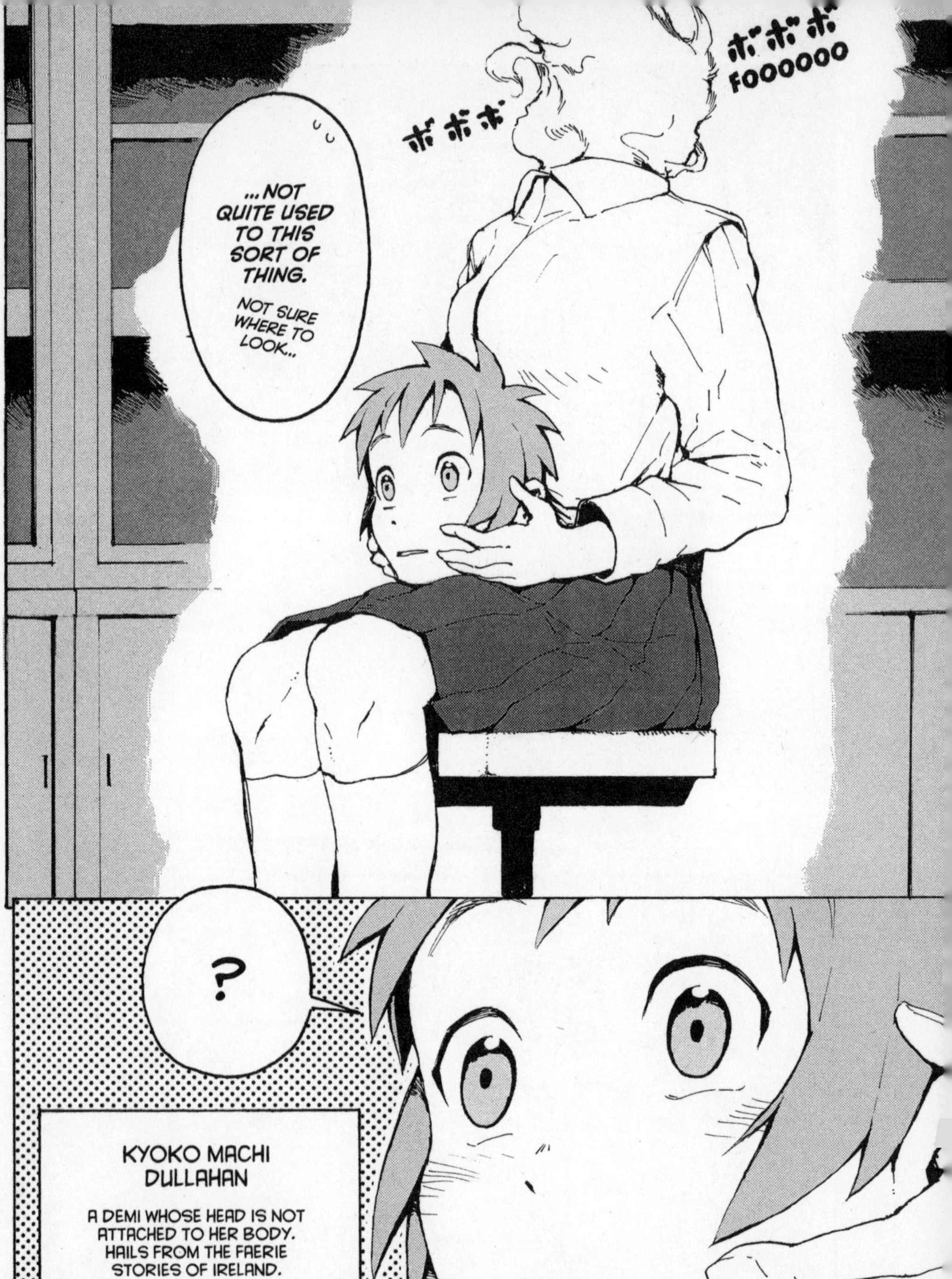
ボボボ
FOOOOOO
ボボボ
...NOT QUITE USED TO THIS SORT OF THING.
NOT SURE WHERE TO LOOK...
?
KYOKO MACHI
DULLAHAN
A DEMI WHOSE HEAD IS NOT ATTACHED TO HER BODY. HAILS FROM THE FAERIE STORIES OF IRELAND.

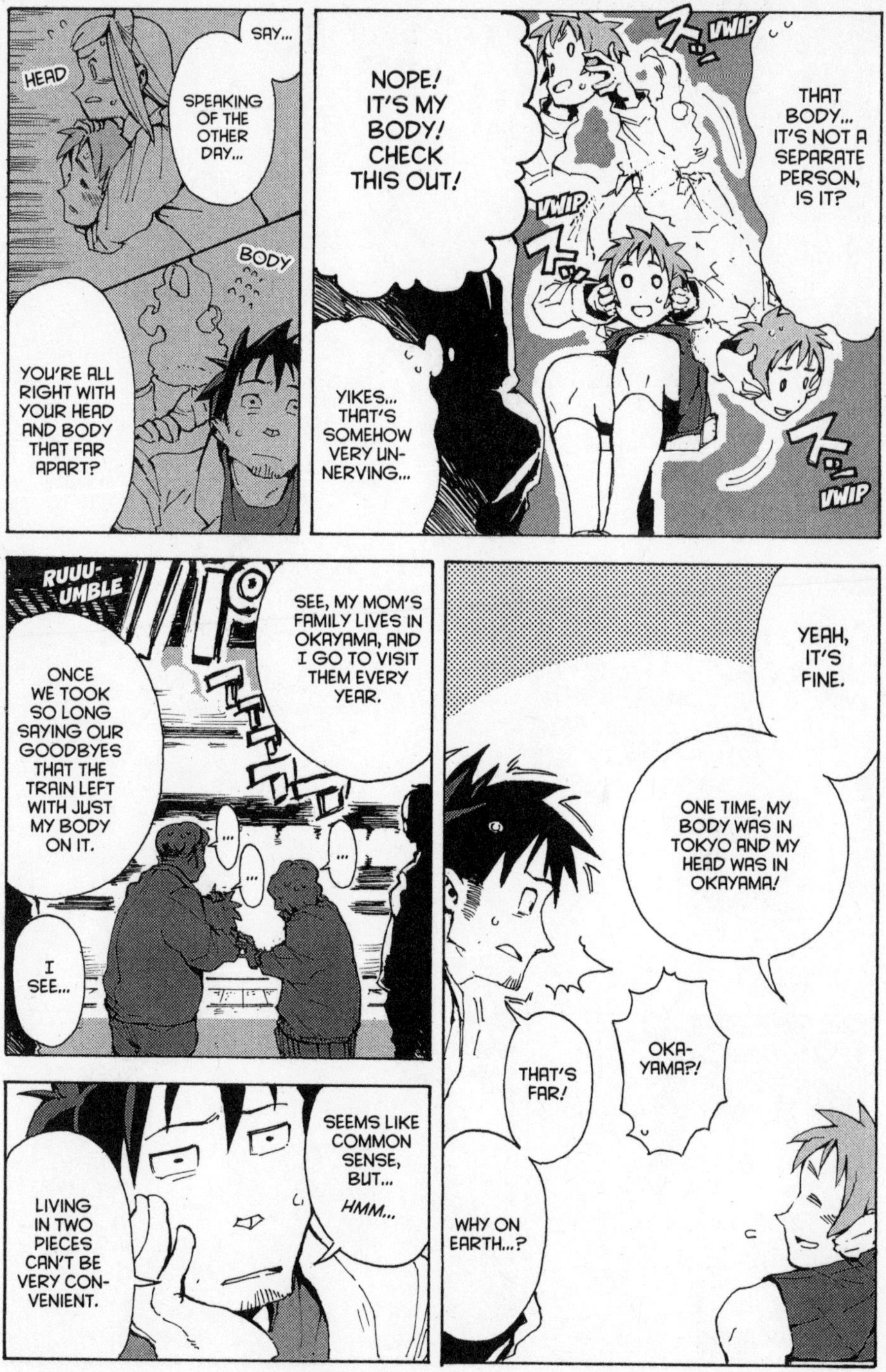
VWIP
THAT BODY... IT'S NOT A SEPARATE PERSON, IS IT?
NOPE! IT'S MY BODY! CHECK THIS OUT!
VWIP
VWIP
YIKES... THAT'S SOMEHOW VERY UN-NERVING...
SAY...
SPEAKING OF THE OTHER DAY...
HEAD
BODY
YOU'RE ALL RIGHT WITH YOUR HEAD AND BODY THAT FAR APART?
YEAH, IT'S FINE.
ONE TIME, MY BODY WAS IN TOKYO AND MY HEAD WAS IN OKAYAMA!
OKA-YAMA?!
THAT'S FAR!
WHY ON EARTH...?
RUUU-UMBLE
SEE, MY MOM'S FAMILY LIVES IN OKAYAMA, AND I GO TO VISIT THEM EVERY YEAR.
ONCE WE TOOK SO LONG SAYING OUR GOODBYES THAT THE TRAIN LEFT WITH JUST MY BODY ON IT.
...
...
...
I SEE...
SEEMS LIKE COMMON SENSE, BUT...
HMM...
LIVING IN TWO PIECES CAN'T BE VERY CON-VENIENT.

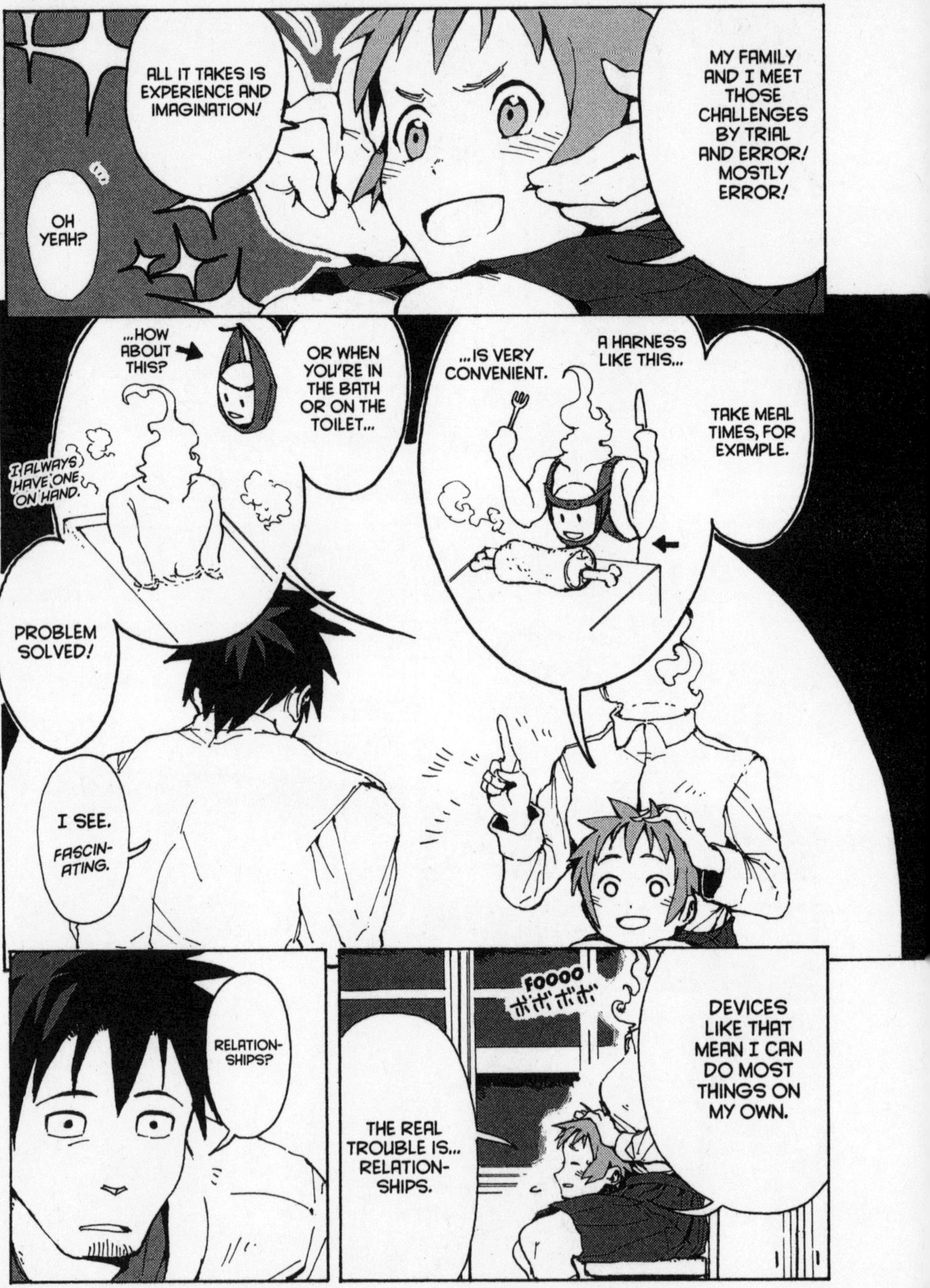
MY FAMILY AND I MEET THOSE CHALLENGES BY TRIAL AND ERROR! MOSTLY ERROR!
ALL IT TAKES IS EXPERIENCE AND IMAGINATION!
OH YEAH?
TAKE MEAL TIMES, FOR EXAMPLE.
A HARNESS LIKE THIS...
...IS VERY CONVENIENT.
OR WHEN YOU'RE IN THE BATH OR ON THE TOILET...
...HOW ABOUT THIS?
I ALWAYS HAVE ONE ON HAND.
PROBLEM SOLVED!
I SEE.
FASCIN-ATING.
FOOOO
ボボボボ
DEVICES LIKE THAT MEAN I CAN DO MOST THINGS ON MY OWN.
THE REAL TROUBLE IS... RELATION-SHIPS.
RELATION-SHIPS?

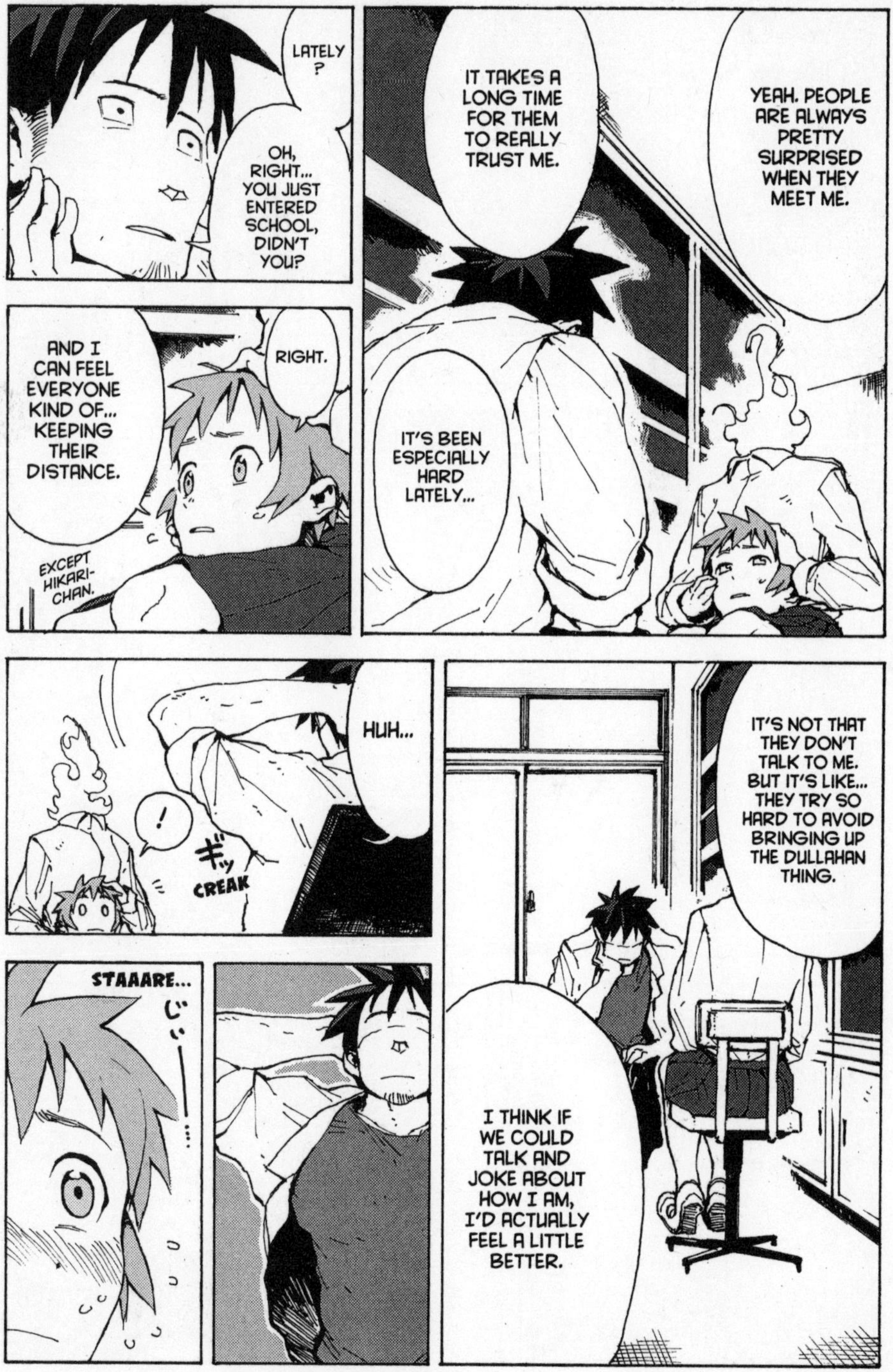
YEAH. PEOPLE ARE ALWAYS PRETTY SURPRISED WHEN THEY MEET ME.
IT TAKES A LONG TIME FOR THEM TO REALLY TRUST ME.
IT'S BEEN ESPECIALLY HARD LATELY...
LATELY?
OH, RIGHT... YOU JUST ENTERED SCHOOL, DIDN'T YOU?
RIGHT.
AND I CAN FEEL EVERYONE KIND OF... KEEPING THEIR DISTANCE.
EXCEPT HIKARI-CHAN.
IT'S NOT THAT THEY DON'T TALK TO ME. BUT IT'S LIKE... THEY TRY SO HARD TO AVOID BRINGING UP THE DULLAHAN THING.
I THINK IF WE COULD TALK AND JOKE ABOUT HOW I AM, I'D ACTUALLY FEEL A LITTLE BETTER.
HUH...
!
ギッ
CREAK
STAAARE...
じぃーー…

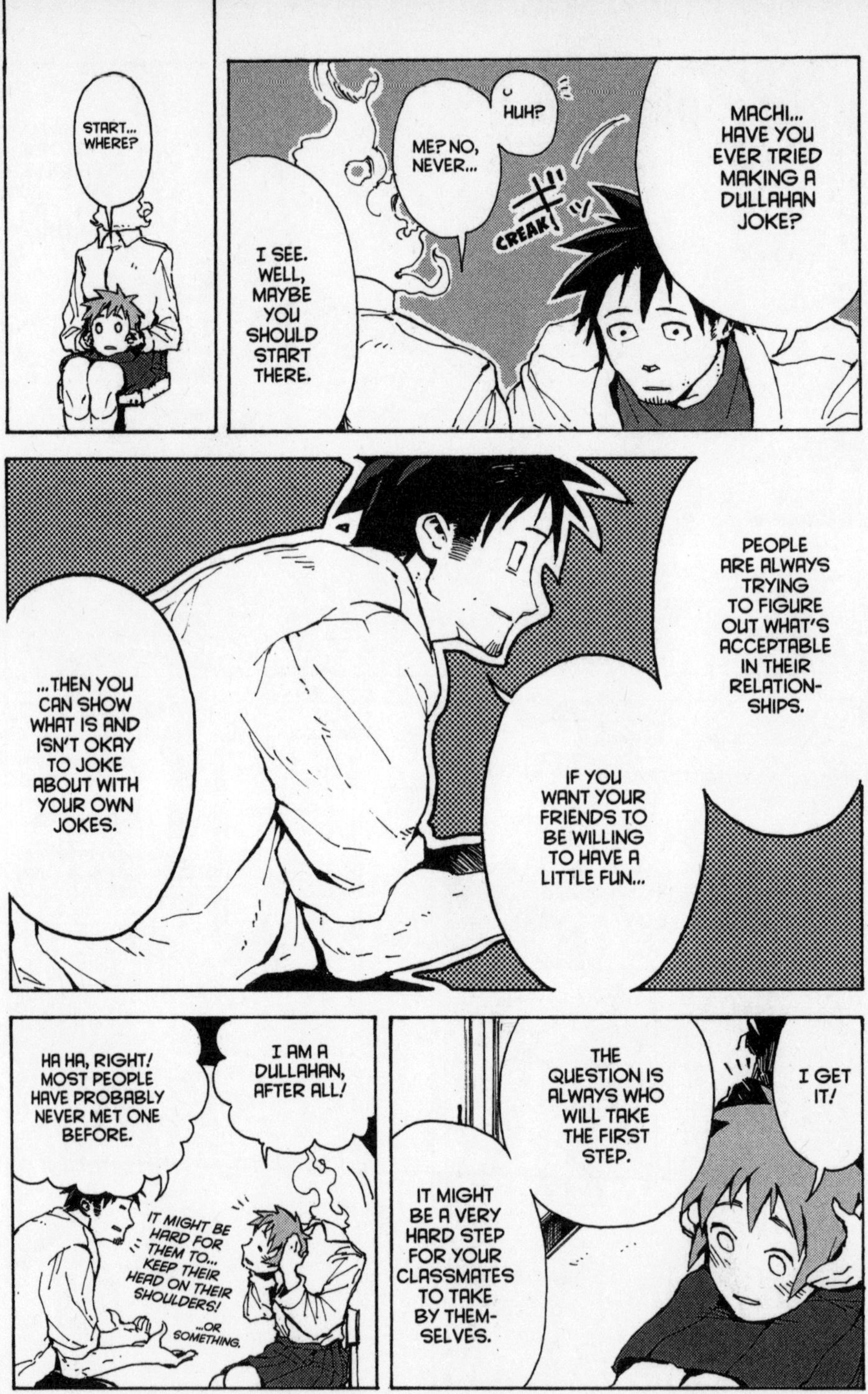
MACHI... HAVE YOU EVER TRIED MAKING A DULLAHAN JOKE?
ギッ
CREAK
HUH?
ME? NO, NEVER...
I SEE. WELL, MAYBE YOU SHOULD START THERE.
START... WHERE?
PEOPLE ARE ALWAYS TRYING TO FIGURE OUT WHAT'S ACCEPTABLE IN THEIR RELATION-SHIPS.
IF YOU WANT YOUR FRIENDS TO BE WILLING TO HAVE A LITTLE FUN...
...THEN YOU CAN SHOW WHAT IS AND ISN'T OKAY TO JOKE ABOUT WITH YOUR OWN JOKES.
I GET IT!
THE QUESTION IS ALWAYS WHO WILL TAKE THE FIRST STEP.
IT MIGHT BE A VERY HARD STEP FOR YOUR CLASSMATES TO TAKE BY THEM-SELVES.
I AM A DULLAHAN, AFTER ALL!
HA HA, RIGHT! MOST PEOPLE HAVE PROBABLY NEVER MET ONE BEFORE.
IT MIGHT BE HARD FOR THEM TO... KEEP THEIR HEAD ON THEIR SHOULDERS!
...OR SOMETHING.

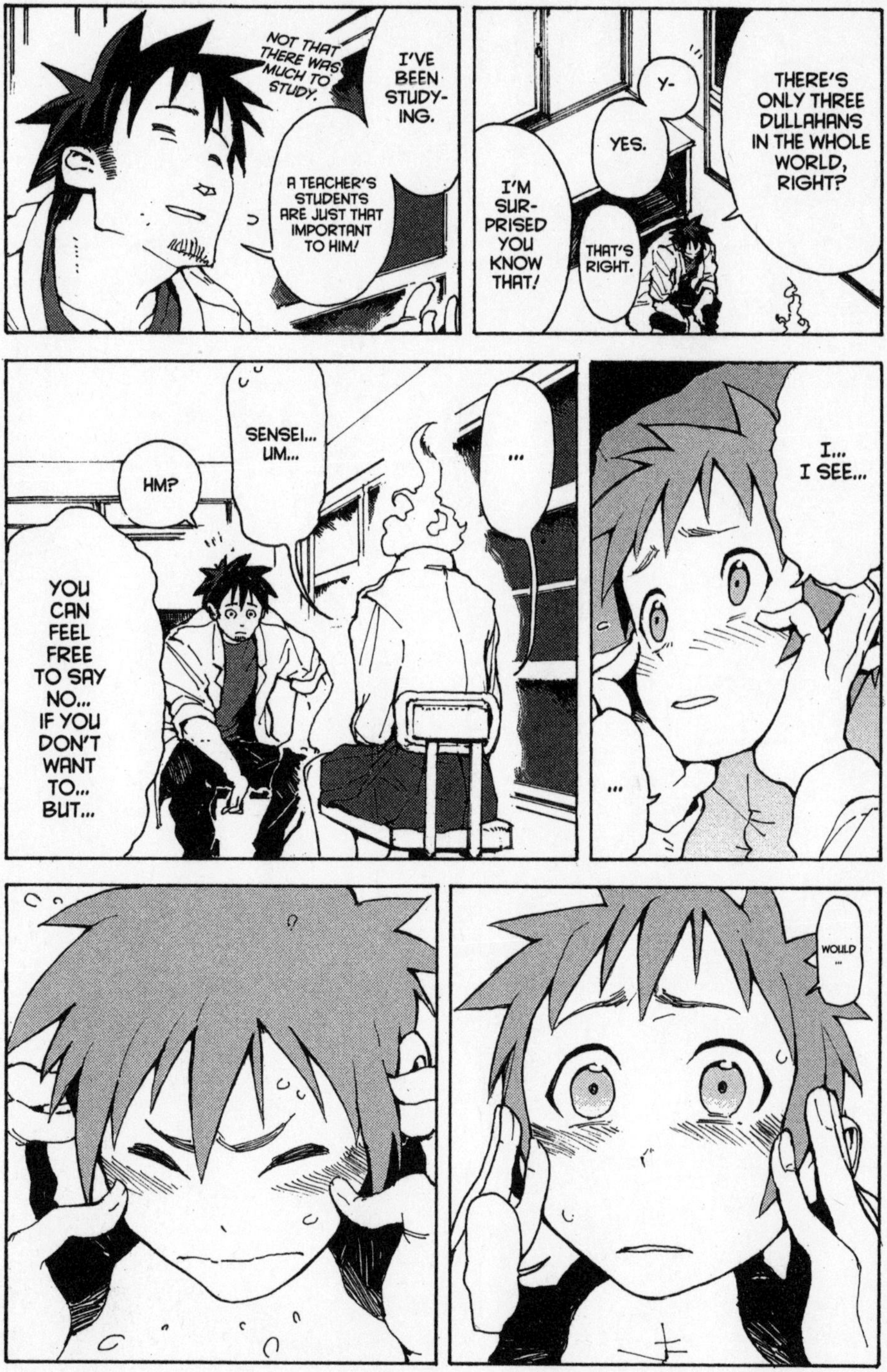
THERE'S ONLY THREE DULLAHANS IN THE WHOLE WORLD, RIGHT?
Y-
YES.
I'M SURPRISED YOU KNOW THAT!
THAT'S RIGHT.
I'VE BEEN STUDYING.
NOT THAT THERE WAS MUCH TO STUDY.
A TEACHER'S STUDENTS ARE JUST THAT IMPORTANT TO HIM!
I... I SEE...
...
...
SENSEI... UM...
HM?
YOU CAN FEEL FREE TO SAY NO... IF YOU DON'T WANT TO... BUT...
WOULD...

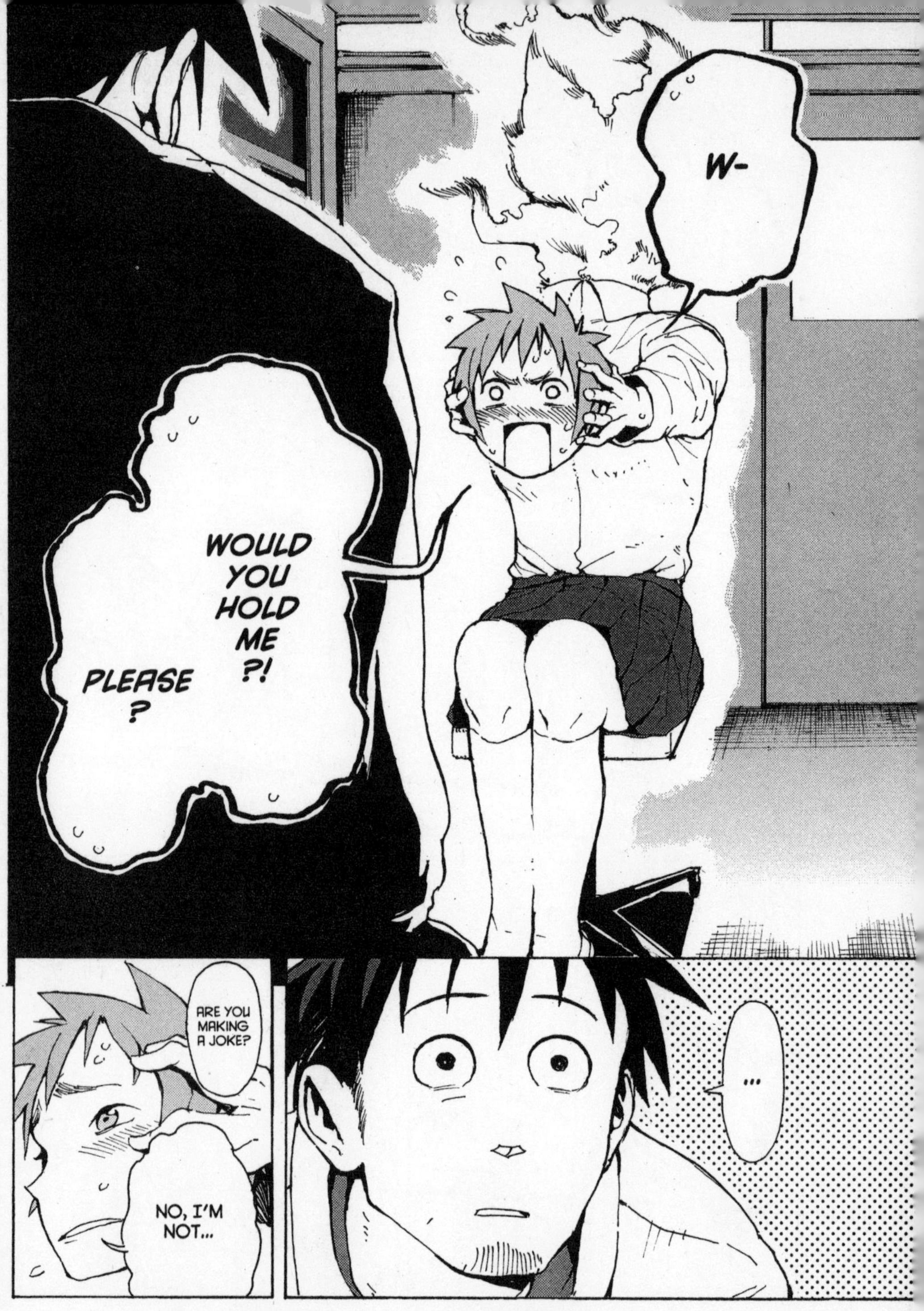
W-
WOULD YOU HOLD ME ?!
PLEASE ?
...
ARE YOU MAKING A JOKE?
NO, I'M NOT...

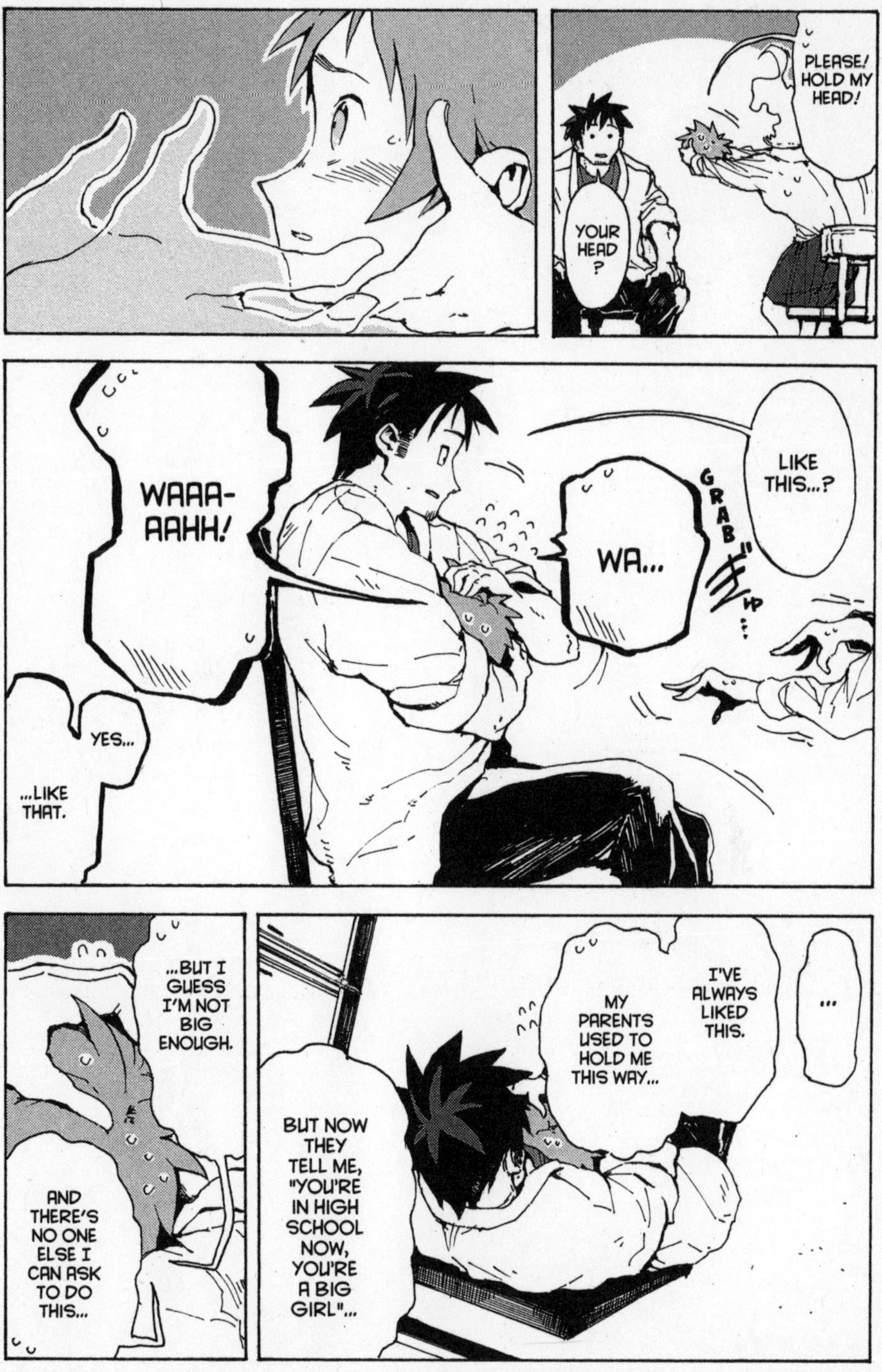
PLEASE! HOLD MY HEAD!
YOUR HEAD?
LIKE THIS...?
GRAB
WA...
WAAA-AAHH!
YES...
...LIKE THAT.
...
I'VE ALWAYS LIKED THIS.
MY PARENTS USED TO HOLD ME THIS WAY...
BUT NOW THEY TELL ME, "YOU'RE IN HIGH SCHOOL NOW, YOU'RE A BIG GIRL"...
...BUT I GUESS I'M NOT BIG ENOUGH.
AND THERE'S NO ONE ELSE I CAN ASK TO DO THIS...

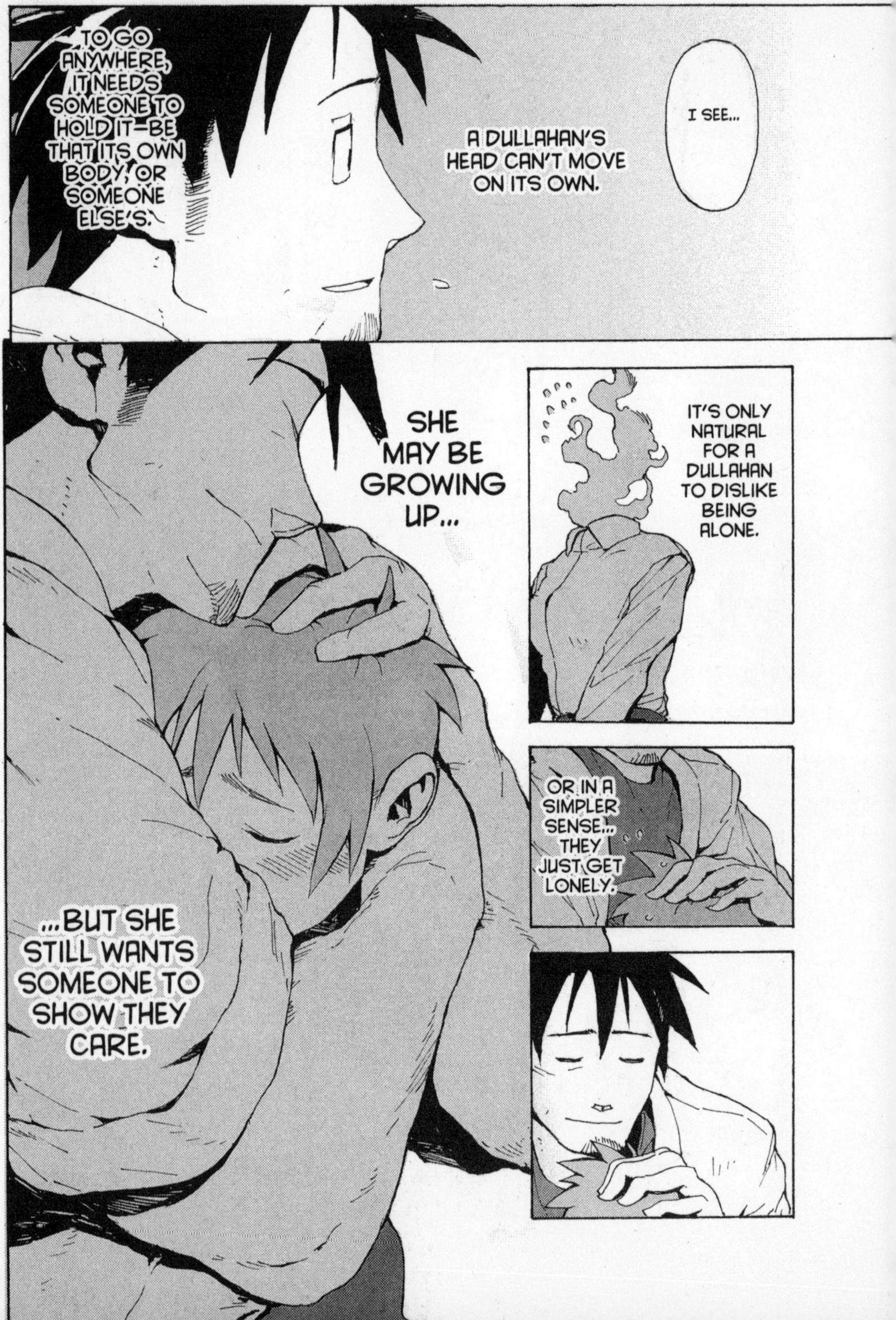
I SEE...
A DULLAHAN'S HEAD CAN'T MOVE ON ITS OWN.
TO GO ANYWHERE, IT NEEDS SOMEONE TO HOLD IT—BE THAT ITS OWN BODY, OR SOMEONE ELSE'S.
IT'S ONLY NATURAL FOR A DULLAHAN TO DISLIKE BEING ALONE.
OR IN A SIMPLER SENSE... THEY JUST GET LONELY.
SHE MAY BE GROWING UP...
...BUT SHE STILL WANTS SOMEONE TO SHOW THEY CARE.

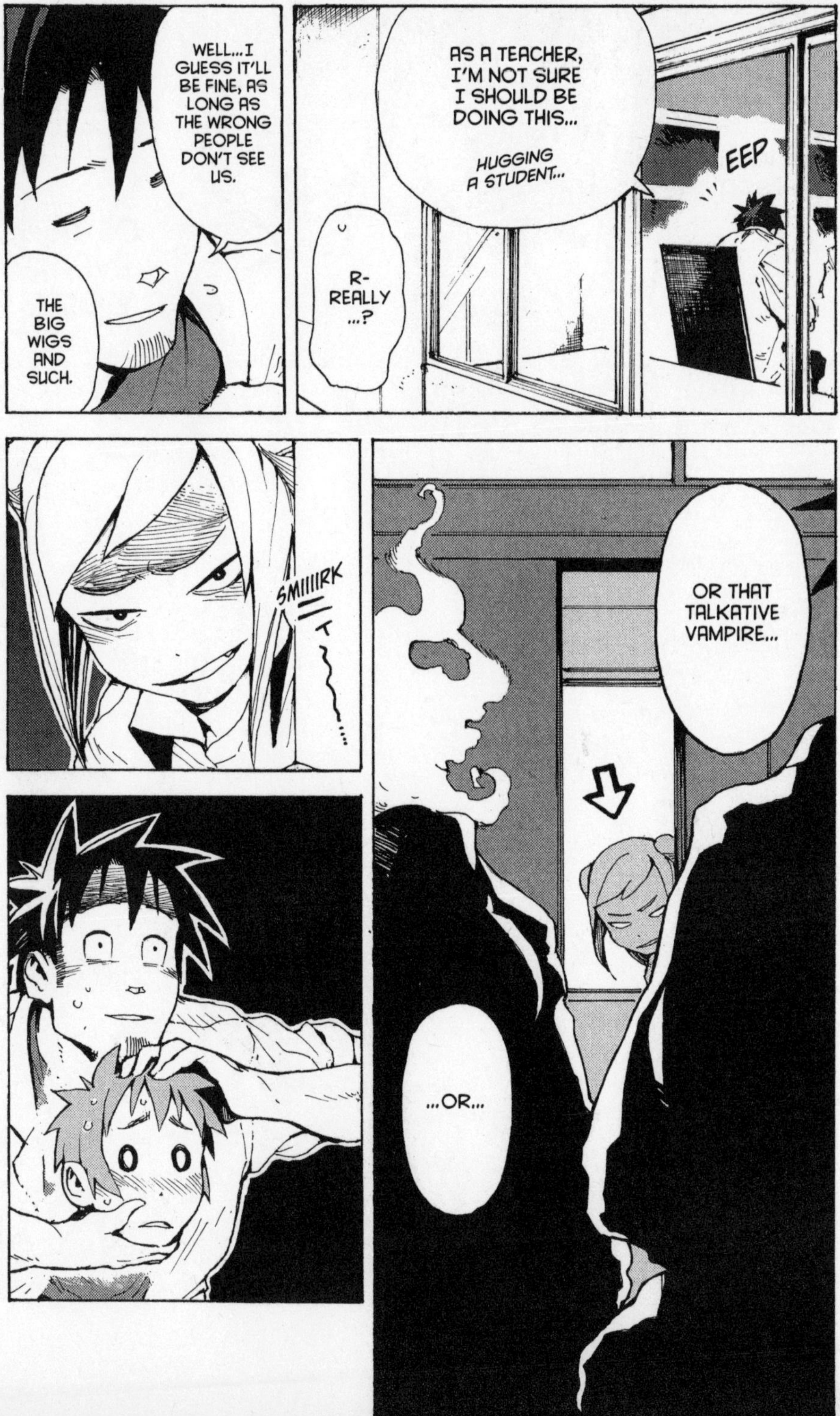

AS A TEACHER, I'M NOT SURE I SHOULD BE DOING THIS...
HUGGING A STUDENT...
EEP
R-REALLY ...?
WELL...I GUESS IT'LL BE FINE, AS LONG AS THE WRONG PEOPLE DON'T SEE US.
THE BIG WIGS AND SUCH.
OR THAT TALKATIVE VAMPIRE...
...OR...
SMIIIIRK

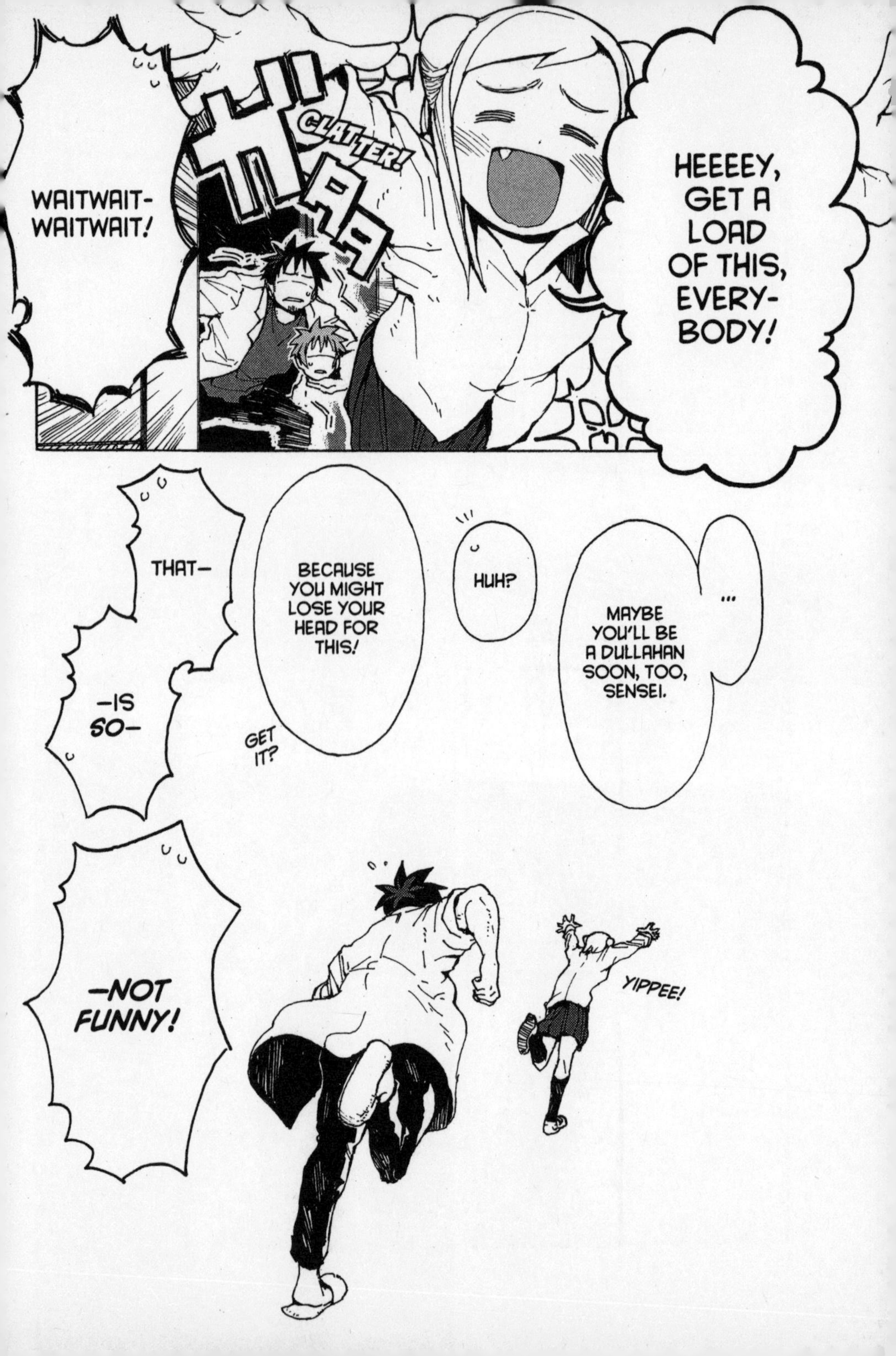
HEEEEY, GET A LOAD OF THIS, EVERY-BODY!
CLATTER!
WAITWAIT-WAITWAIT!
...
MAYBE YOU'LL BE A DULLAHAN SOON, TOO, SENSEI.
HUH?
BECAUSE YOU MIGHT LOSE YOUR HEAD FOR THIS!
GET IT?
THAT-
-IS SO-
YIPPEE!
-NOT FUNNY!

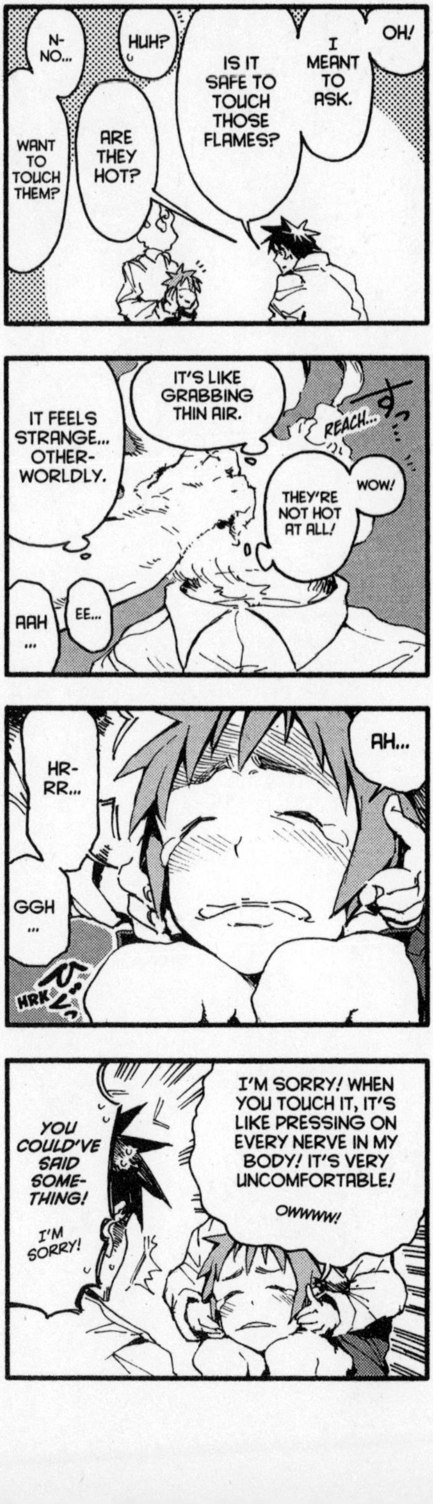
OH!
I MEANT TO ASK.
IS IT SAFE TO TOUCH THOSE FLAMES?
HUH?
N-NO...
ARE THEY HOT?
WANT TO TOUCH THEM?
すっ
REACH...
WOW!
THEY'RE NOT HOT AT ALL!
IT'S LIKE GRABBING THIN AIR.
IT FEELS STRANGE... OTHER-WORLDLY.
EE...
AAH...
AH...
HR-RR...
GGH...
ぴくっ
HRK
I'M SORRY! WHEN YOU TOUCH IT, IT'S LIKE PRESSING ON EVERY NERVE IN MY BODY! IT'S VERY UNCOMFORTABLE!
OWWWW!
YOU COULD'VE SAID SOME-THING!
I'M SORRY!

INTERVIEWS WITH MONSTER GIRLS

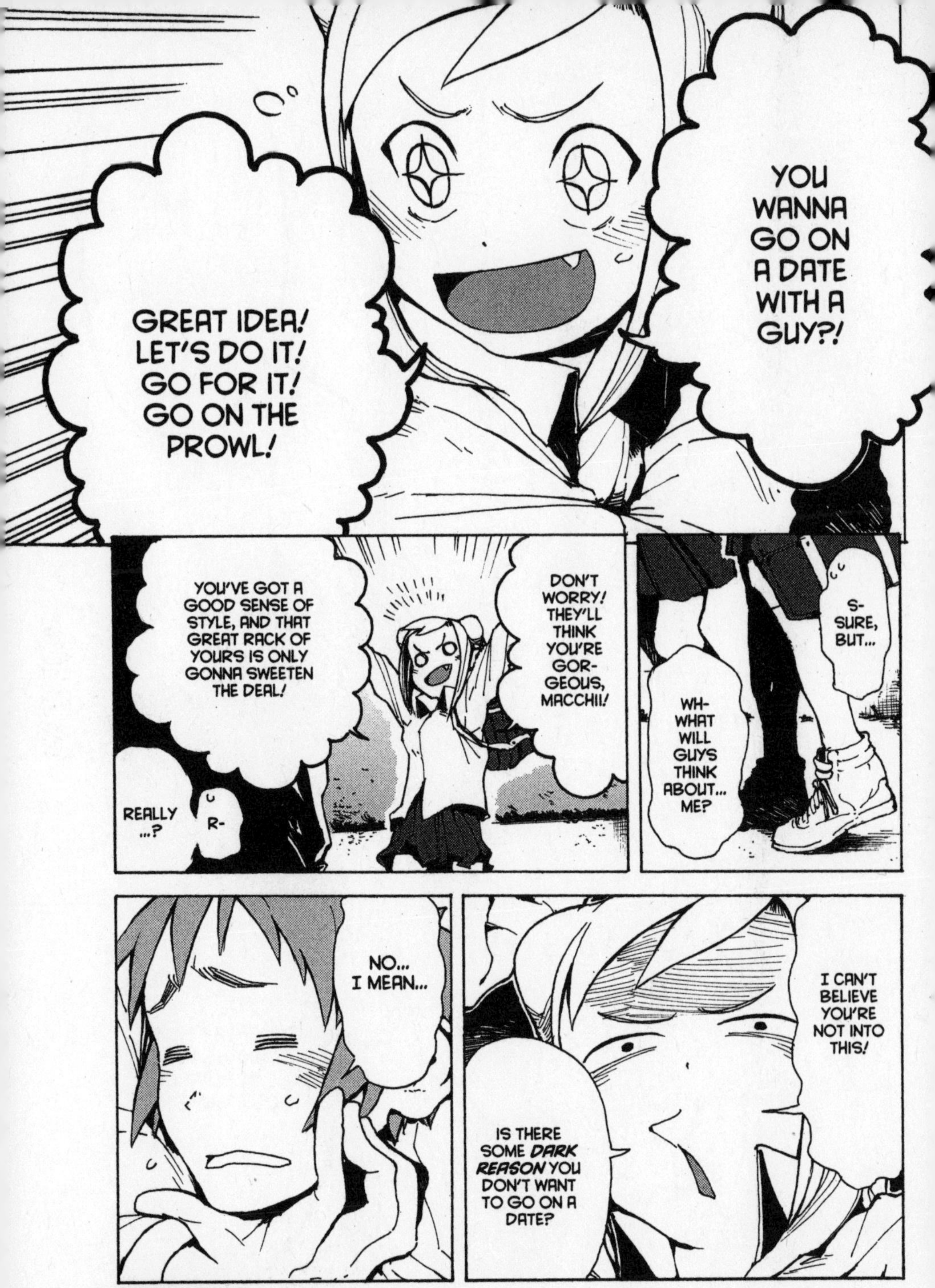
YOU WANNA GO ON A DATE WITH A GUY?!
GREAT IDEA! LET'S DO IT! GO FOR IT! GO ON THE PROWL!
S-SURE, BUT...
WH-WHAT WILL GUYS THINK ABOUT... ME?
DON'T WORRY! THEY'LL THINK YOU'RE GORGEOUS, MACCHII!
YOU'VE GOT A GOOD SENSE OF STYLE, AND THAT GREAT RACK OF YOURS IS ONLY GONNA SWEETEN THE DEAL!
R- REALLY ...?
I CAN'T BELIEVE YOU'RE NOT INTO THIS!
IS THERE SOME DARK REASON YOU DON'T WANT TO GO ON A DATE?
NO... I MEAN...

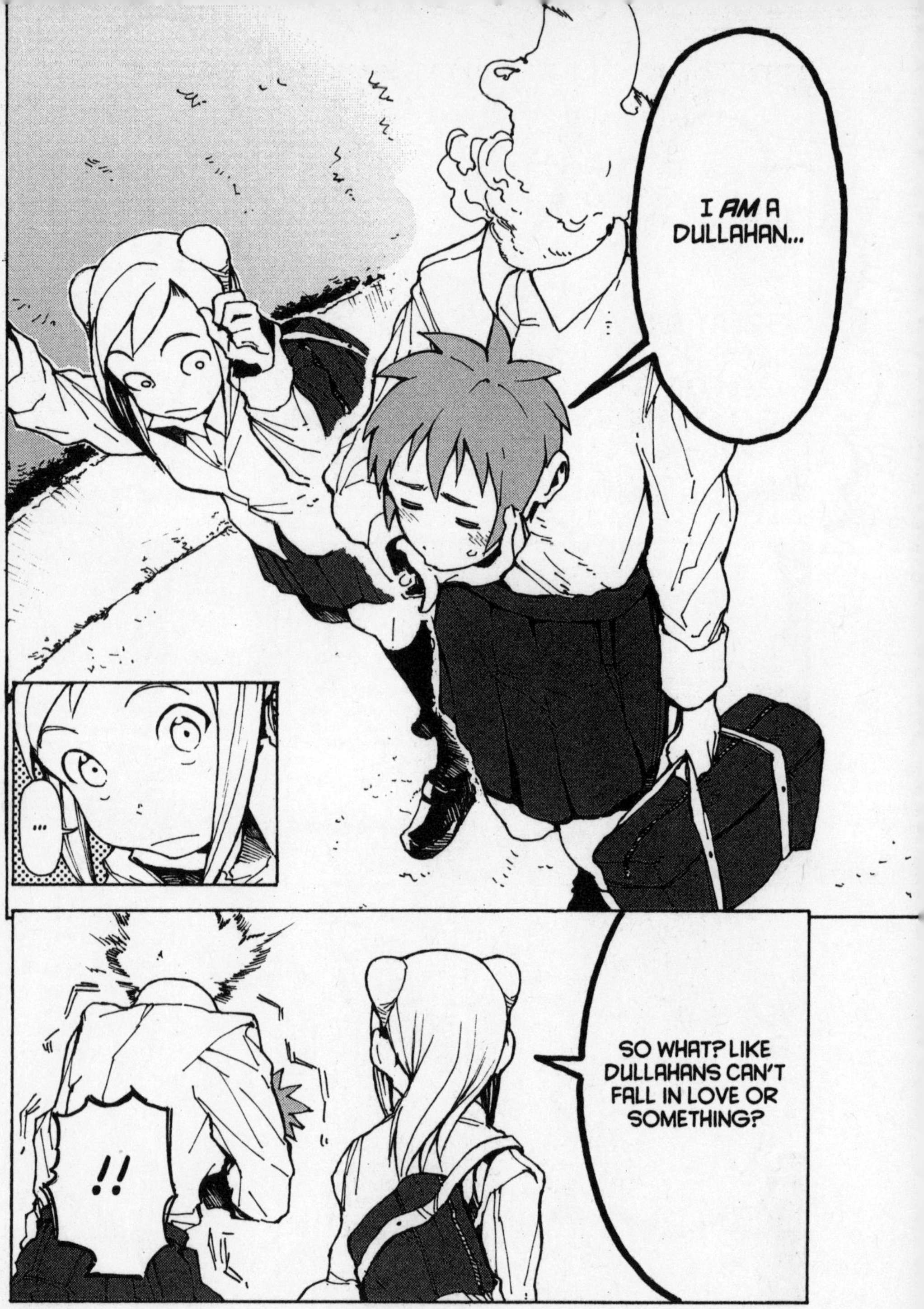
I *AM* A DULLAHAN...
...
SO WHAT? LIKE DULLAHANS CAN'T FALL IN LOVE OR SOMETHING?
!!

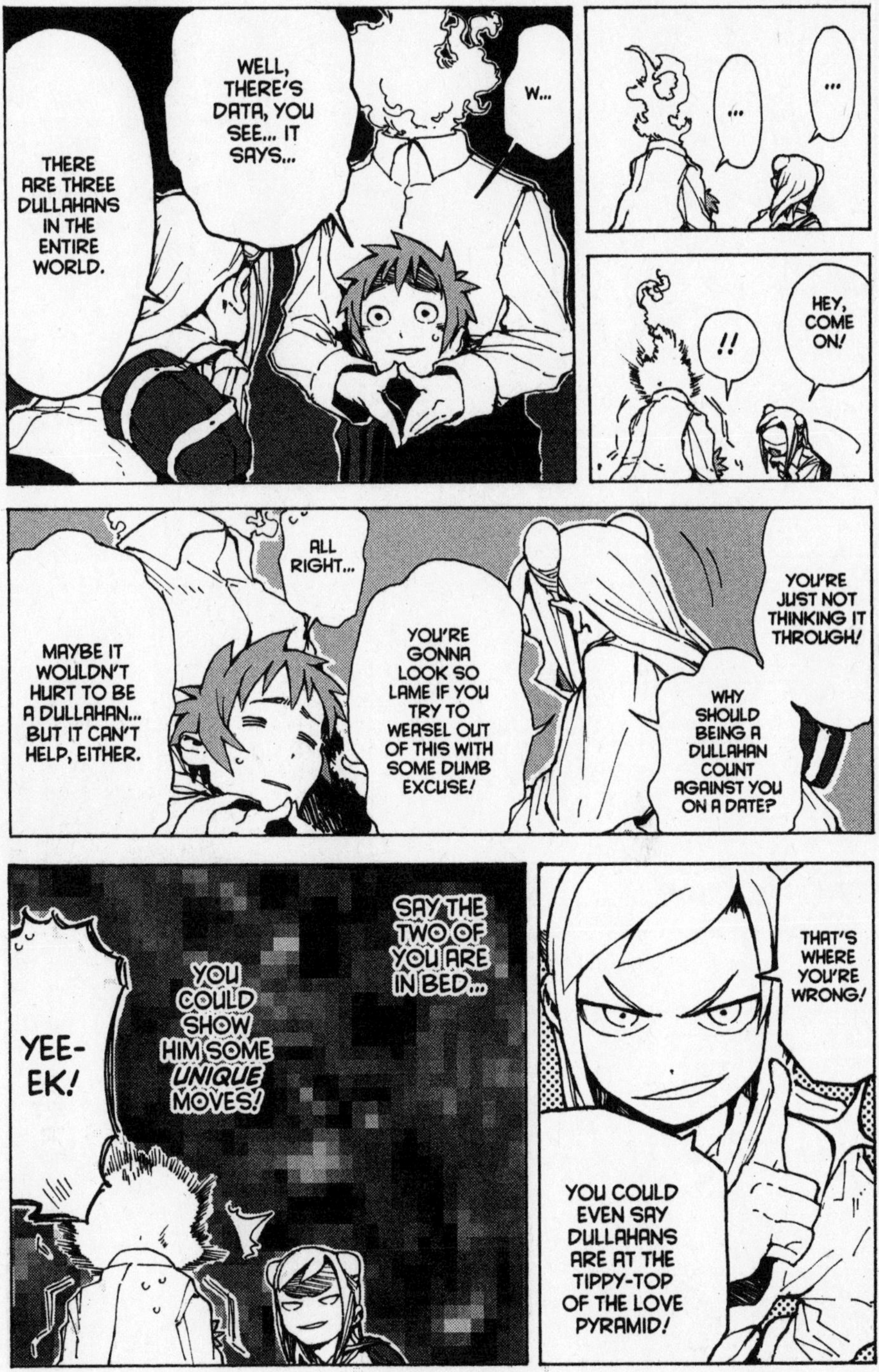
...
...
HEY, COME ON!
!!
W...
WELL, THERE'S DATA, YOU SEE... IT SAYS...
THERE ARE THREE DULLAHANS IN THE ENTIRE WORLD.
YOU'RE JUST NOT THINKING IT THROUGH!
WHY SHOULD BEING A DULLAHAN COUNT AGAINST YOU ON A DATE?
YOU'RE GONNA LOOK SO LAME IF YOU TRY TO WEASEL OUT OF THIS WITH SOME DUMB EXCUSE!
ALL RIGHT...
MAYBE IT WOULDN'T HURT TO BE A DULLAHAN... BUT IT CAN'T HELP, EITHER.
THAT'S WHERE YOU'RE WRONG!
YOU COULD EVEN SAY DULLAHANS ARE AT THE TIPPY-TOP OF THE LOVE PYRAMID!
SAY THE TWO OF YOU ARE IN BED...
YOU COULD SHOW HIM SOME *UNIQUE* MOVES!
YEE-EK!

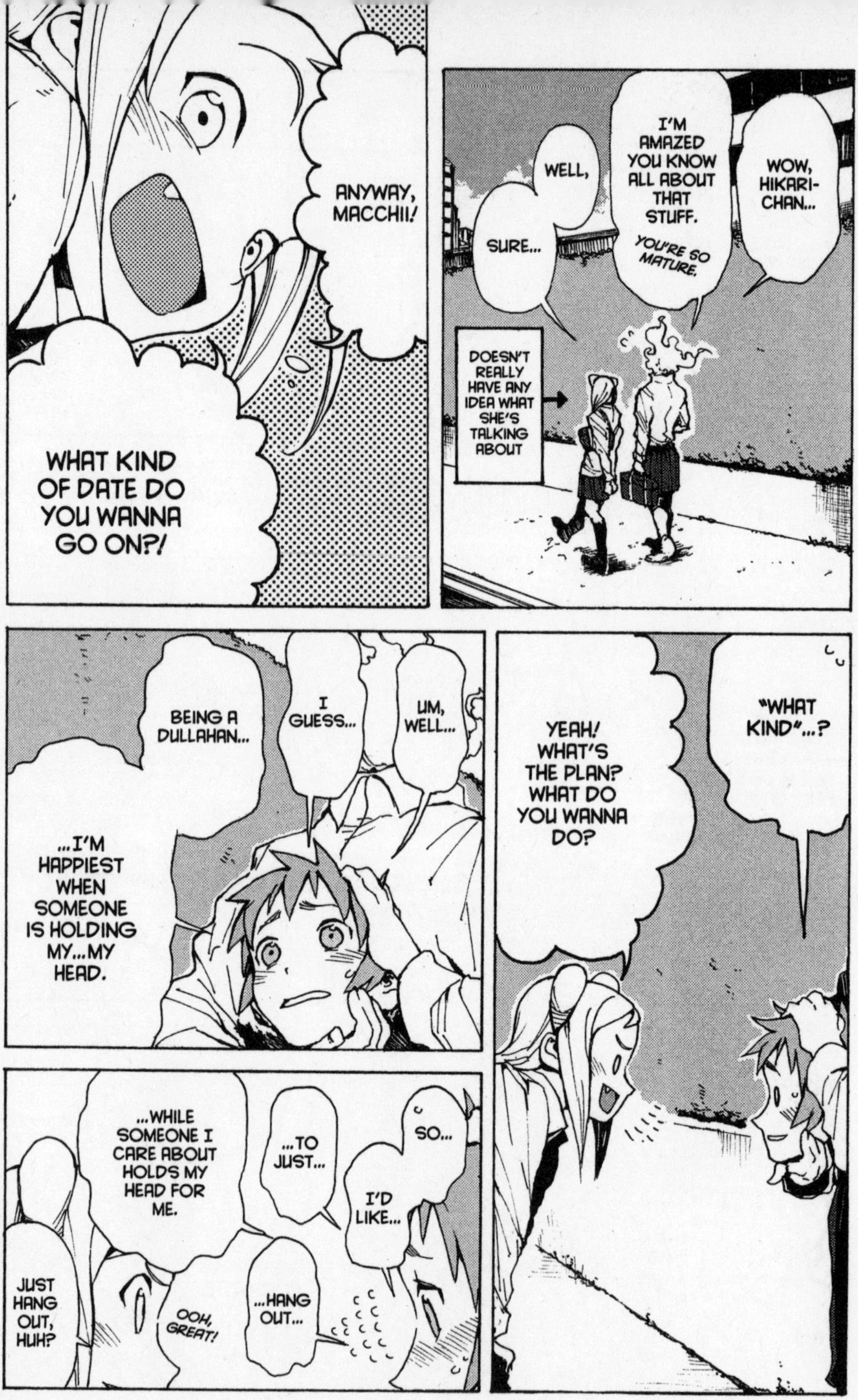
WOW, HIKARI-CHAN...
I'M AMAZED YOU KNOW ALL ABOUT THAT STUFF.
YOU'RE SO MATURE.
WELL,
SURE...
DOESN'T REALLY HAVE ANY IDEA WHAT SHE'S TALKING ABOUT
ANYWAY, MACCHII!
WHAT KIND OF DATE DO YOU WANNA GO ON?!
"WHAT KIND"...?
YEAH! WHAT'S THE PLAN? WHAT DO YOU WANNA DO?
UM, WELL...
I GUESS...
BEING A DULLAHAN...
...I'M HAPPIEST WHEN SOMEONE IS HOLDING MY...MY HEAD.
SO...
...TO JUST...
...WHILE SOMEONE I CARE ABOUT HOLDS MY HEAD FOR ME.
I'D LIKE...
...HANG OUT...
OOH, GREAT!
JUST HANG OUT, HUH?

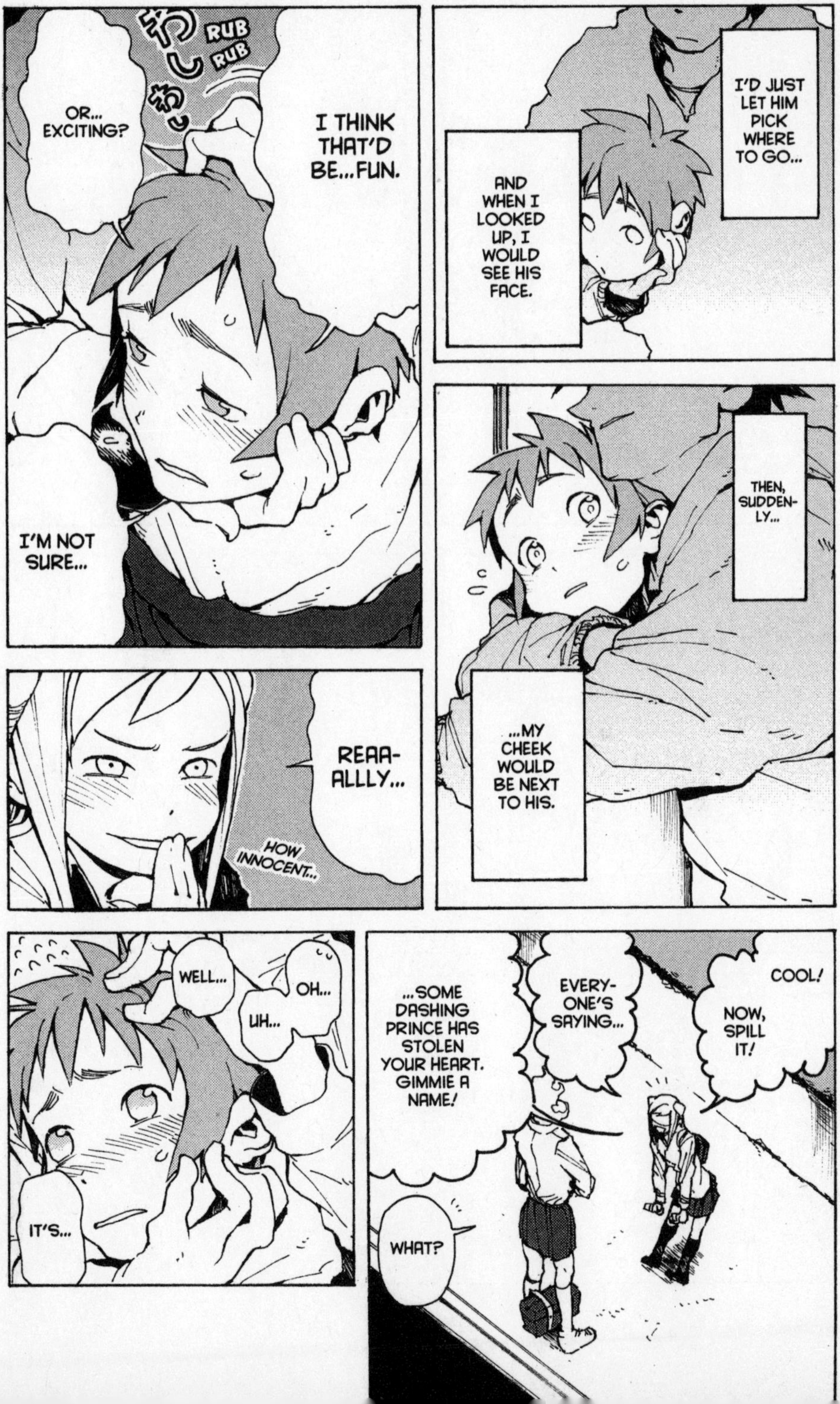
I'D JUST LET HIM PICK WHERE TO GO...
AND WHEN I LOOKED UP, I WOULD SEE HIS FACE.
THEN, SUDDEN-LY...
...MY CHEEK WOULD BE NEXT TO HIS.
わしわし
RUB RUB
I THINK THAT'D BE...FUN.
OR... EXCITING?
I'M NOT SURE...
REAA-ALLLY...
HOW INNOCENT...
COOL!
NOW, SPILL IT!
EVERY-ONE'S SAYING...
...SOME DASHING PRINCE HAS STOLEN YOUR HEART. GIMMIE A NAME!
WHAT?
OH...
UH...
WELL...
IT'S...

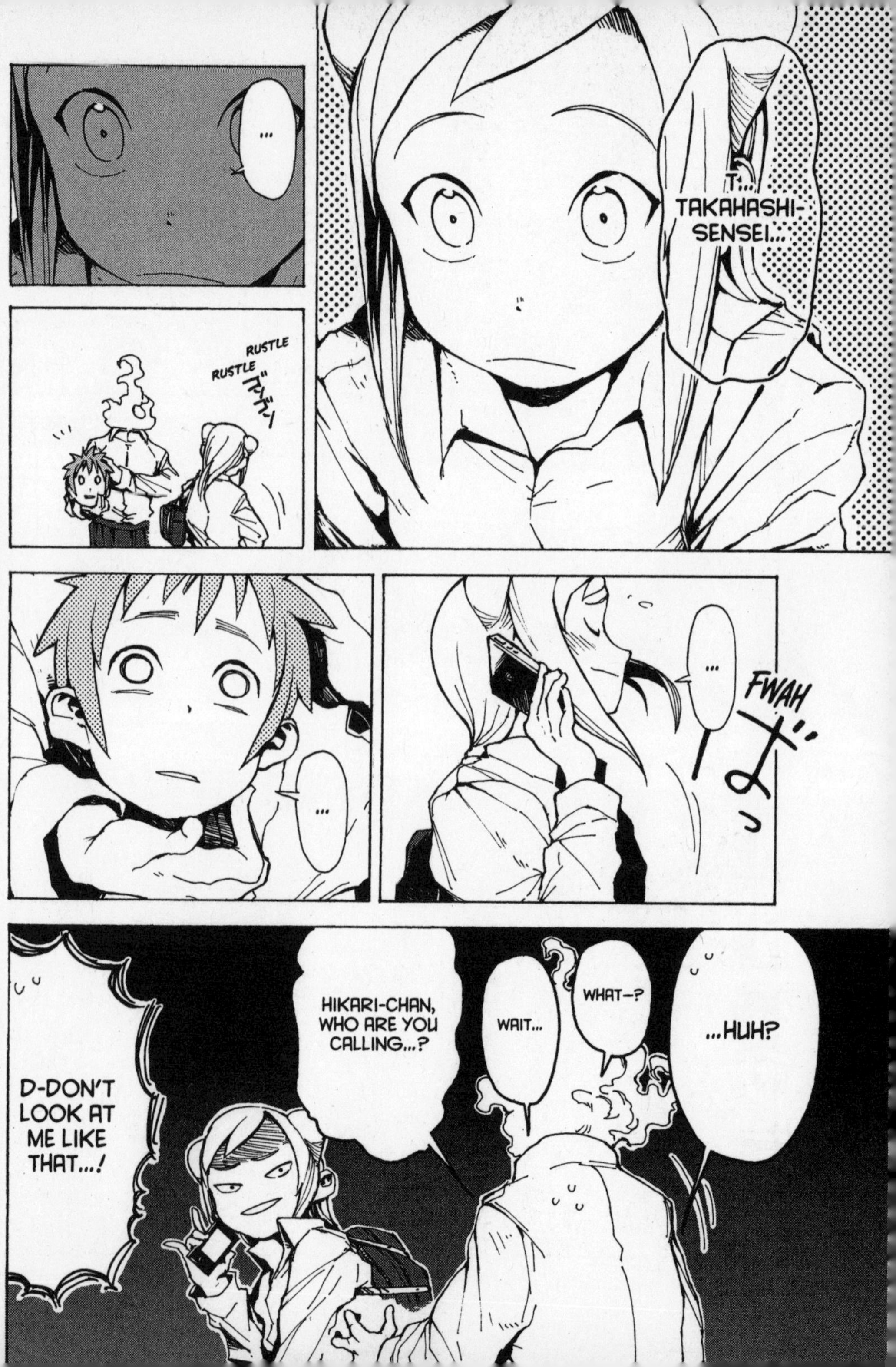
T... TAKAHASHI-SENSEI...
...
RUSTLE
RUSTLE
...
FWAH
...
...HUH?
WHAT-?
WAIT...
HIKARI-CHAN, WHO ARE YOU CALLING...?
D-DON'T LOOK AT ME LIKE THAT...!

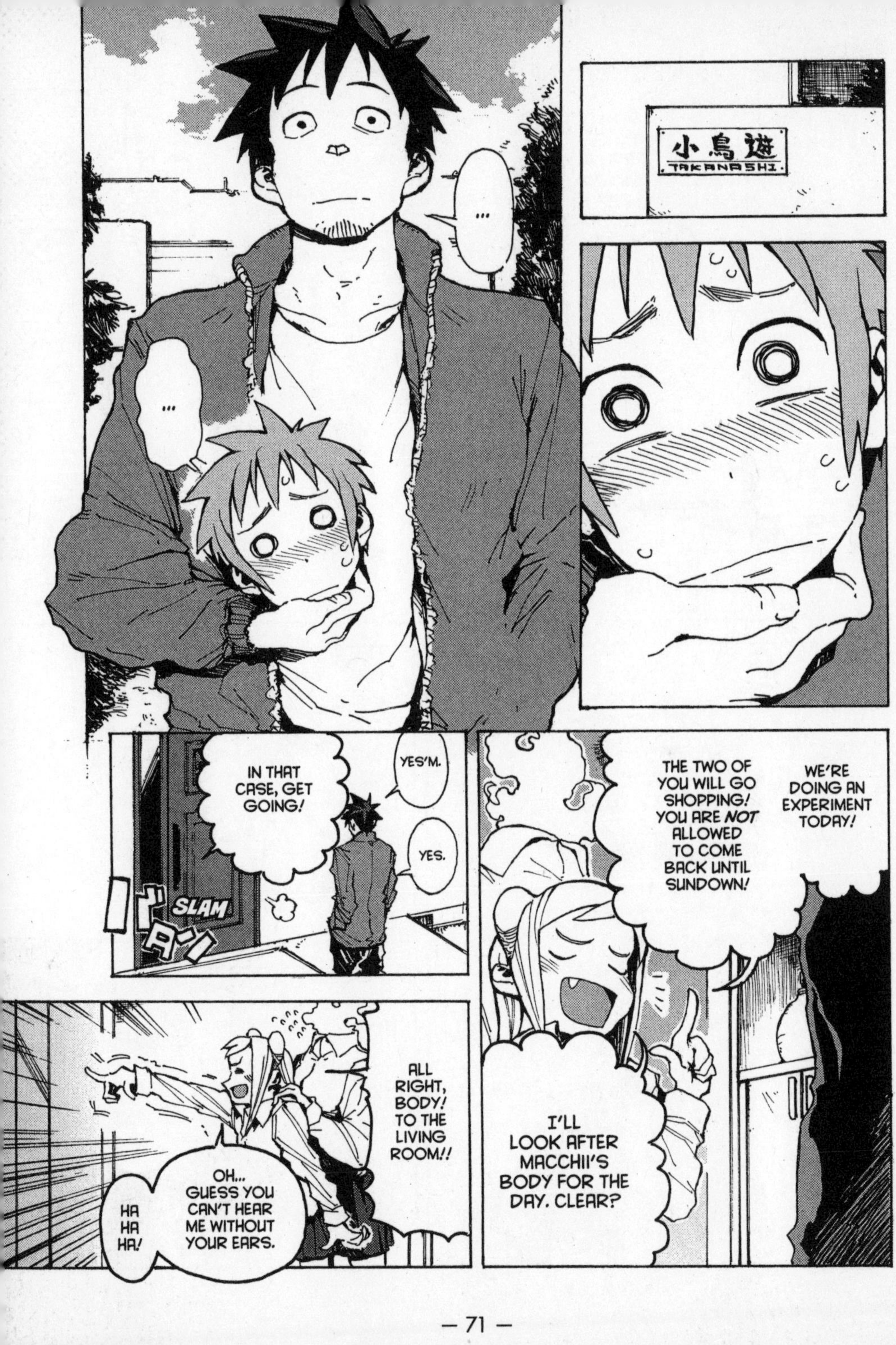

小鳥遊
TAKANASHI
...
...
WE'RE DOING AN EXPERIMENT TODAY!
THE TWO OF YOU WILL GO SHOPPING! YOU ARE *NOT* ALLOWED TO COME BACK UNTIL SUNDOWN!
I'LL LOOK AFTER MACCHII'S BODY FOR THE DAY. CLEAR?
IN THAT CASE, GET GOING!
YES'M.
YES.
SLAM
ALL RIGHT, BODY! TO THE LIVING ROOM!!
OH... GUESS YOU CAN'T HEAR ME WITHOUT YOUR EARS.
HA HA HA!

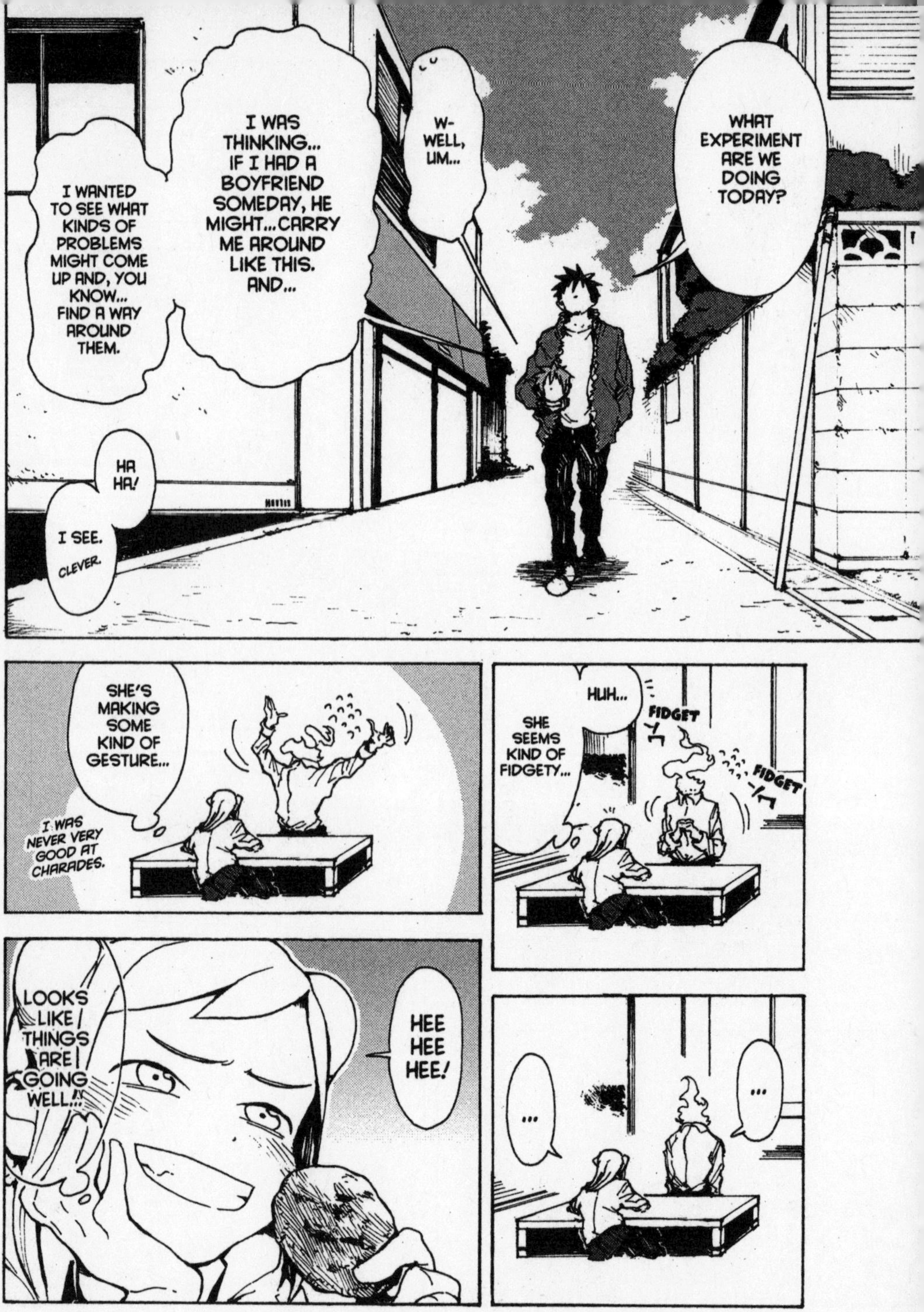
WHAT EXPERIMENT ARE WE DOING TODAY?
W-WELL, UM...
I WAS THINKING... IF I HAD A BOYFRIEND SOMEDAY, HE MIGHT...CARRY ME AROUND LIKE THIS. AND...
I WANTED TO SEE WHAT KINDS OF PROBLEMS MIGHT COME UP AND, YOU KNOW... FIND A WAY AROUND THEM.
HA HA!
I SEE.
CLEVER.
HUH...
SHE SEEMS KIND OF FIDGETY...
FIDGET
FIDGET
SHE'S MAKING SOME KIND OF GESTURE...
I WAS NEVER VERY GOOD AT CHARADES.
...
...
HEE HEE HEE!
LOOKS LIKE THINGS ARE GOING WELL!!

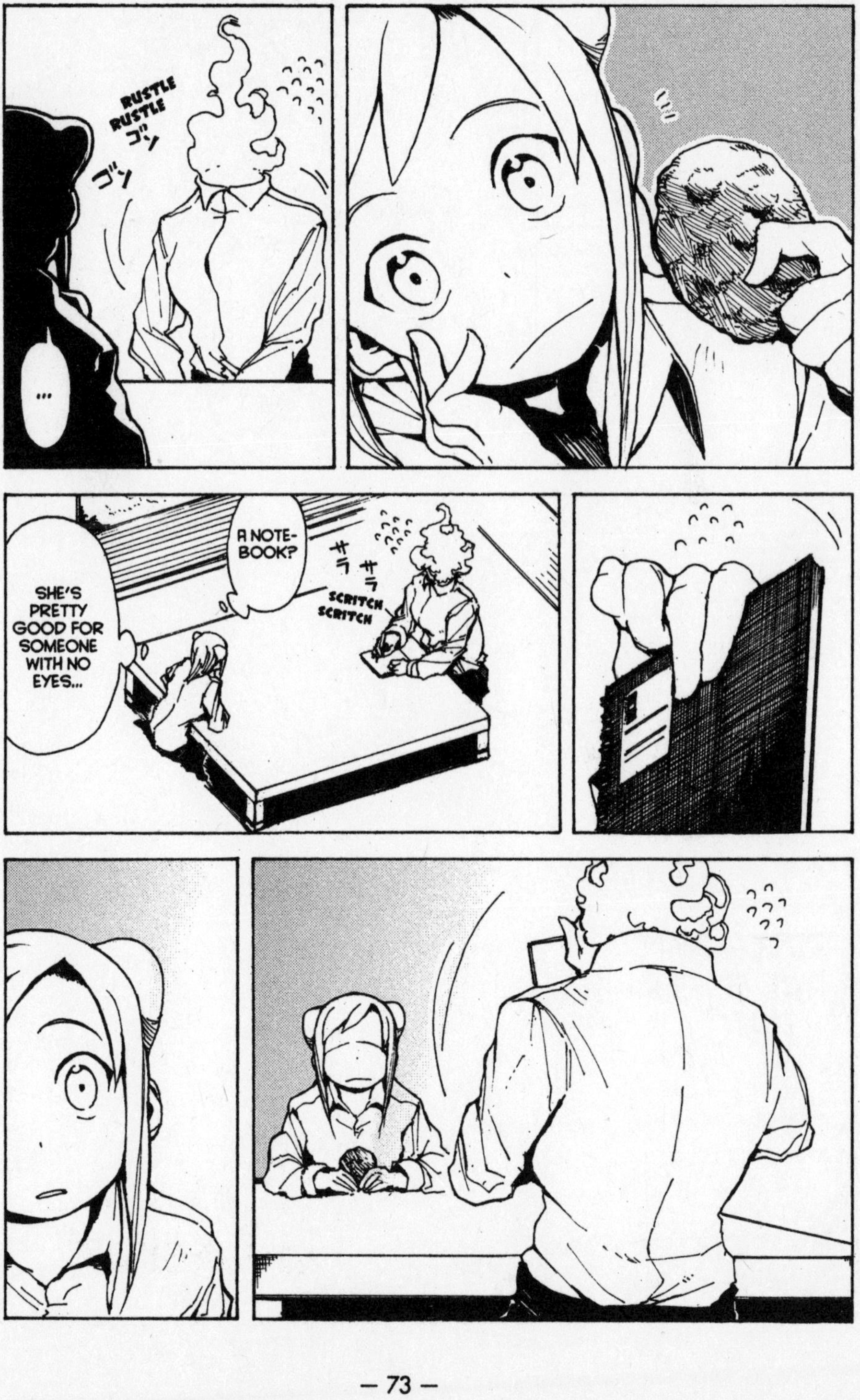
RUSTLE RUSTLE
ゴソ ゴソ
...
サラ サラ
SCRITCH SCRITCH
A NOTE-BOOK?
SHE'S PRETTY GOOD FOR SOMEONE WITH NO EYES...

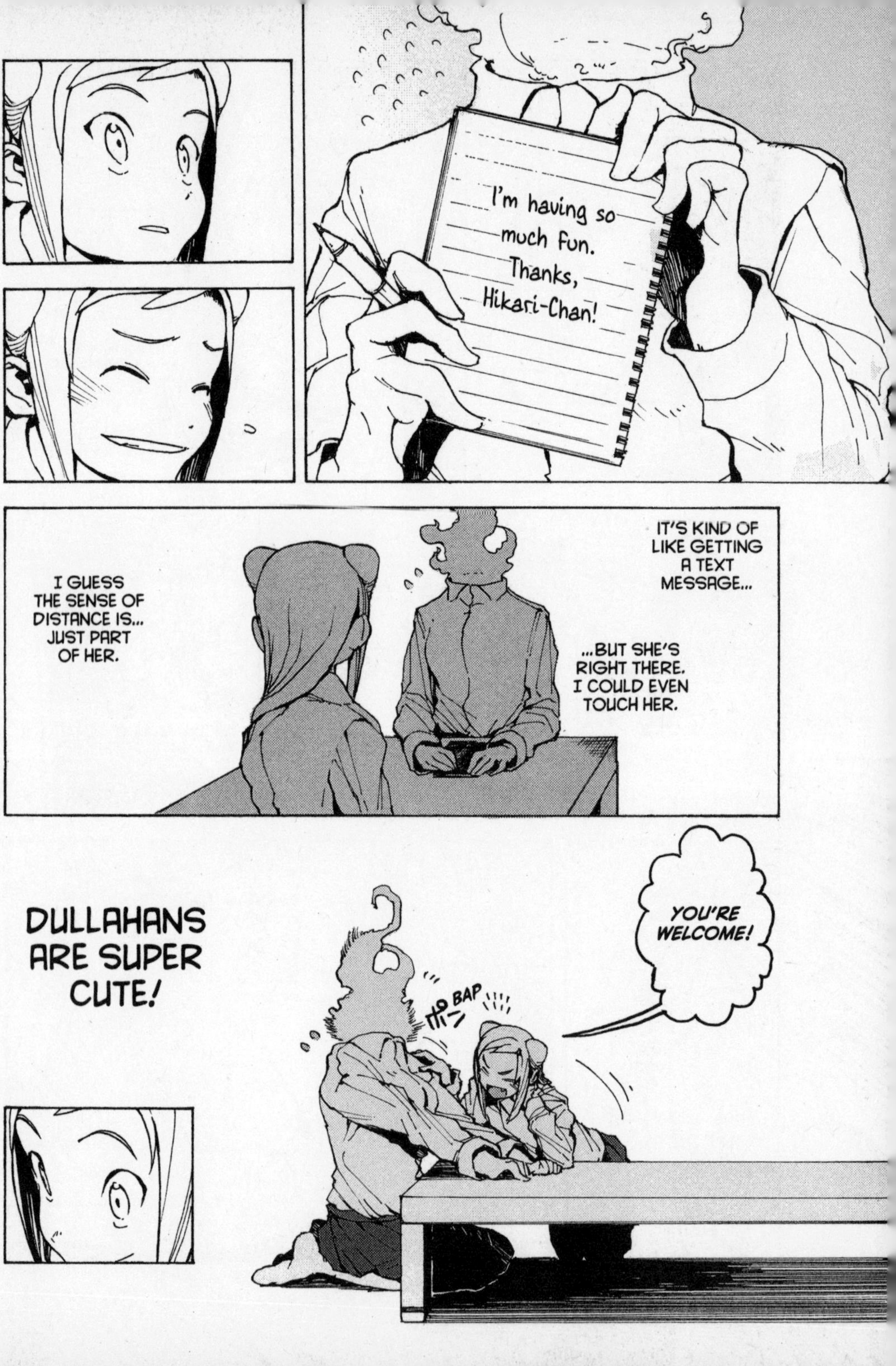
I'm having so much fun. Thanks, Hikari-Chan!
IT'S KIND OF LIKE GETTING A TEXT MESSAGE...
...BUT SHE'S RIGHT THERE. I COULD EVEN TOUCH HER.
I GUESS THE SENSE OF DISTANCE IS... JUST PART OF HER.
YOU'RE WELCOME!
BAP
DULLAHANS ARE SUPER CUTE!

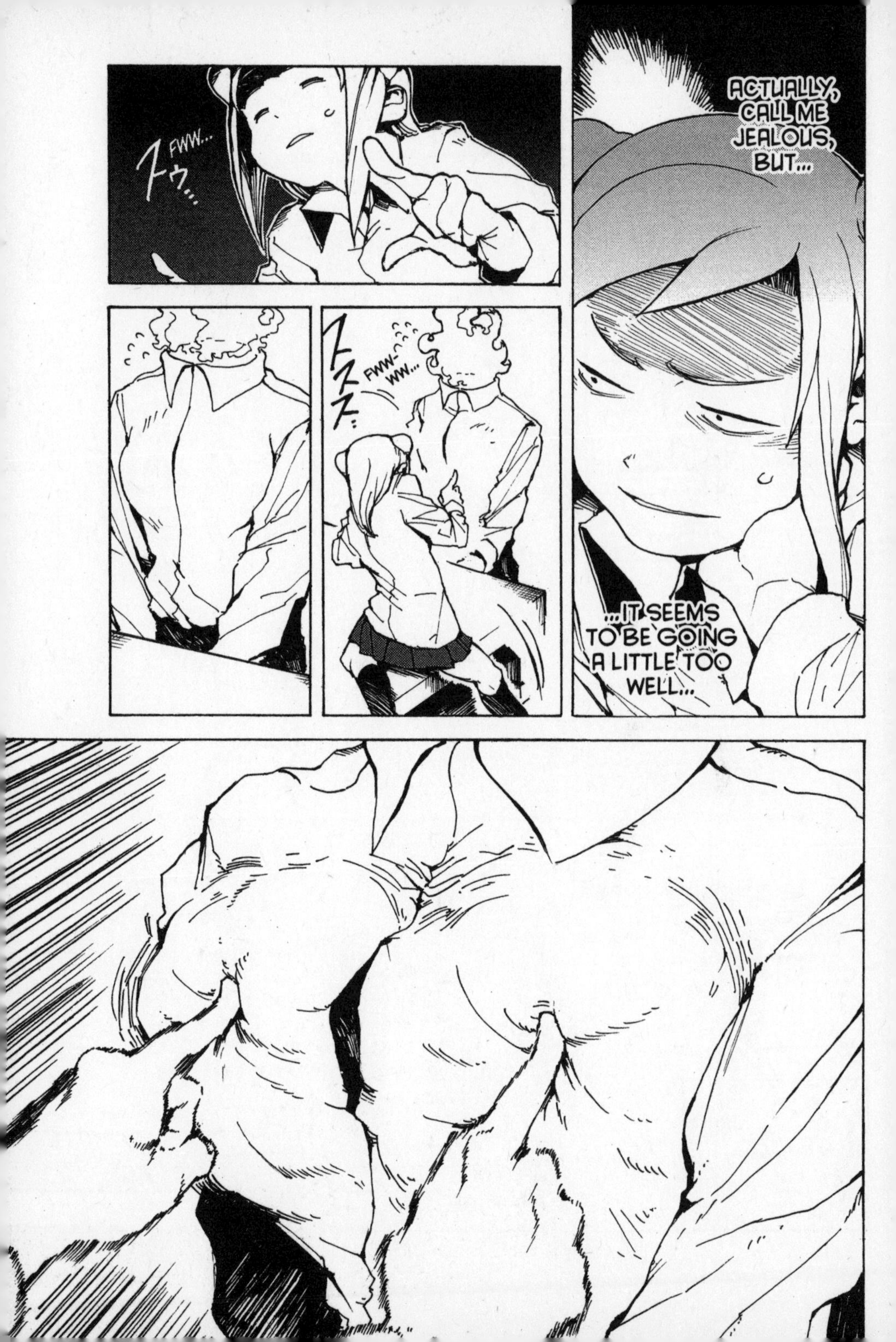
ACTUALLY, CALL ME JEALOUS, BUT...
...IT SEEMS TO BE GOING A LITTLE TOO WELL...
FWW...
FWW-WW...

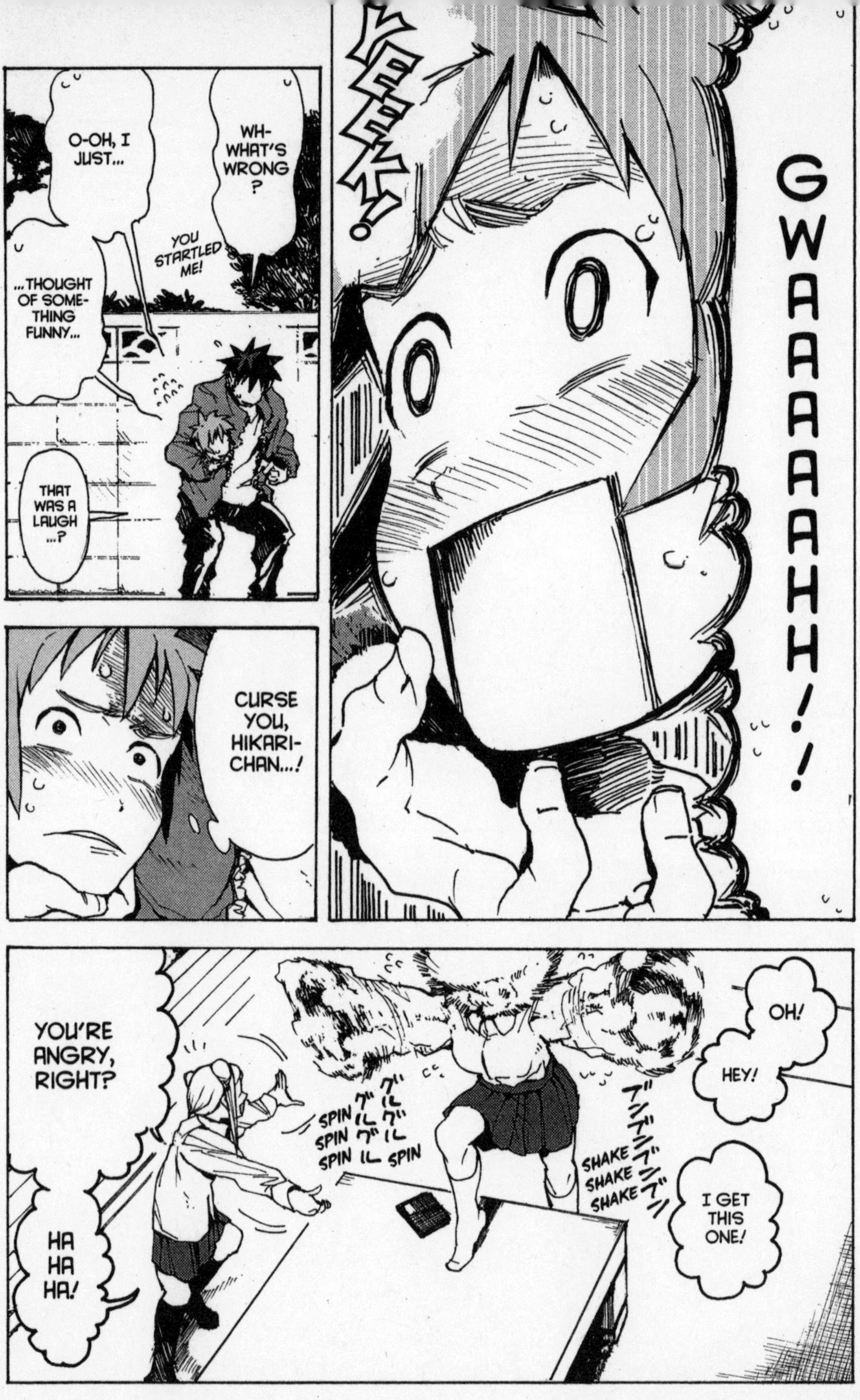
YEEEK!
GWAAAAAAH!!
WH-WHAT'S WRONG?
YOU STARTLED ME!
O-OH, I JUST...
...THOUGHT OF SOME-THING FUNNY...
THAT WAS A LAUGH...?
CURSE YOU, HIKARI-CHAN...!
OH!
HEY!
I GET THIS ONE!
SHAKE SHAKE SHAKE
SPIN SPIN SPIN SPIN
YOU'RE ANGRY, RIGHT?
HA HA HA!

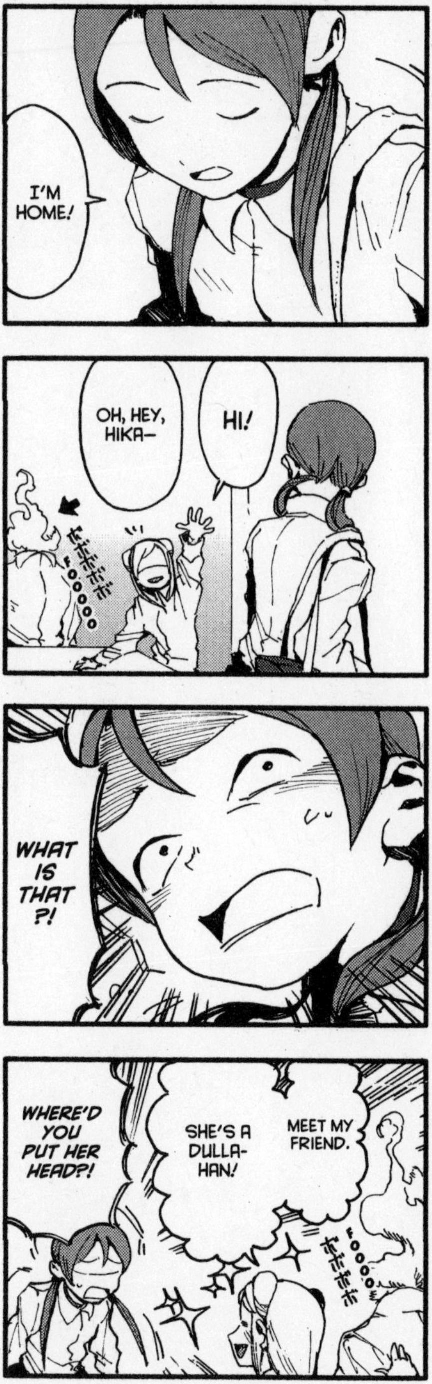
I'M HOME!
HI!
OH, HEY, HIKA—
ボボボボ
FOOOOOO
WHAT IS THAT?!
MEET MY FRIEND.
SHE'S A DULLA-HAN!
WHERE'D YOU PUT HER HEAD?!
ボボボボ
FOOOOM

INTERVIEWS WITH MONSTER GIRLS

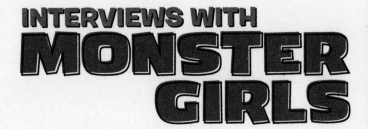

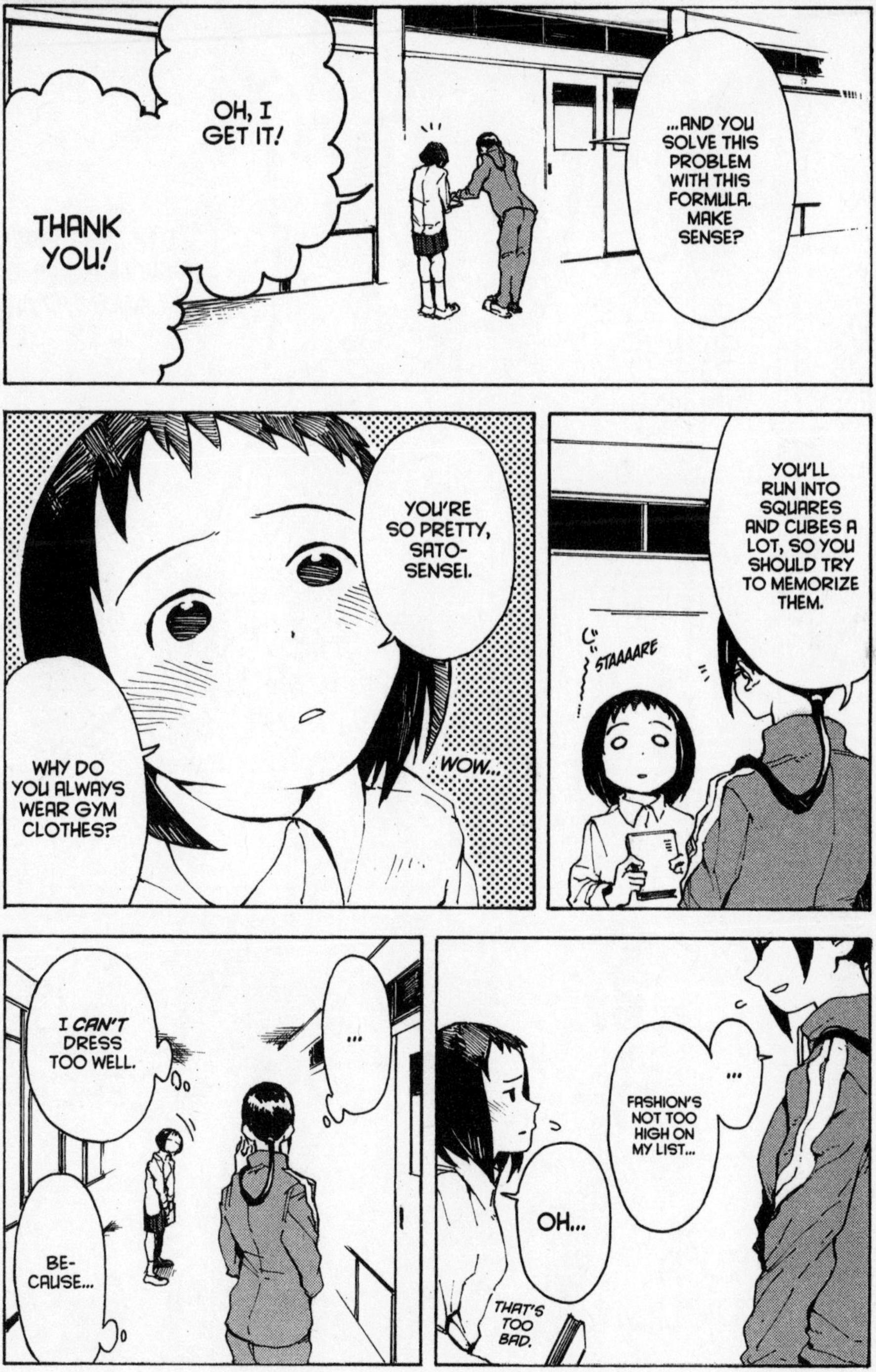
...AND YOU SOLVE THIS PROBLEM WITH THIS FORMULA. MAKE SENSE?
OH, I GET IT!
THANK YOU!
YOU'LL RUN INTO SQUARES AND CUBES A LOT, SO YOU SHOULD TRY TO MEMORIZE THEM.
STAAAARE
YOU'RE SO PRETTY, SATO-SENSEI.
WOW...
WHY DO YOU ALWAYS WEAR GYM CLOTHES?
...
FASHION'S NOT TOO HIGH ON MY LIST...
OH...
THAT'S TOO BAD.
...
I CAN'T DRESS TOO WELL.
BE-CAUSE...

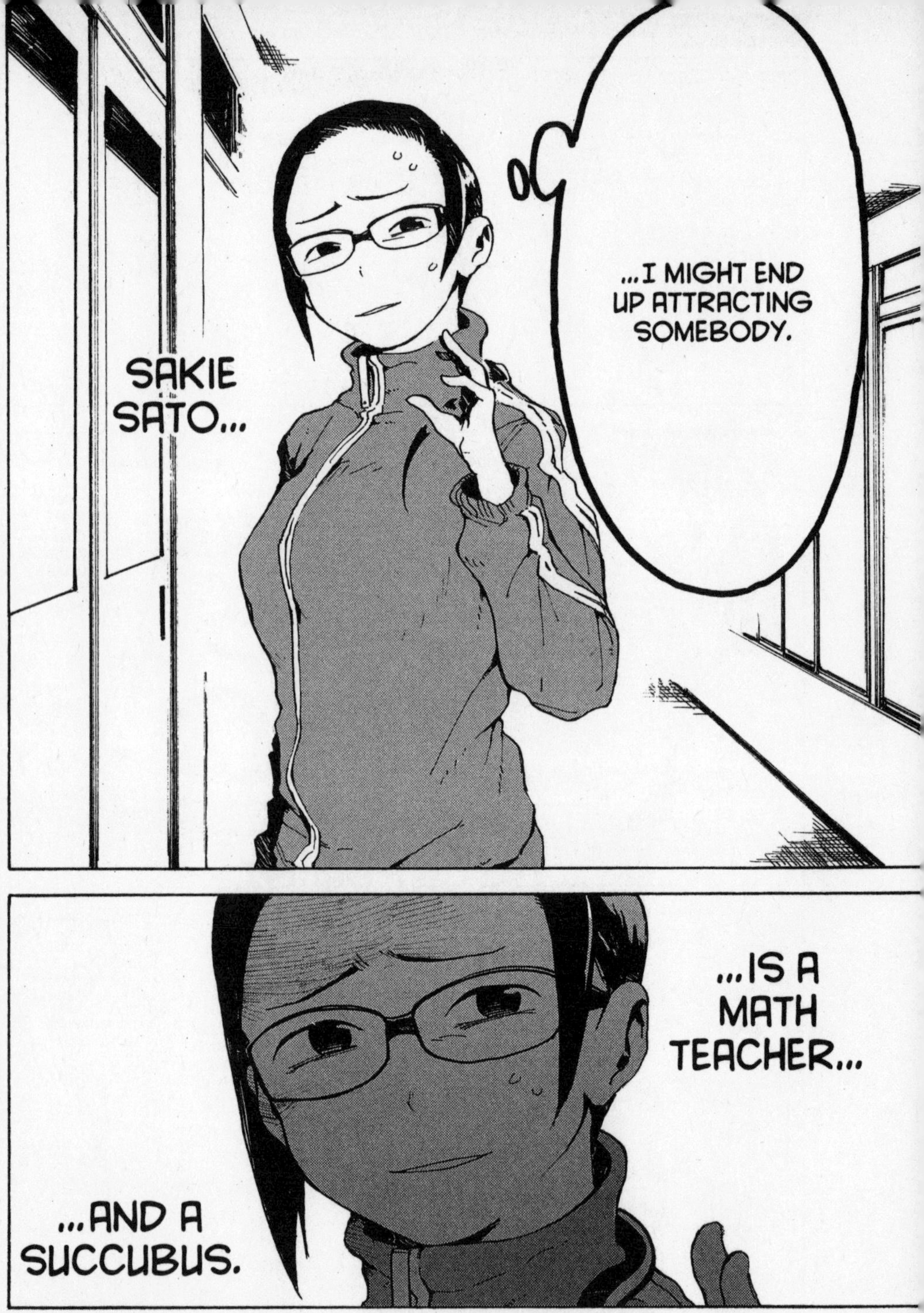
...I MIGHT END UP ATTRACTING SOMEBODY.
SAKIE SATO...
...IS A MATH TEACHER...
...AND A SUCCUBUS.

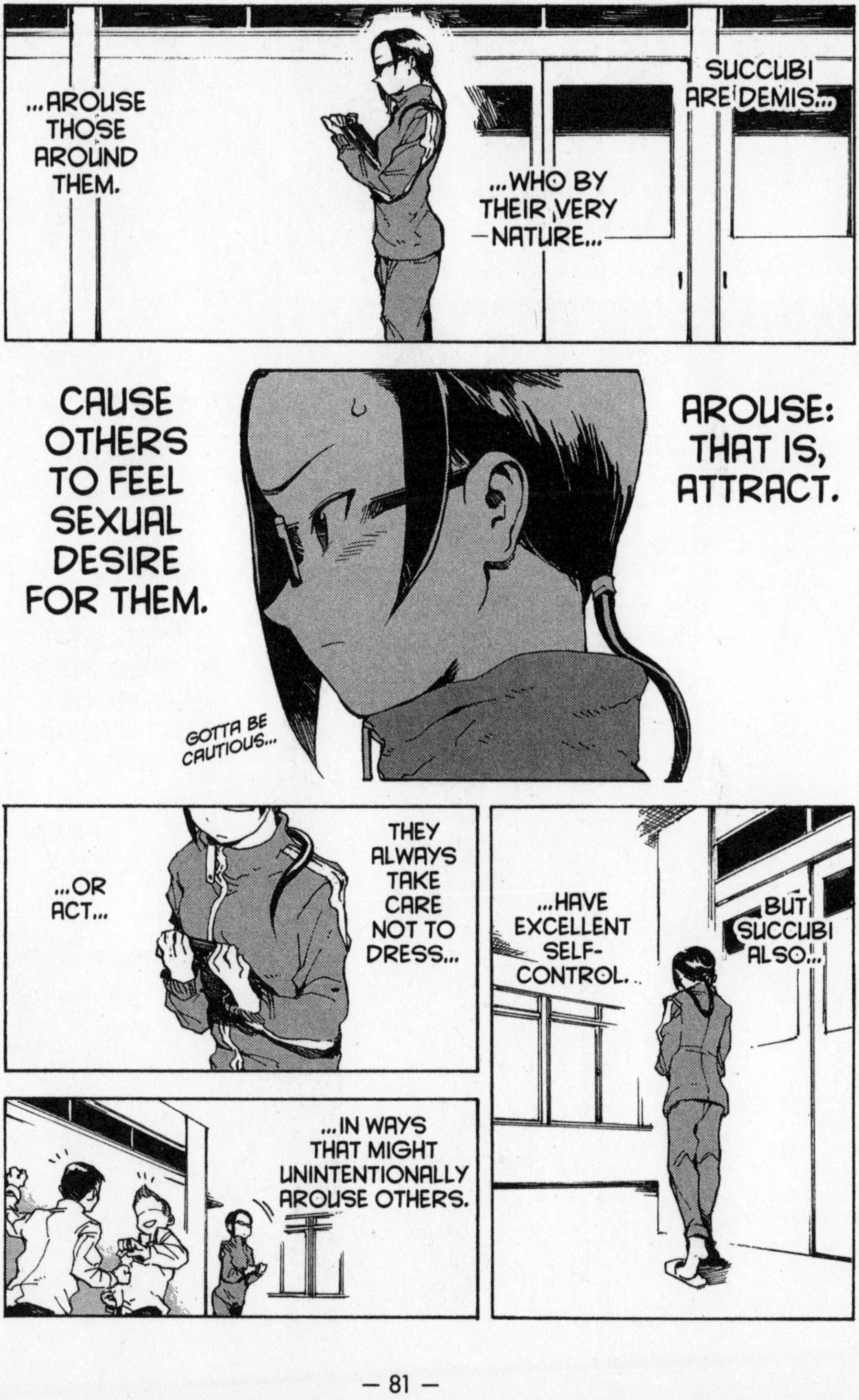
SUCCUBI ARE DEMIS...
...WHO BY THEIR VERY NATURE...
...AROUSE THOSE AROUND THEM.
AROUSE: THAT IS, ATTRACT.
CAUSE OTHERS TO FEEL SEXUAL DESIRE FOR THEM.
GOTTA BE CAUTIOUS...
BUT SUCCUBI ALSO...
...HAVE EXCELLENT SELF-CONTROL..
THEY ALWAYS TAKE CARE NOT TO DRESS...
...OR ACT...
...IN WAYS THAT MIGHT UNINTENTIONALLY AROUSE OTHERS.

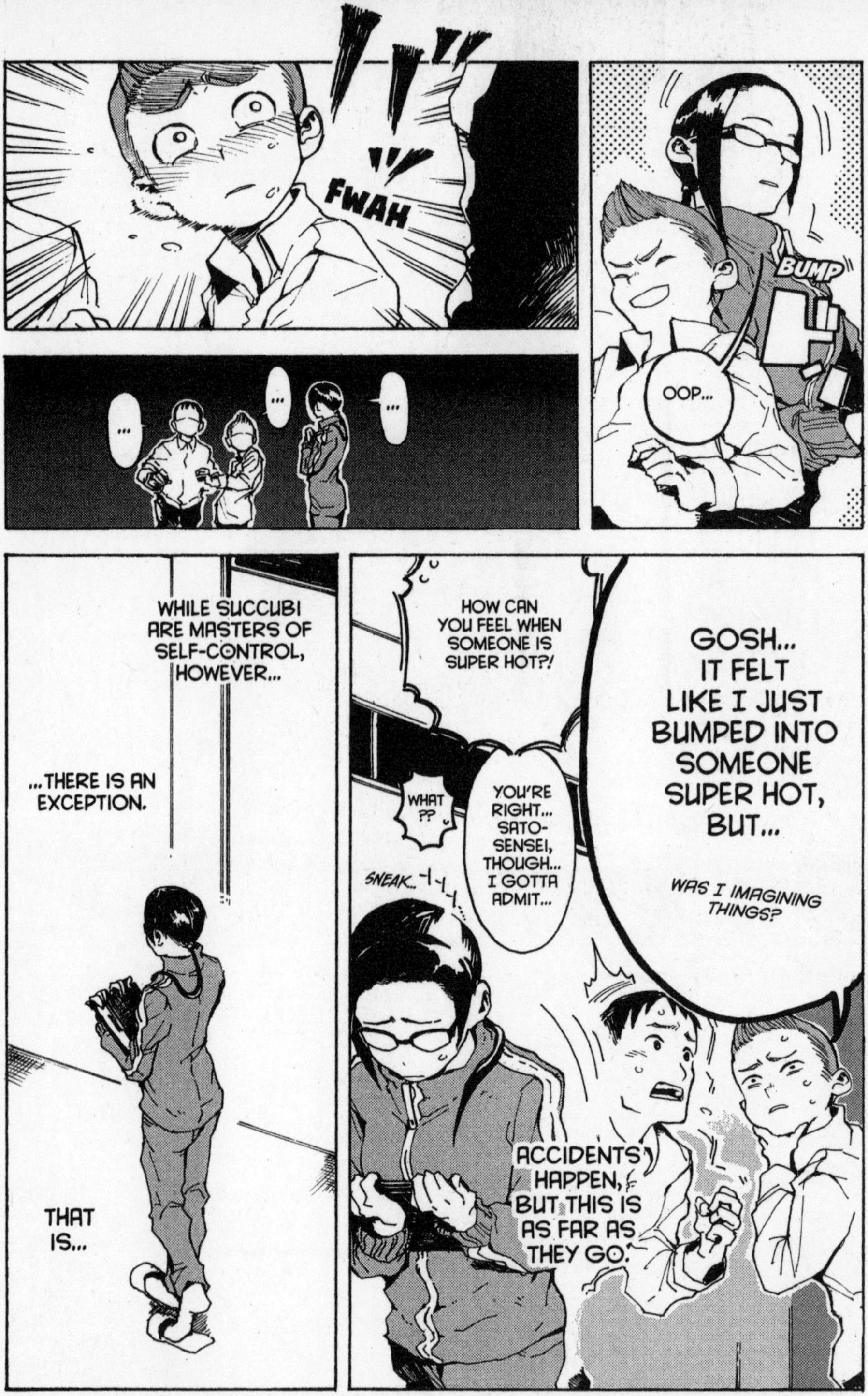
BUMP
OOP...
FWAH
...
...
...
GOSH... IT FELT LIKE I JUST BUMPED INTO SOMEONE SUPER HOT, BUT...
WAS I IMAGINING THINGS?
HOW CAN YOU FEEL WHEN SOMEONE IS SUPER HOT?!
YOU'RE RIGHT... SATO-SENSEI, THOUGH... I GOTTA ADMIT...
WHAT ??
SNEAK...
ACCIDENTS HAPPEN, BUT THIS IS AS FAR AS THEY GO.
WHILE SUCCUBI ARE MASTERS OF SELF-CONTROL, HOWEVER...
...THERE IS AN EXCEPTION.
THAT IS...

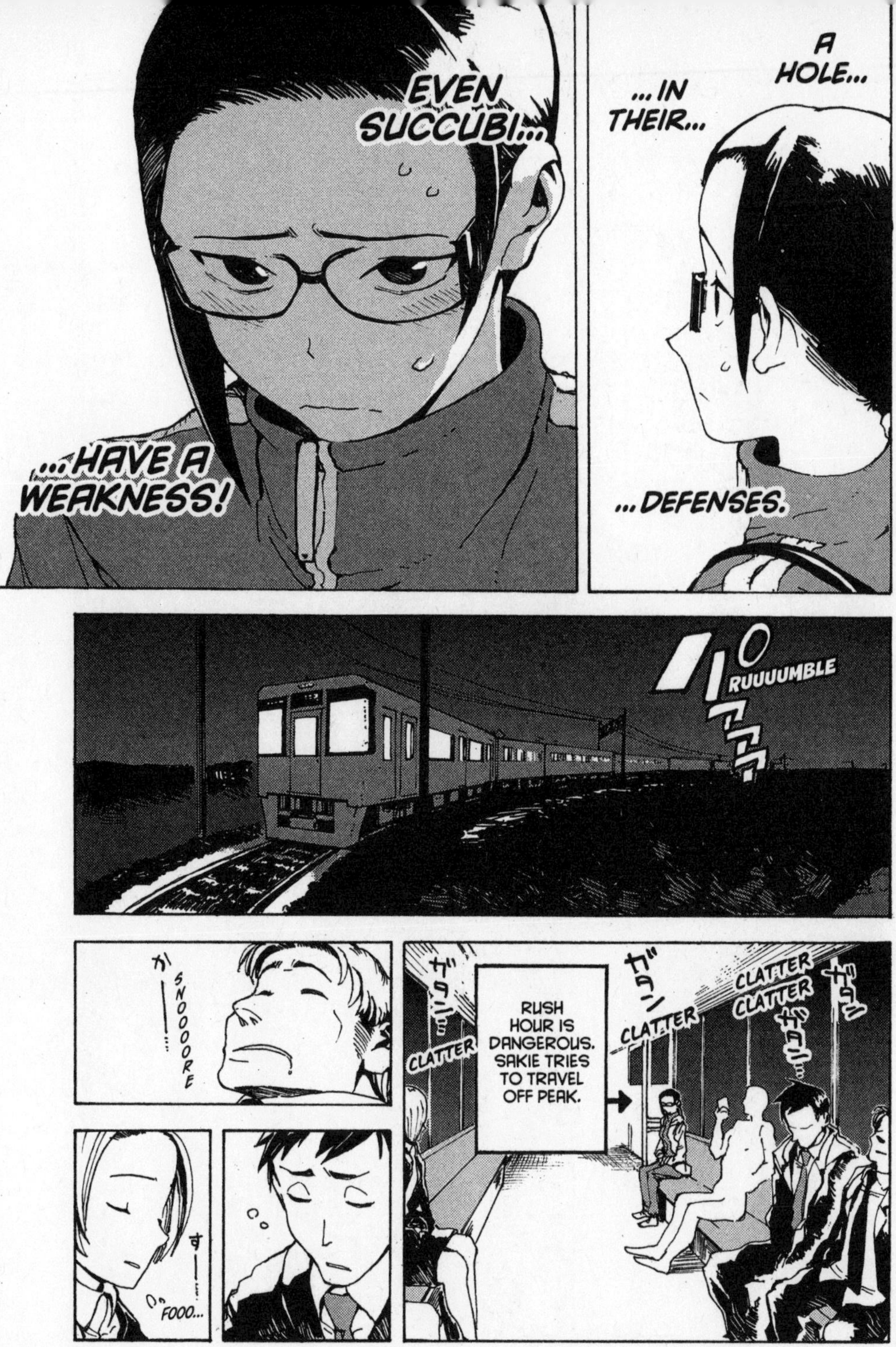
A HOLE...
...IN THEIR...
...DEFENSES.
EVEN SUCCUBI...
...HAVE A WEAKNESS!
パアア
RUUUUMBLE
RUSH HOUR IS DANGEROUS. SAKIE TRIES TO TRAVEL OFF PEAK.
ガタン
CLATTER
CLATTER
CLATTER
ガタン
CLATTER
CLATTER
SNOOOORE
FOOO...

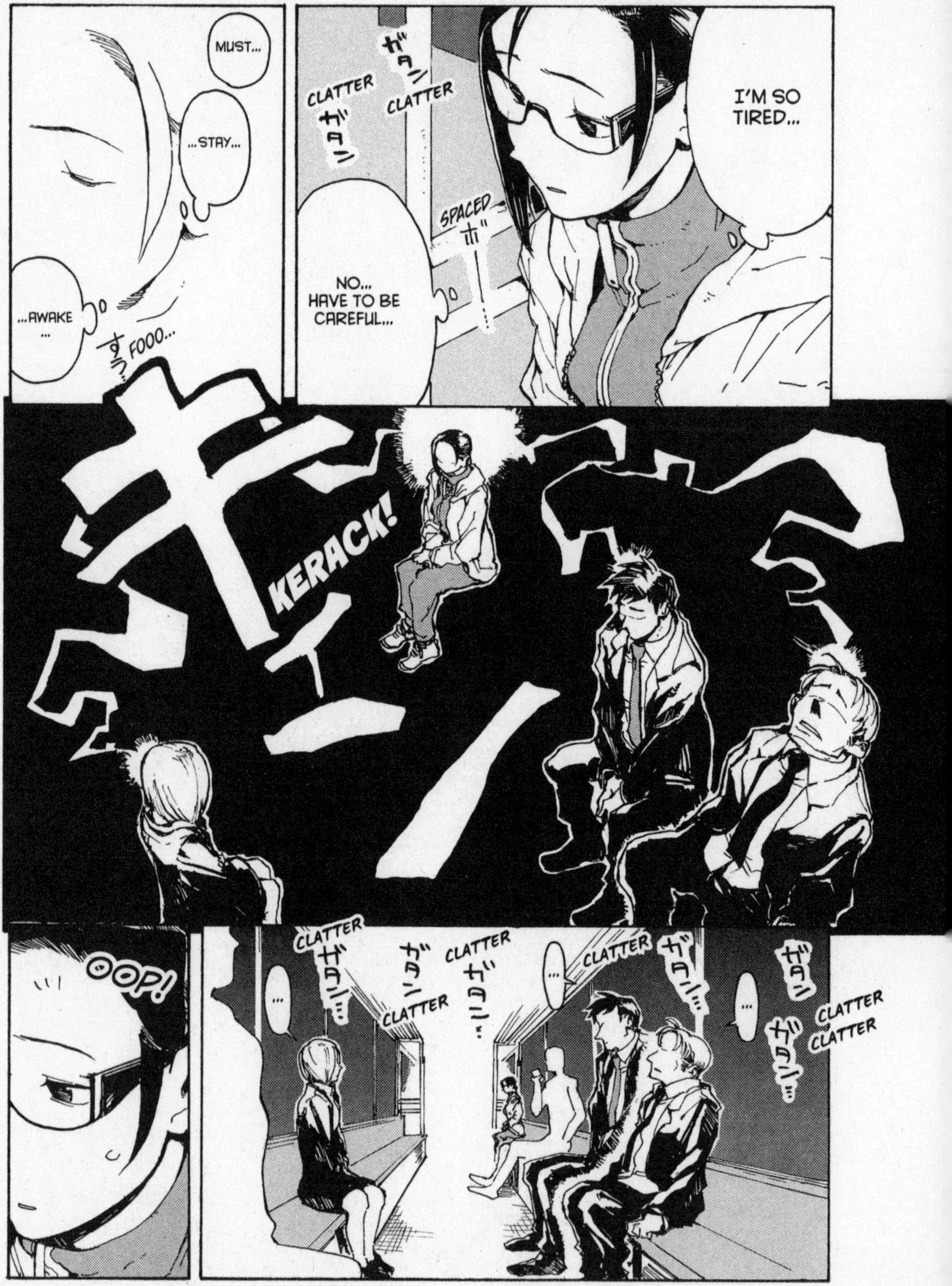
CLATTER
ガタン
CLATTER
ガタン
I'M SO TIRED...
SPACED
ボー
NO... HAVE TO BE CAREFUL...
MUST...
...STAY...
...AWAKE ...
すう FOOO...
KERACK!
CLATTER
ガタン
CLATTER
CLATTER
ガタン
...
ガタン
CLATTER
CLATTER
...
ガタン
CLATTER
ガタン
CLATTER
...
...
CLATTER
ガタン
CLATTER
OOP!

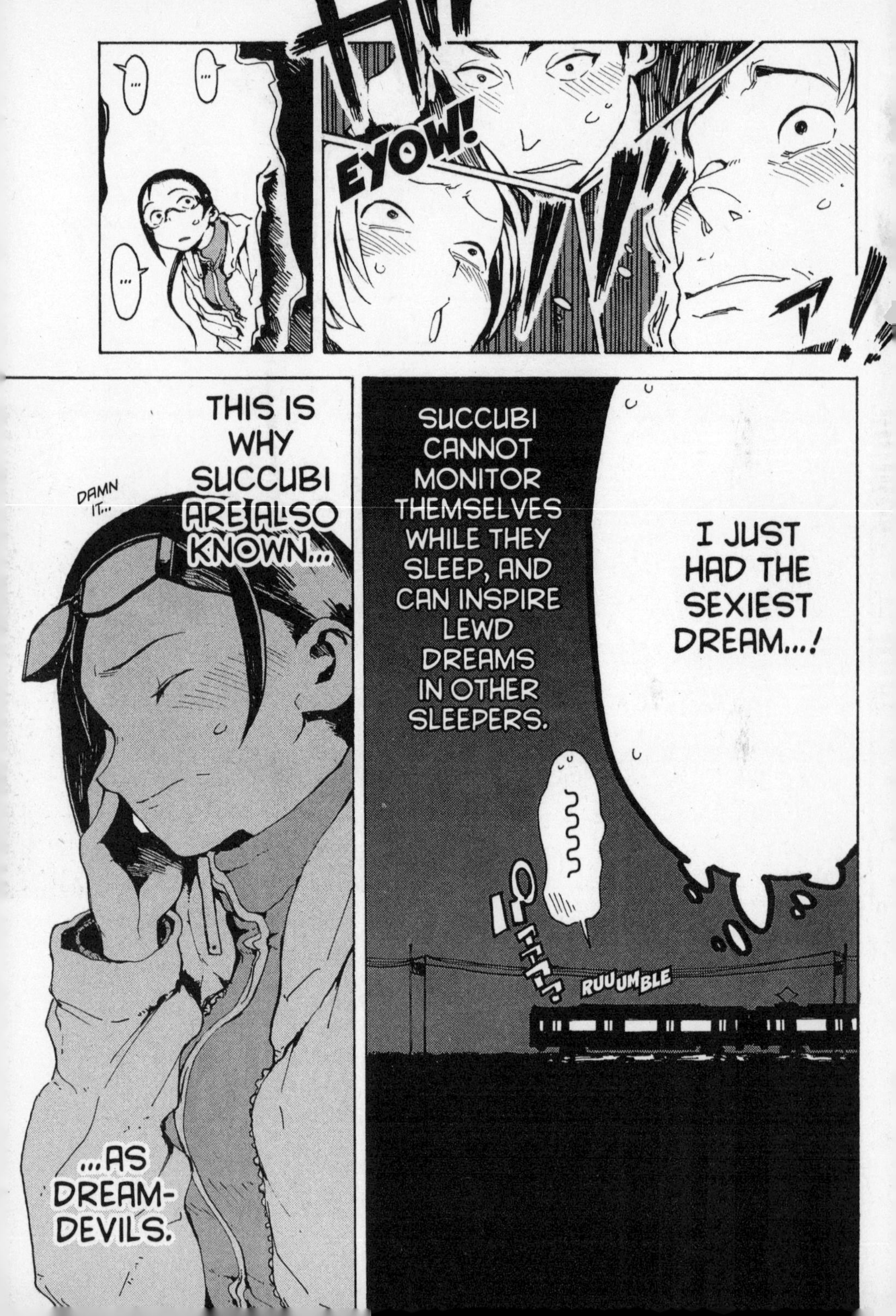

EYOW!
...
...
...
I JUST HAD THE SEXIEST DREAM...!
SUCCUBI CANNOT MONITOR THEMSELVES WHILE THEY SLEEP, AND CAN INSPIRE LEWD DREAMS IN OTHER SLEEPERS.
RUUUMBLE
THIS IS WHY SUCCUBI ARE ALSO KNOWN...
DAMN IT...
...AS DREAM-DEVILS.

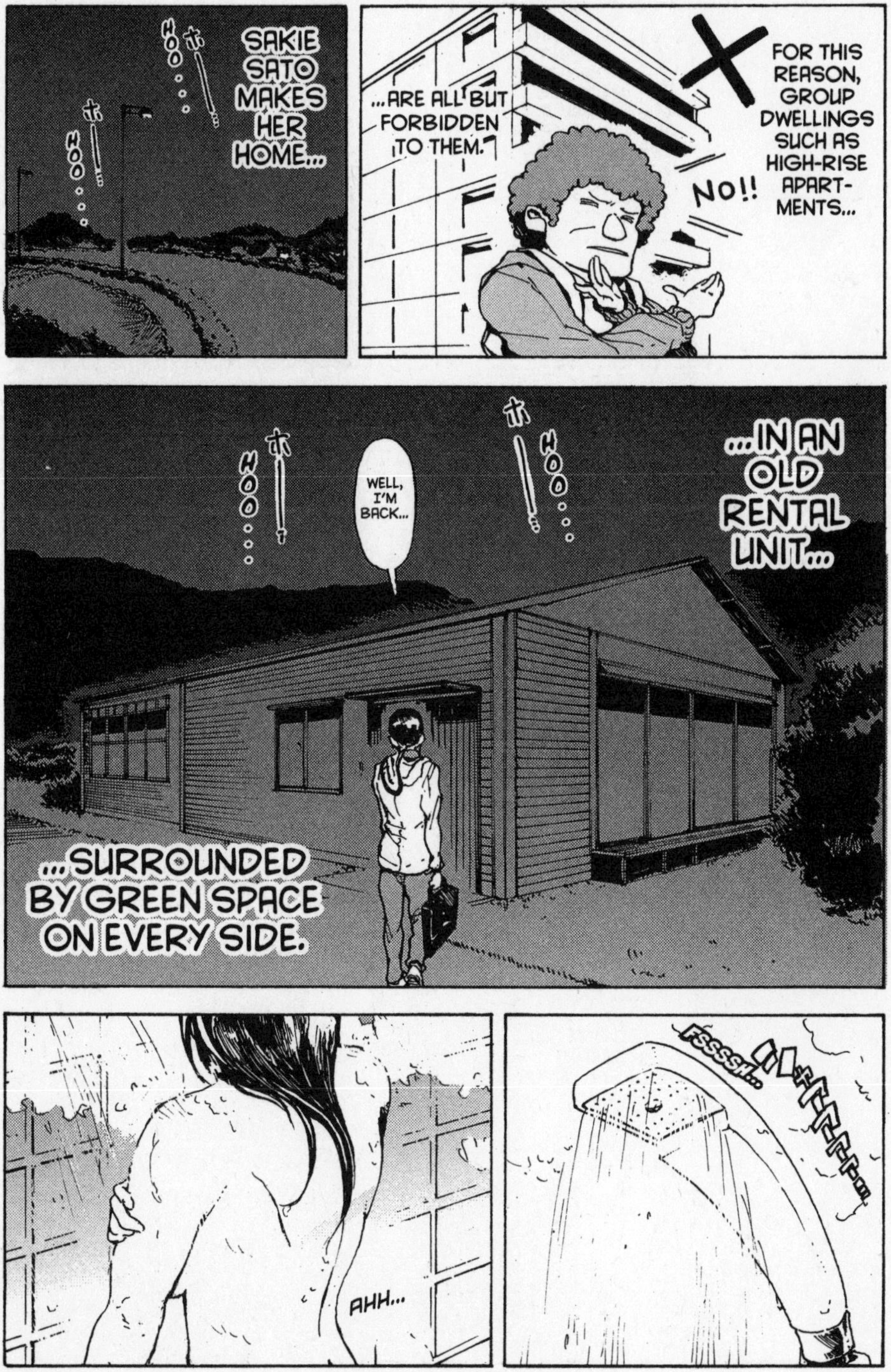
FOR THIS REASON, GROUP DWELLINGS SUCH AS HIGH-RISE APARTMENTS...
No!!
...ARE ALL BUT FORBIDDEN TO THEM.
HOO...
HOO...
SAKIE SATO MAKES HER HOME...
...IN AN OLD RENTAL UNIT...
HOO...
WELL, I'M BACK...
HOO...
...SURROUNDED BY GREEN SPACE ON EVERY SIDE.
FSSSSH...
AHH...

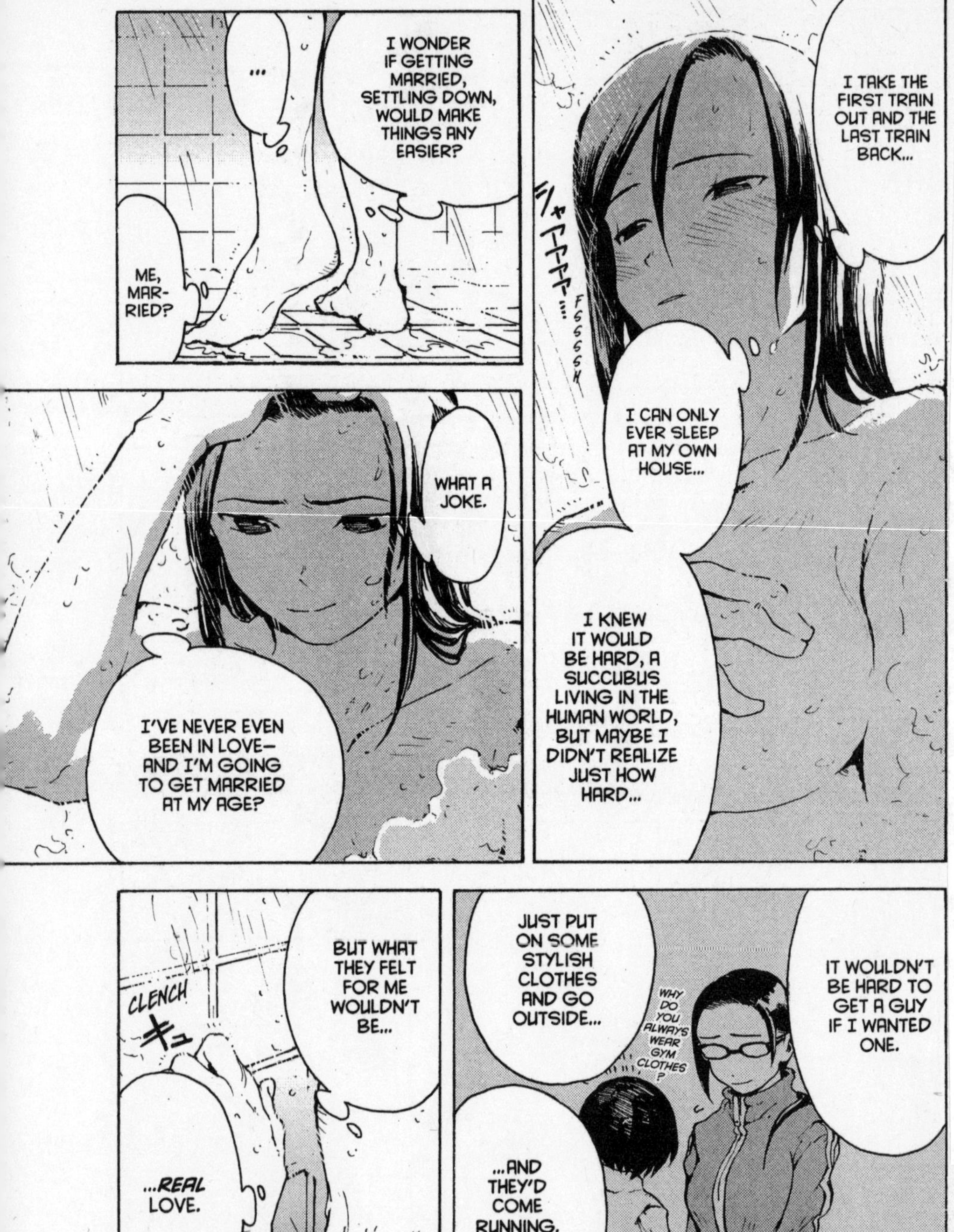
I TAKE THE FIRST TRAIN OUT AND THE LAST TRAIN BACK...
シャアアアア… FSSSSH
I CAN ONLY EVER SLEEP AT MY OWN HOUSE...
I KNEW IT WOULD BE HARD, A SUCCUBUS LIVING IN THE HUMAN WORLD, BUT MAYBE I DIDN'T REALIZE JUST HOW HARD...
I WONDER IF GETTING MARRIED, SETTLING DOWN, WOULD MAKE THINGS ANY EASIER?
...
ME, MAR-RIED?
WHAT A JOKE.
I'VE NEVER EVEN BEEN IN LOVE— AND I'M GOING TO GET MARRIED AT MY AGE?
IT WOULDN'T BE HARD TO GET A GUY IF I WANTED ONE.
JUST PUT ON SOME STYLISH CLOTHES AND GO OUTSIDE...
WHY DO YOU ALWAYS WEAR GYM CLOTHES?
...AND THEY'D COME RUNNING.
BUT WHAT THEY FELT FOR ME WOULDN'T BE...
CLENCH キュ
...*REAL* LOVE.

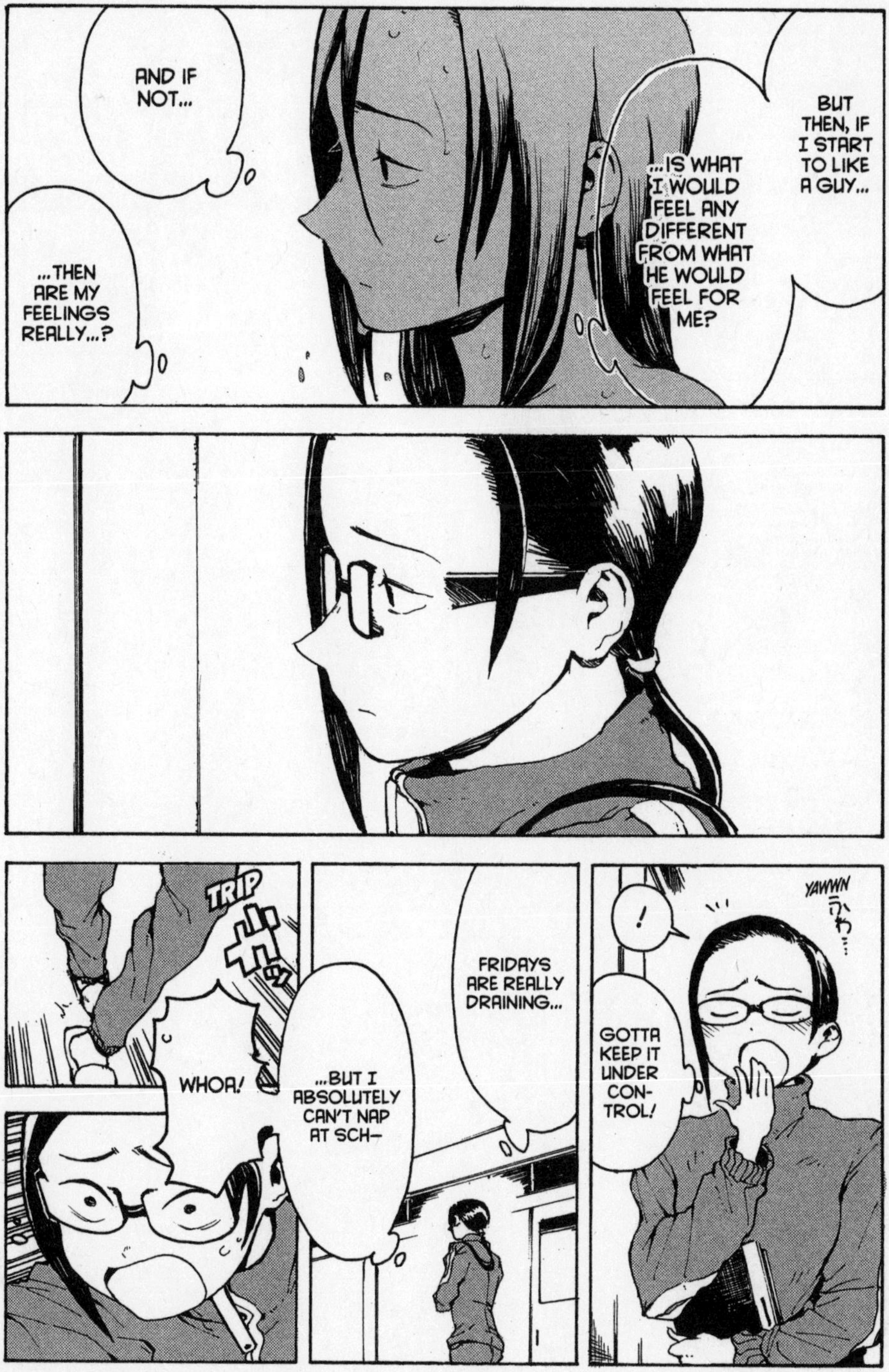
BUT THEN, IF I START TO LIKE A GUY...
...IS WHAT I WOULD FEEL ANY DIFFERENT FROM WHAT HE WOULD FEEL FOR ME?
AND IF NOT...
...THEN ARE MY FEELINGS REALLY...?
YAWWN
ふわ…
!
GOTTA KEEP IT UNDER CON-TROL!
FRIDAYS ARE REALLY DRAINING...
...BUT I ABSOLUTELY CAN'T NAP AT SCH–
TRIP
WHOA!

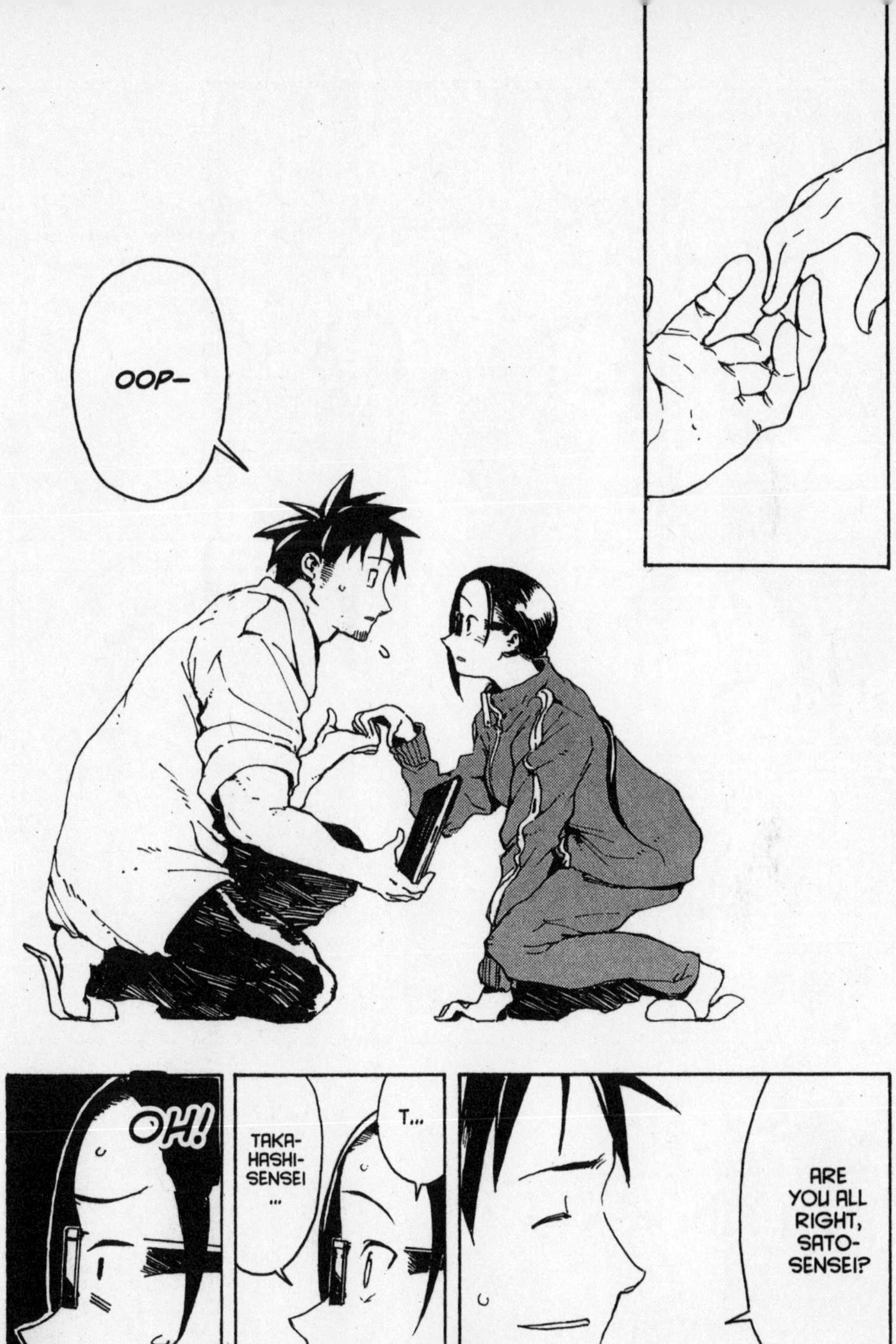
OOP–
ARE YOU ALL RIGHT, SATO-SENSEI?
T...
TAKA-HASHI-SENSEI ...
OH!

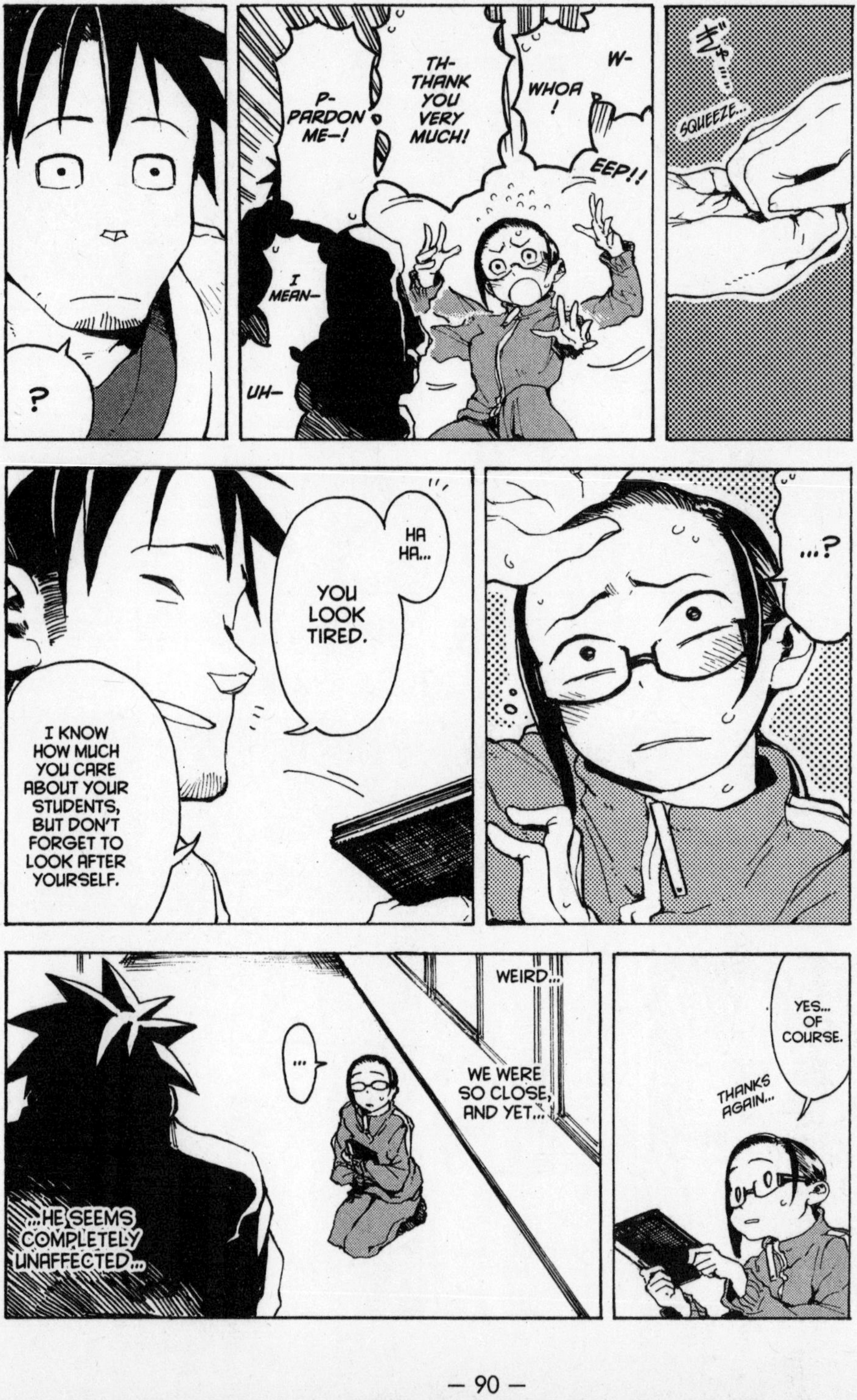
ぎゅ…
SQUEEZE...
W- WHOA!
EEP!!
TH- THANK YOU VERY MUCH!
P- PARDON ME-!
I MEAN-
UH-
?
...?
HA HA...
YOU LOOK TIRED.
I KNOW HOW MUCH YOU CARE ABOUT YOUR STUDENTS, BUT DON'T FORGET TO LOOK AFTER YOURSELF.
YES... OF COURSE.
THANKS AGAIN...
WEIRD...
WE WERE SO CLOSE, AND YET...
...
...HE SEEMS COMPLETELY UNAFFECTED...

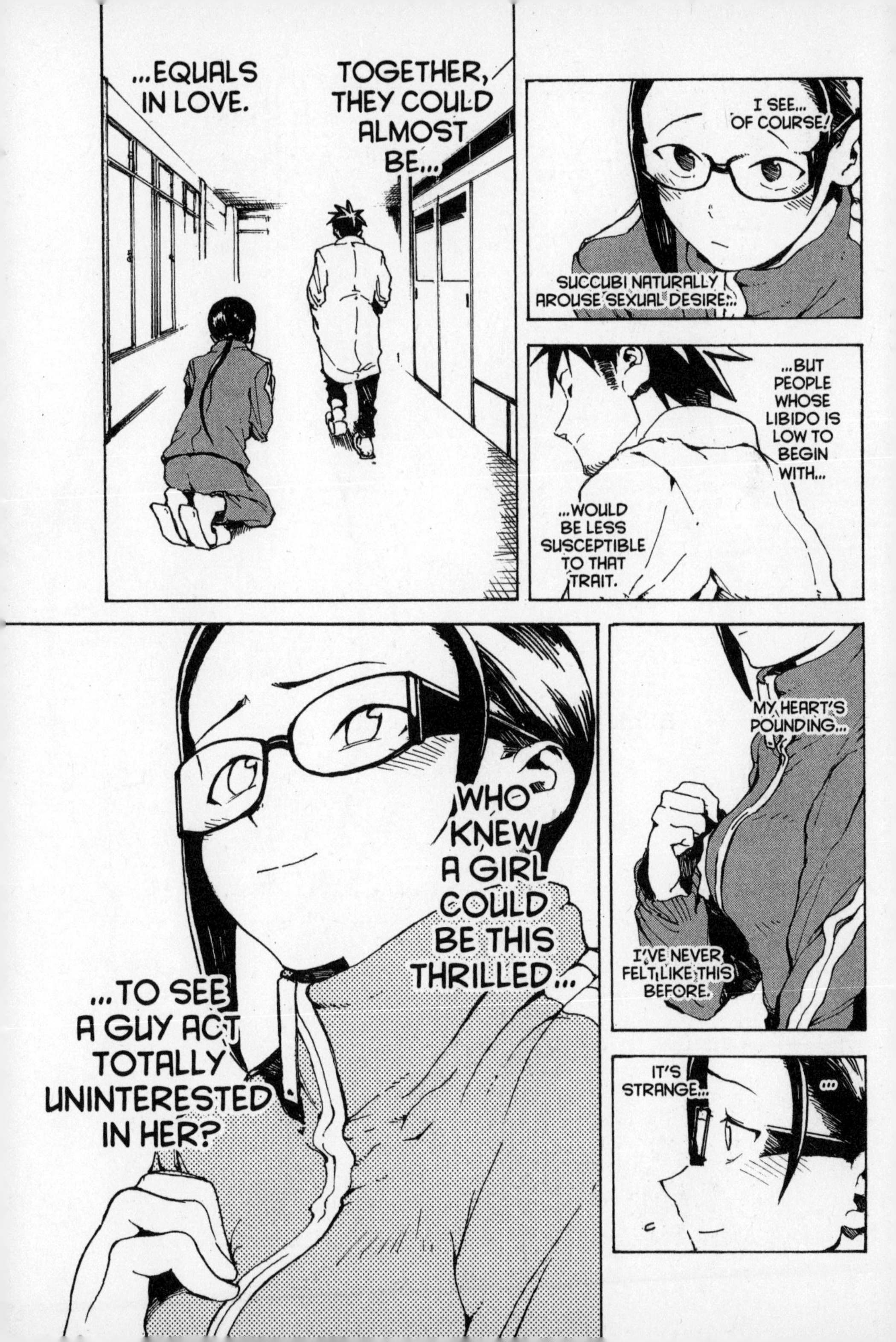
I SEE... OF COURSE!
SUCCUBI NATURALLY AROUSE SEXUAL DESIRE...
...BUT PEOPLE WHOSE LIBIDO IS LOW TO BEGIN WITH...
...WOULD BE LESS SUSCEPTIBLE TO THAT TRAIT.
TOGETHER, THEY COULD ALMOST BE...
...EQUALS IN LOVE.
MY HEART'S POUNDING...
I'VE NEVER FELT LIKE THIS BEFORE.
IT'S STRANGE...
...
WHO KNEW A GIRL COULD BE THIS THRILLED...
...TO SEE A GUY ACT TOTALLY UNINTERESTED IN HER?

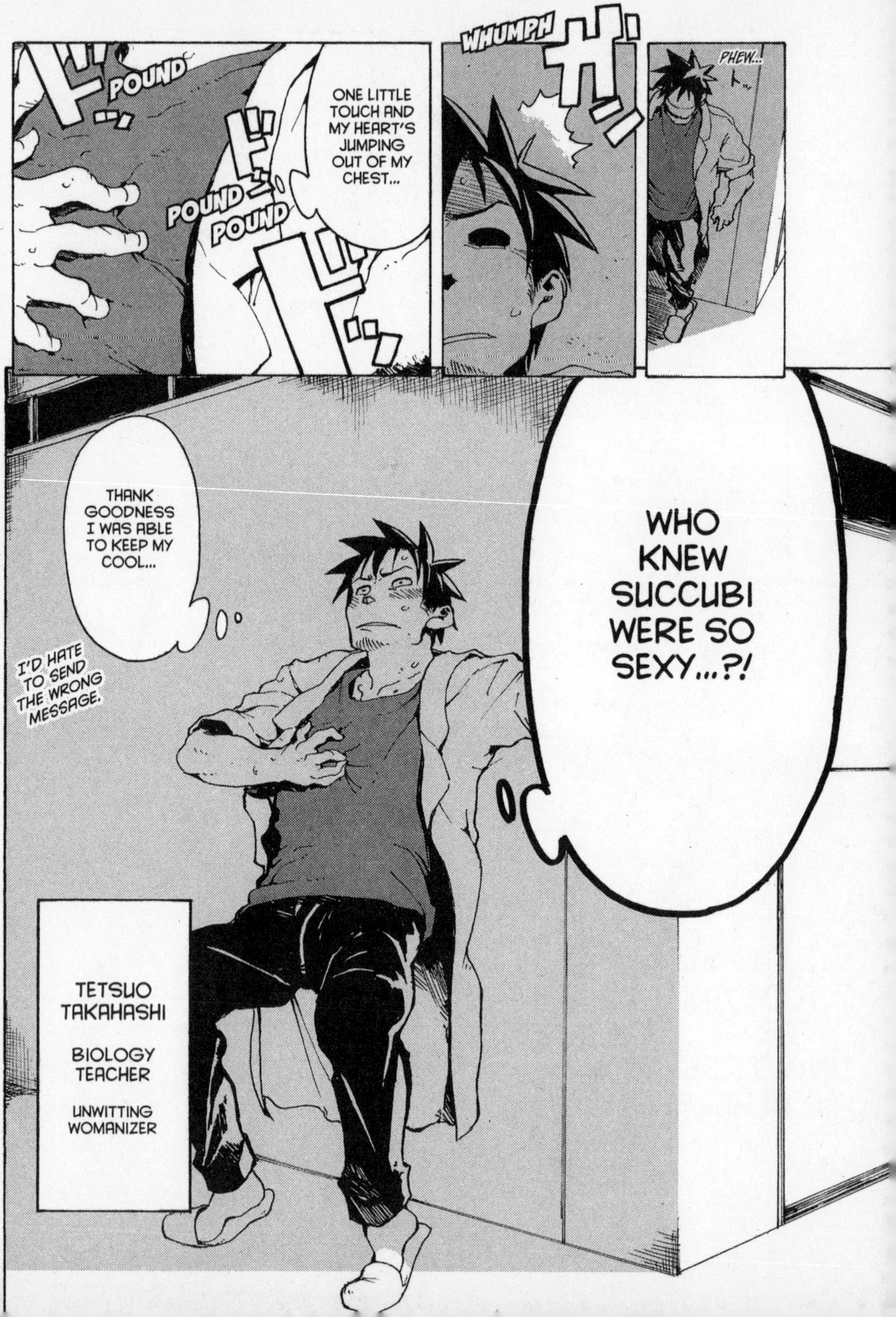
PHEW...
WHUMPH
ONE LITTLE TOUCH AND MY HEART'S JUMPING OUT OF MY CHEST...
POUND
POUND
POUND
WHO KNEW SUCCUBI WERE SO SEXY...?!
THANK GOODNESS I WAS ABLE TO KEEP MY COOL...
I'D HATE TO SEND THE WRONG MESSAGE.
TETSUO TAKAHASHI
BIOLOGY TEACHER
UNWITTING WOMANIZER

BEING A SUCCUBUS IN THE HUMAN WORLD IS TOUGH...
FSS-SSH
THE ONLY TIME I CAN REALLY RELAX IS WHEN I'M AT HOME...
BEER
GLUG
GLUG
KAKI-PEANUTS
THAT'S SOOO
GOO-OOOO-OD!
PERFECTION!
SAKIE SATO
BACHELORETTE

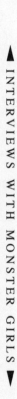

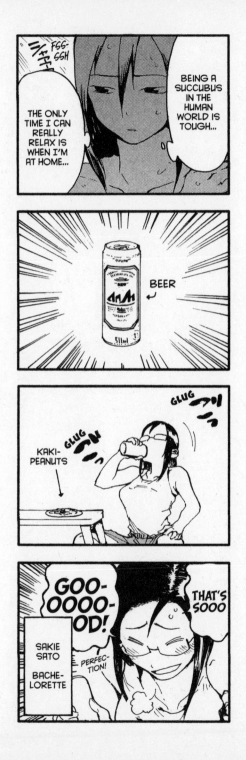

INTERVIEWS WITH MONSTER GIRLS

Chapter 7: Tetsuo Takahashi, Protector of Demis

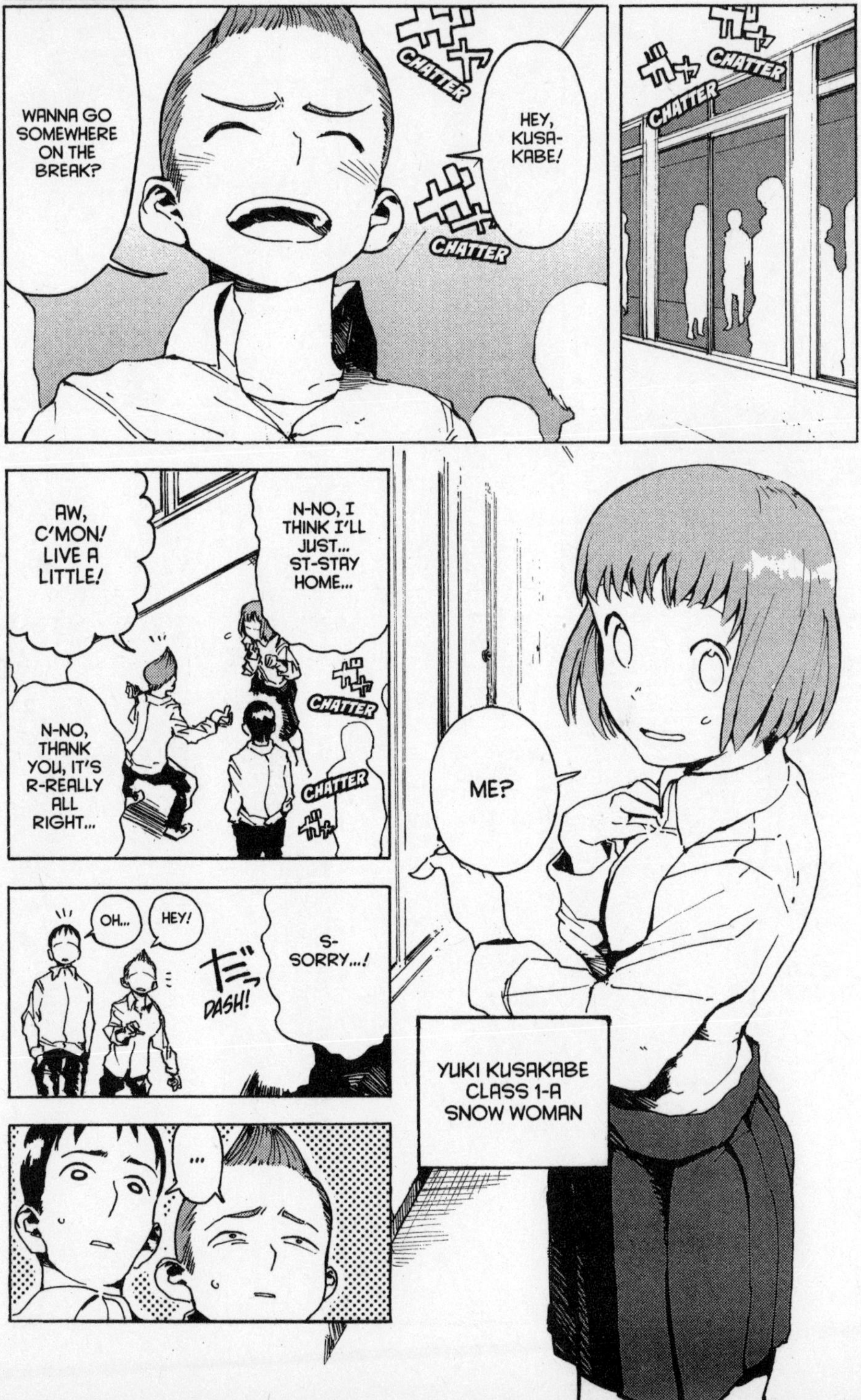
CHATTER
CHATTER
CHATTER
CHATTER
HEY, KUSA-KABE!
WANNA GO SOMEWHERE ON THE BREAK?
ME?
YUKI KUSAKABE CLASS 1-A SNOW WOMAN
N-NO, I THINK I'LL JUST... ST-STAY HOME...
AW, C'MON! LIVE A LITTLE!
N-NO, THANK YOU, IT'S R-REALLY ALL RIGHT...
CHATTER
CHATTER
S-SORRY...!
DASH!
HEY!
OH...
...

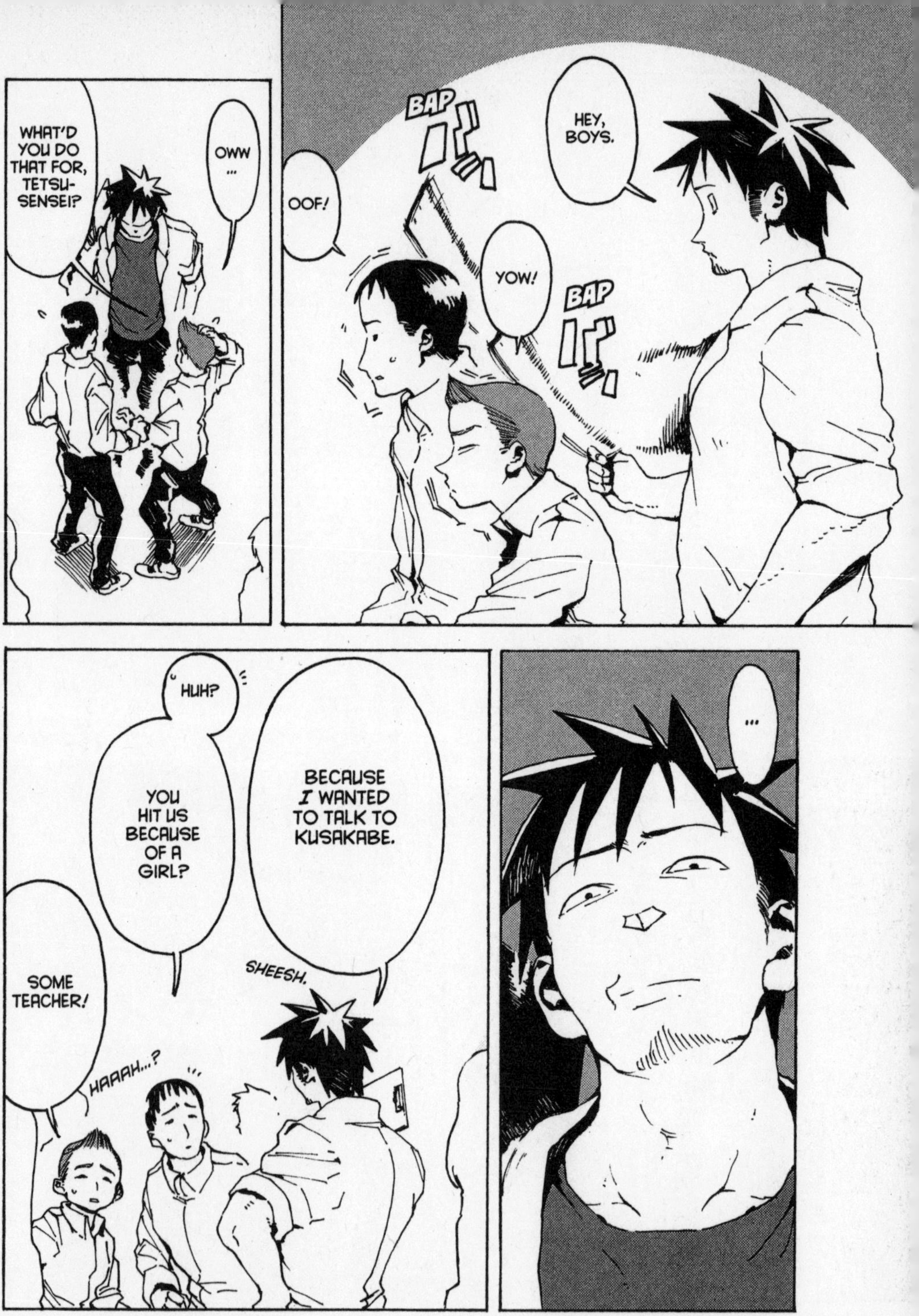
HEY, BOYS.
BAP
OOF!
YOW!
BAP
OWW ...
WHAT'D YOU DO THAT FOR, TETSU-SENSEI?
...
BECAUSE I WANTED TO TALK TO KUSAKABE.
HUH?
YOU HIT US BECAUSE OF A GIRL?
SHEESH.
SOME TEACHER!
HAAAH...?

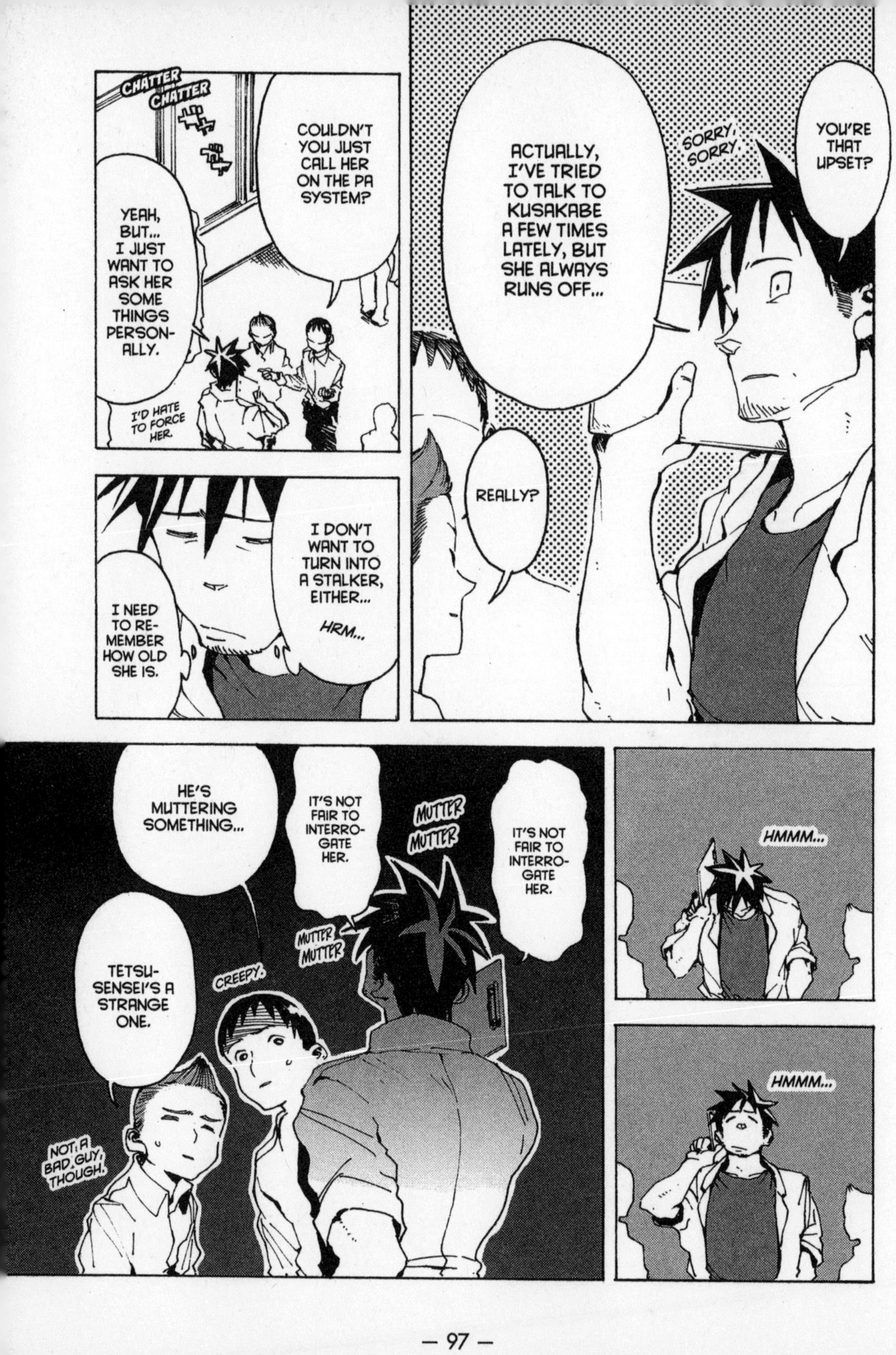
YOU'RE THAT UPSET?
SORRY, SORRY.
ACTUALLY, I'VE TRIED TO TALK TO KUSAKABE A FEW TIMES LATELY, BUT SHE ALWAYS RUNS OFF...
REALLY?
CHATTER CHATTER
COULDN'T YOU JUST CALL HER ON THE PA SYSTEM?
YEAH, BUT... I JUST WANT TO ASK HER SOME THINGS PERSON-ALLY.
I'D HATE TO FORCE HER.
I DON'T WANT TO TURN INTO A STALKER, EITHER...
HRM...
I NEED TO RE-MEMBER HOW OLD SHE IS.
HMMM...
HMMM...
IT'S NOT FAIR TO INTERRO-GATE HER.
MUTTER MUTTER
IT'S NOT FAIR TO INTERRO-GATE HER.
HE'S MUTTERING SOMETHING...
MUTTER MUTTER
CREEPY.
TETSU-SENSEI'S A STRANGE ONE.
NOT A BAD GUY, THOUGH.

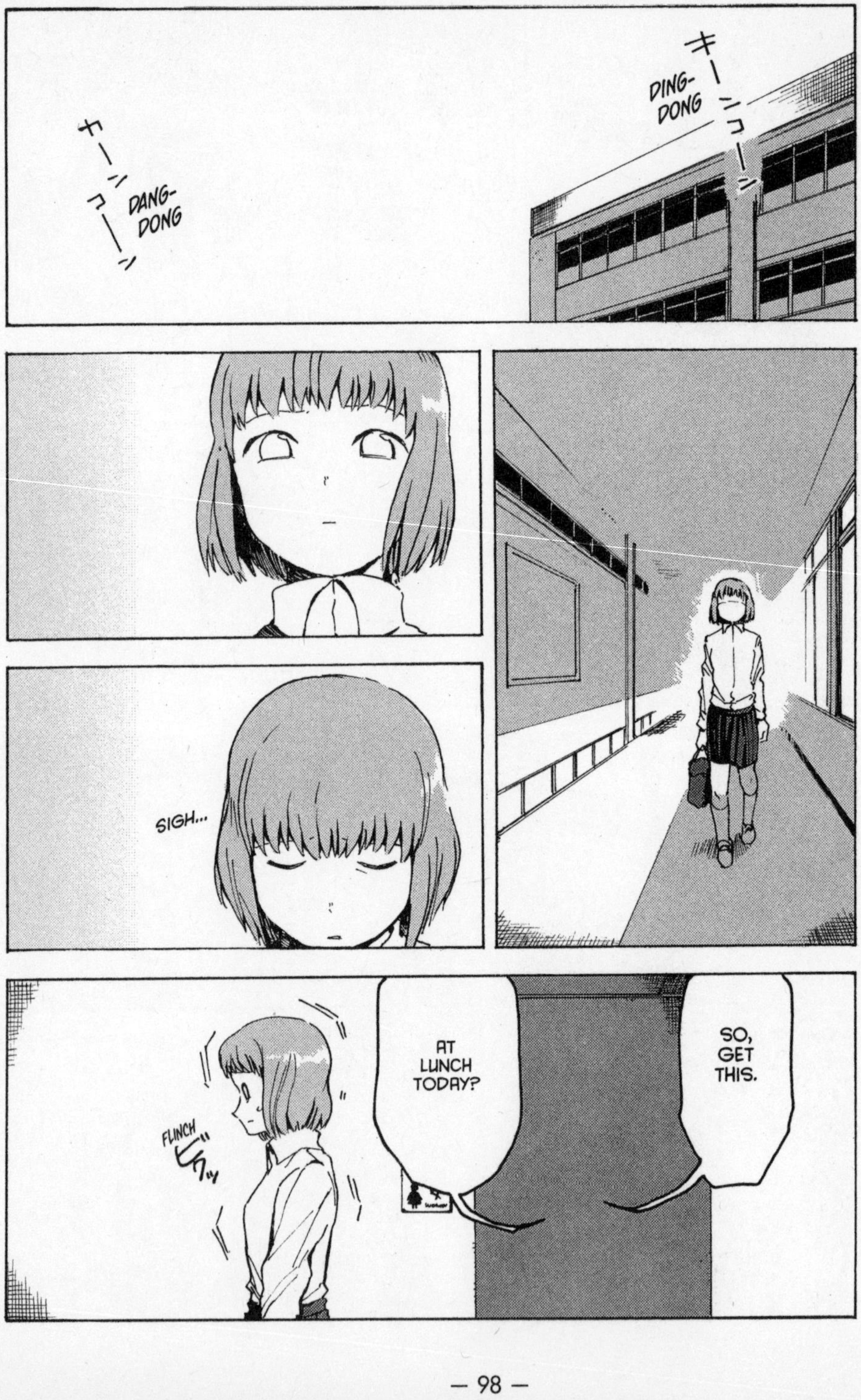
キーンコーン
DING-DONG
カーンコーン
DANG-DONG
SIGH...
SO, GET THIS.
AT LUNCH TODAY?
FLINCH
ビクッ

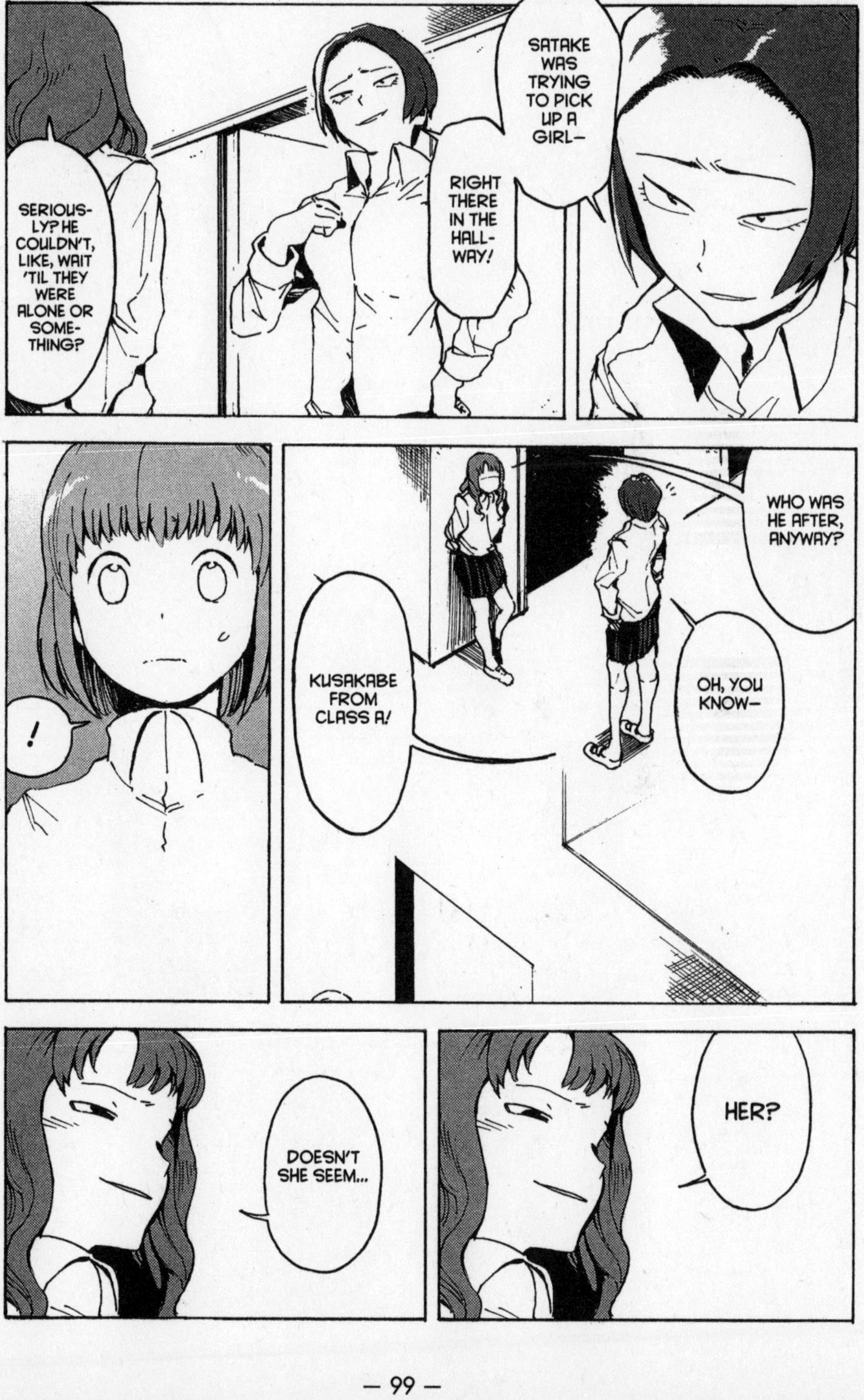
SATAKE WAS TRYING TO PICK UP A GIRL—
RIGHT THERE IN THE HALL-WAY!
SERIOUS-LY? HE COULDN'T, LIKE, WAIT 'TIL THEY WERE ALONE OR SOME-THING?
WHO WAS HE AFTER, ANYWAY?
OH, YOU KNOW—
KUSAKABE FROM CLASS A!
!
HER?
DOESN'T SHE SEEM...

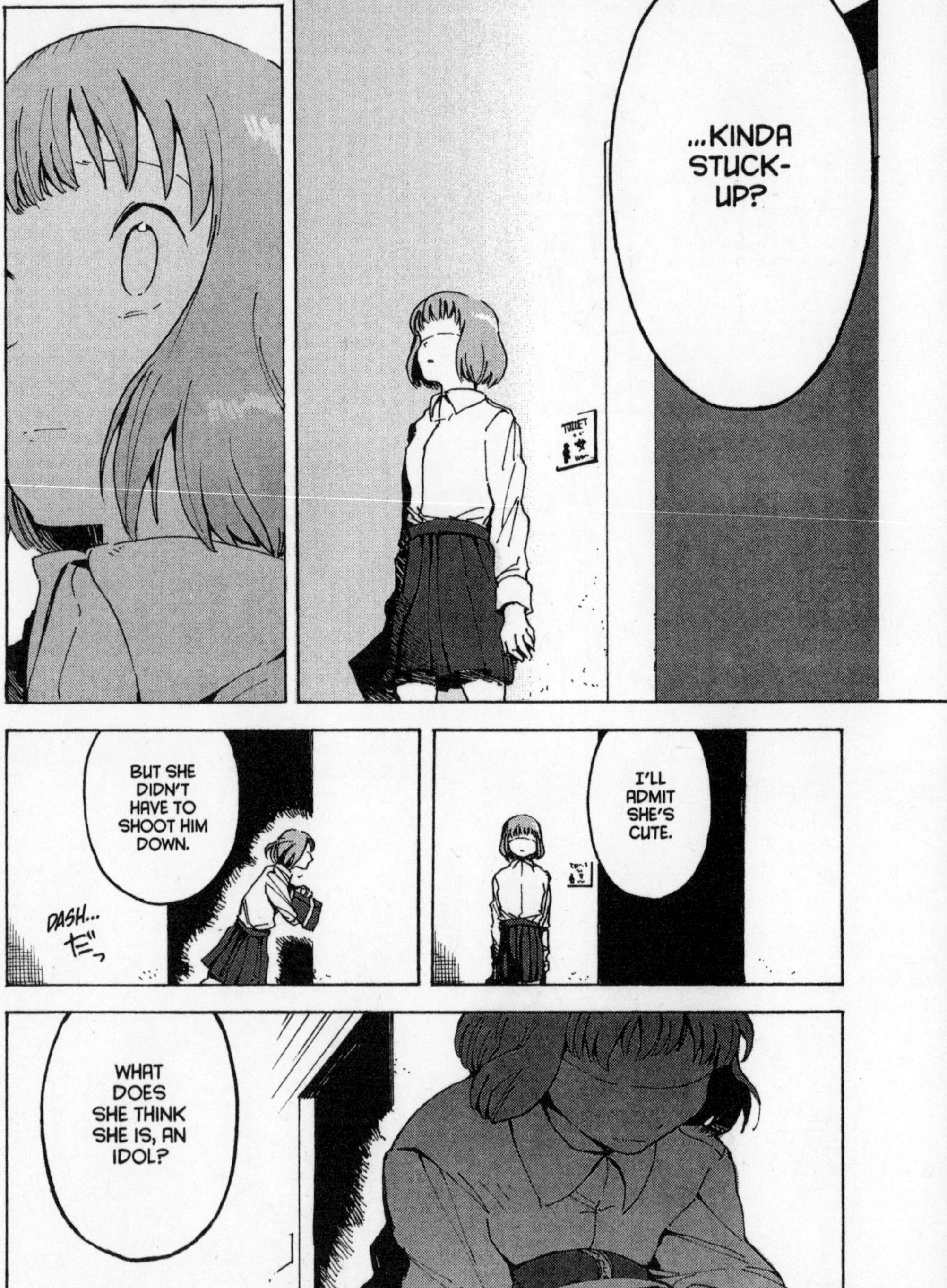
...KINDA STUCK-UP?
I'LL ADMIT SHE'S CUTE.
BUT SHE DIDN'T HAVE TO SHOOT HIM DOWN.
DASH...
WHAT DOES SHE THINK SHE IS, AN IDOL?

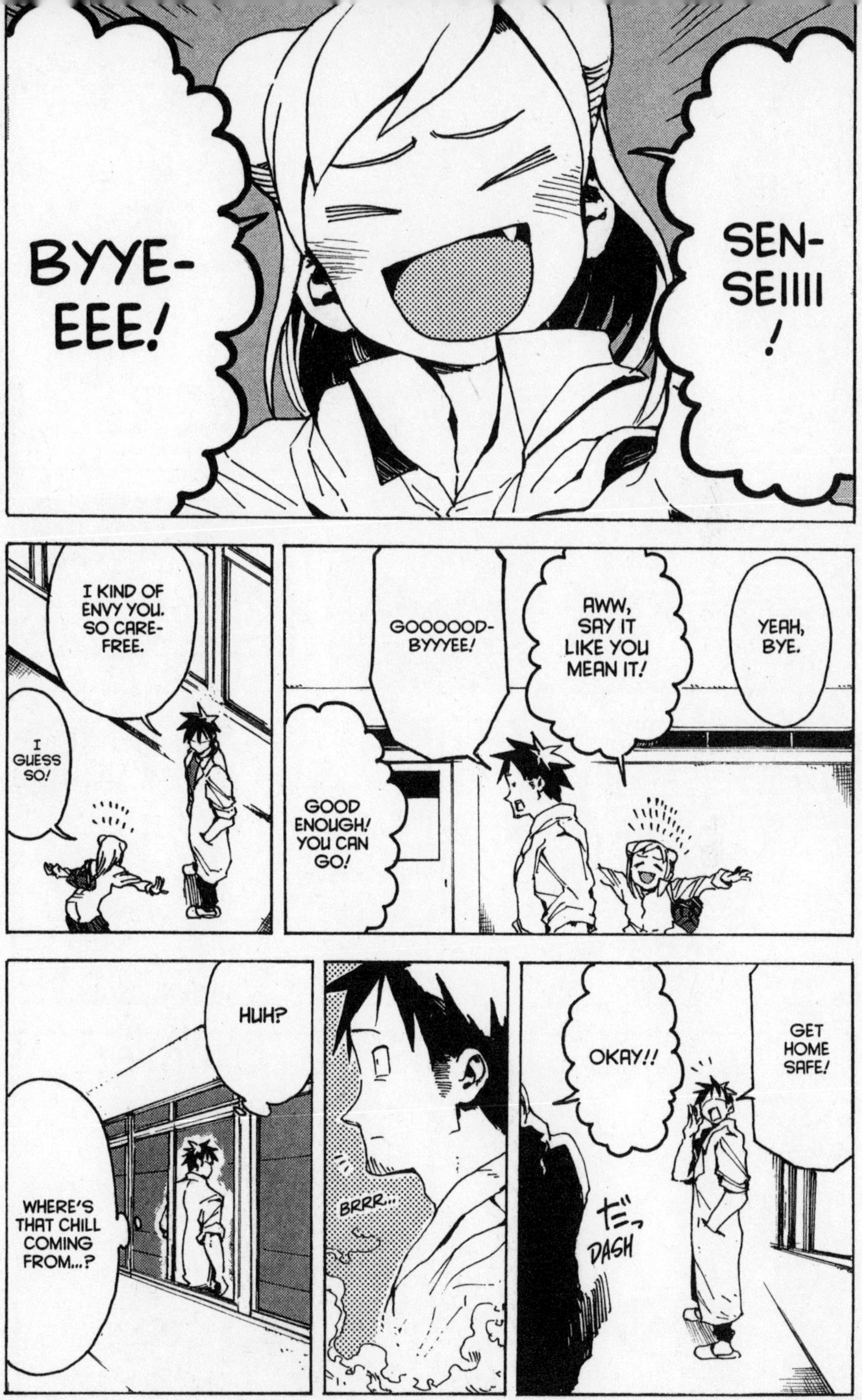
SEN-SEIIII!
BYYE-EEE!
YEAH, BYE.
AWW, SAY IT LIKE YOU MEAN IT!
GOOOOOD-BYYYEE!
GOOD ENOUGH! YOU CAN GO!
I KIND OF ENVY YOU. SO CARE-FREE.
I GUESS SO!
GET HOME SAFE!
OKAY!!
だっ
DASH
BRRR...
HUH?
WHERE'S THAT CHILL COMING FROM...?

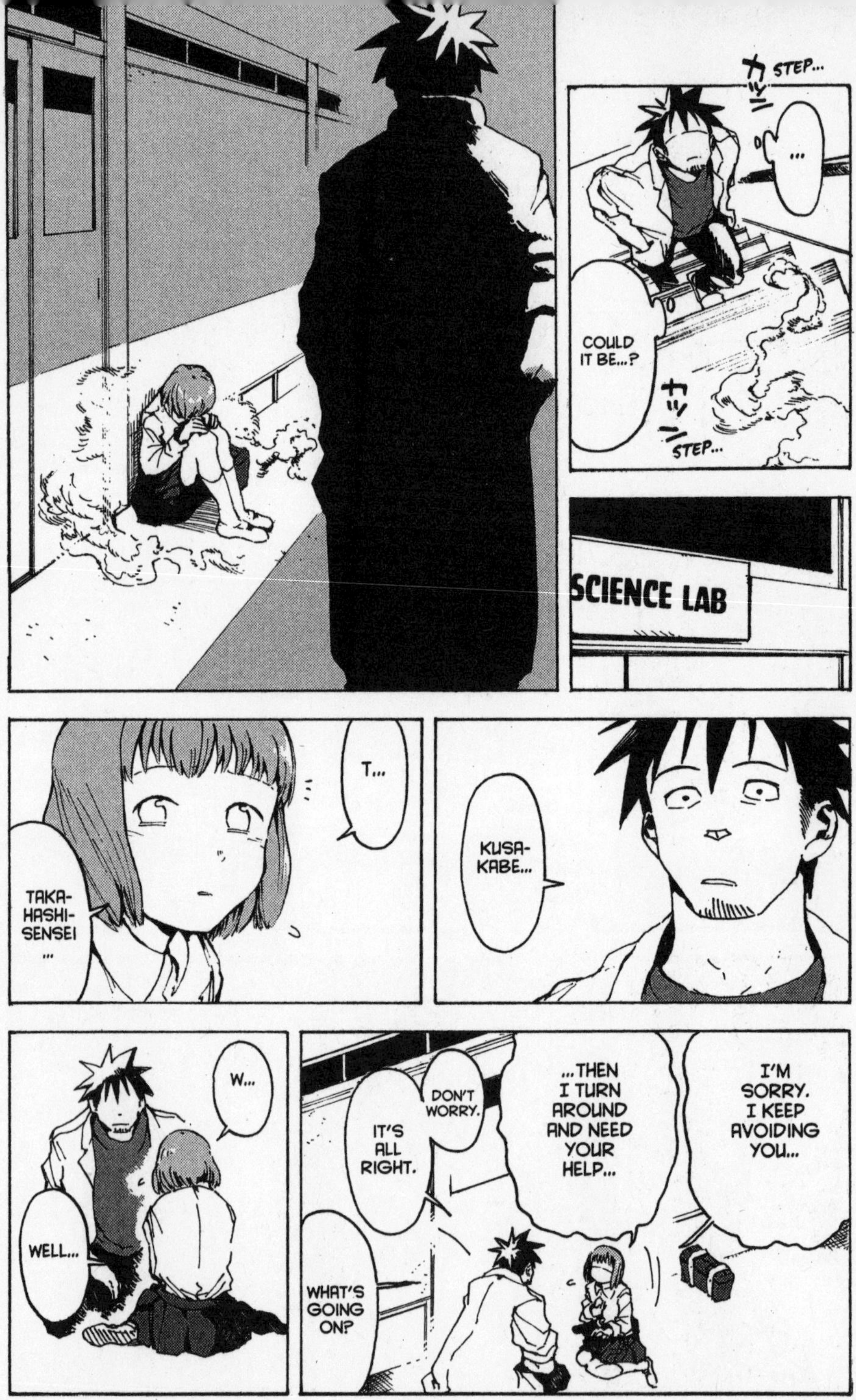
カッ STEP...
...
COULD IT BE...?
カッ STEP...
SCIENCE LAB
KUSA-KABE...
T...
TAKA-HASHI-SENSEI ...
I'M SORRY. I KEEP AVOIDING YOU...
...THEN I TURN AROUND AND NEED YOUR HELP...
DON'T WORRY.
IT'S ALL RIGHT.
WHAT'S GOING ON?
W...
WELL...

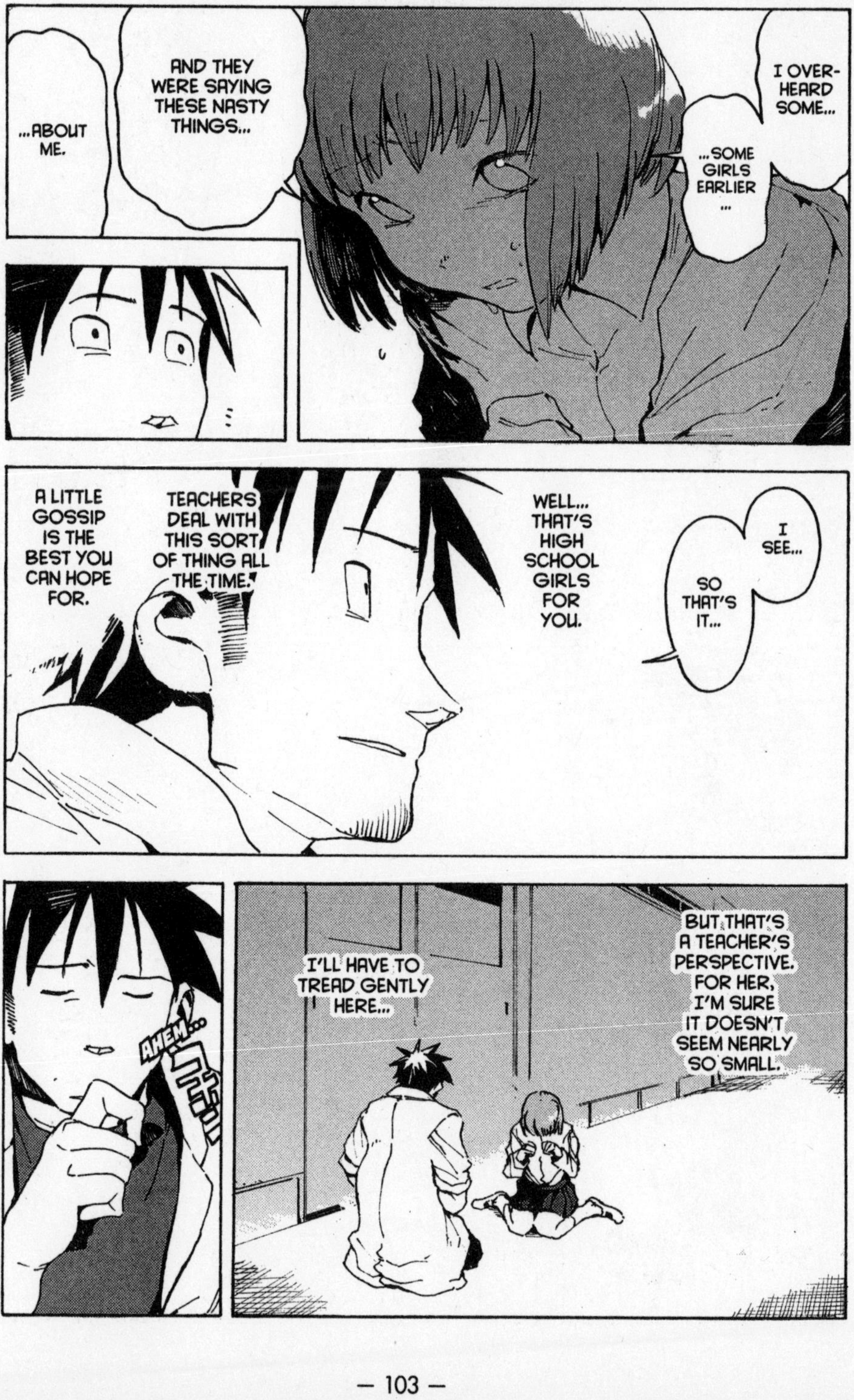
I OVER-HEARD SOME...
...SOME GIRLS EARLIER ...
AND THEY WERE SAYING THESE NASTY THINGS...
...ABOUT ME.
I SEE...
SO THAT'S IT...
WELL... THAT'S HIGH SCHOOL GIRLS FOR YOU.
TEACHERS DEAL WITH THIS SORT OF THING ALL THE TIME.
A LITTLE GOSSIP IS THE BEST YOU CAN HOPE FOR.
BUT THAT'S A TEACHER'S PERSPECTIVE. FOR HER, I'M SURE IT DOESN'T SEEM NEARLY SO SMALL.
I'LL HAVE TO TREAD GENTLY HERE...
AHEM...

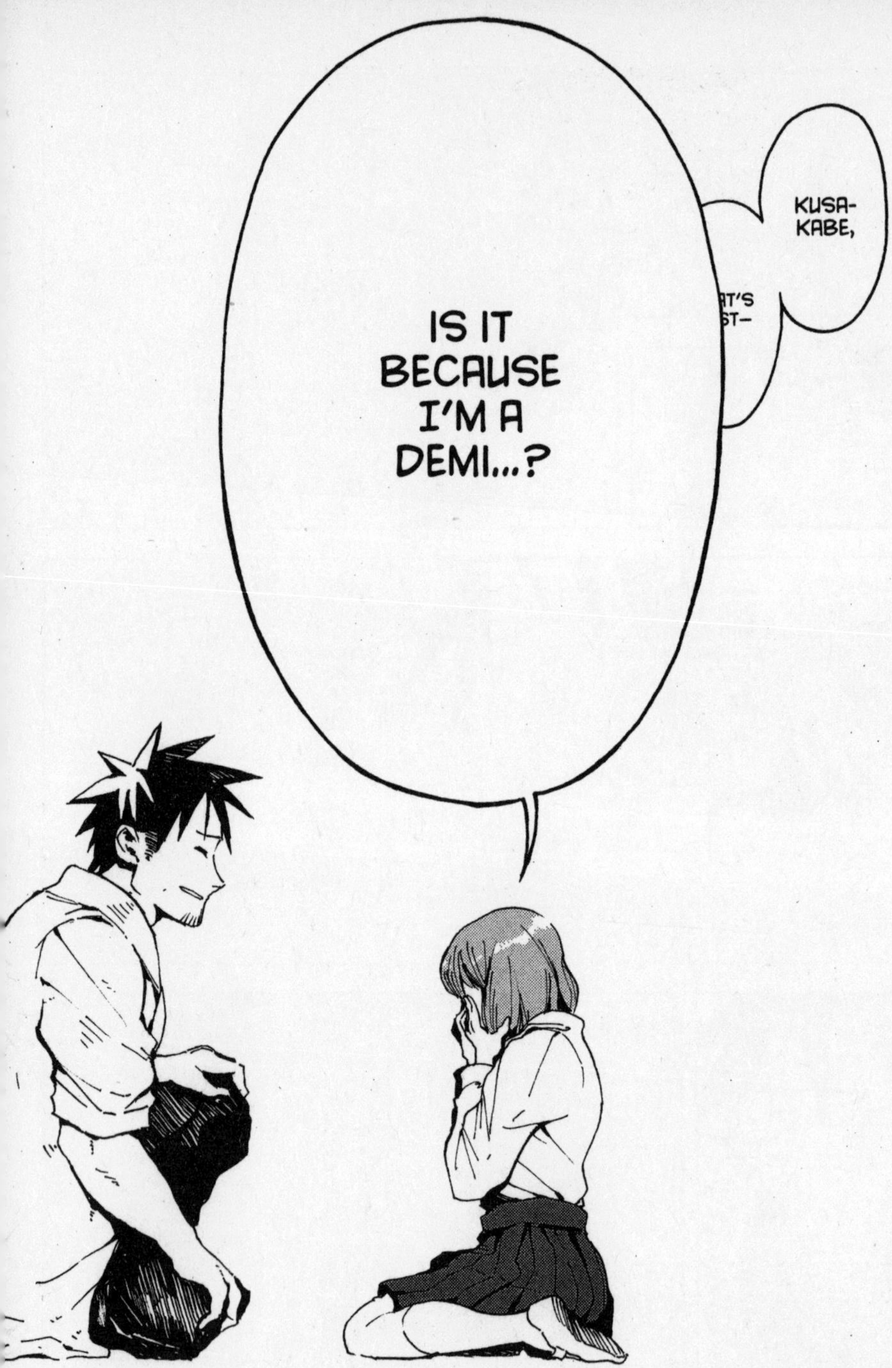
KUSA-KABE,
IS IT BECAUSE I'M A DEMI...?

...
HUH?
IF I WEREN'T...
...THE WAY I AM...
...MAYBE THEY WOULDN'T ...
...MAKE ME FEEL THIS WAY...

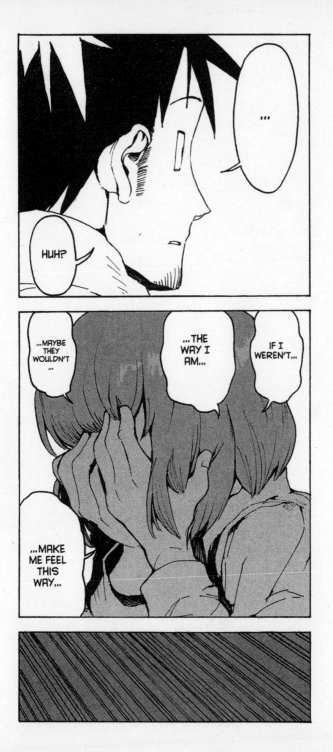

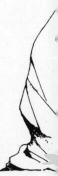

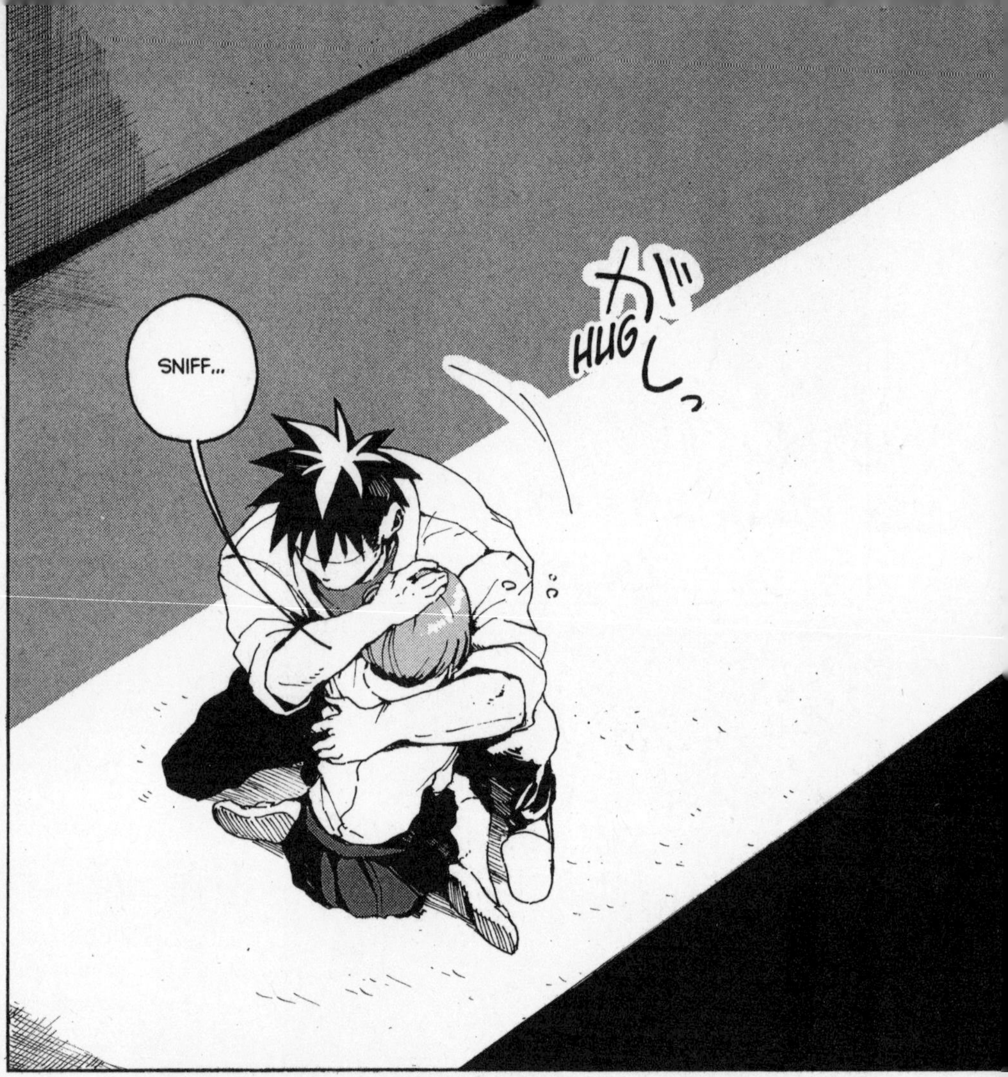
がしっ
HUG
SNIFF...

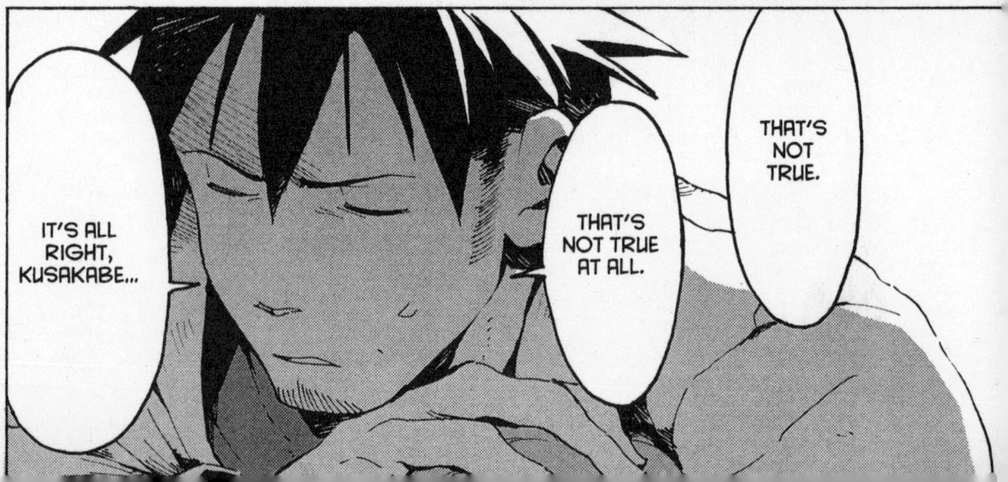
THAT'S NOT TRUE.
THAT'S NOT TRUE AT ALL.
IT'S ALL RIGHT, KUSAKABE...

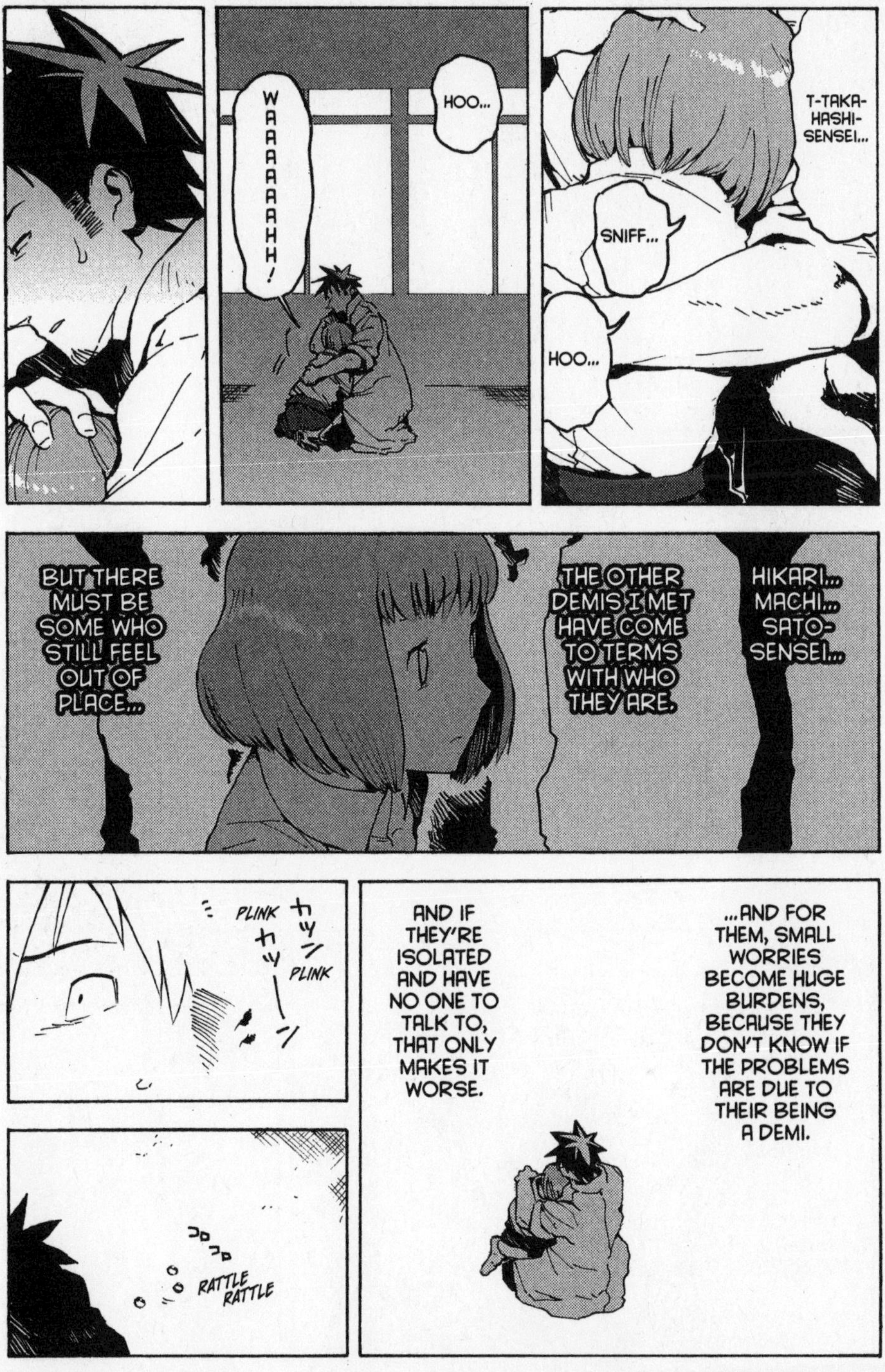
T-TAKAHASHI-SENSEI...
SNIFF...
HOO...
HOO...
WAAAAAAAAHH!
HIKARI... MACHI... SATO-SENSEI...
THE OTHER DEMIS I MET HAVE COME TO TERMS WITH WHO THEY ARE.
BUT THERE MUST BE SOME WHO STILL FEEL OUT OF PLACE...
...AND FOR THEM, SMALL WORRIES BECOME HUGE BURDENS, BECAUSE THEY DON'T KNOW IF THE PROBLEMS ARE DUE TO THEIR BEING A DEMI.
AND IF THEY'RE ISOLATED AND HAVE NO ONE TO TALK TO, THAT ONLY MAKES IT WORSE.
PLINK
PLINK
RATTLE RATTLE

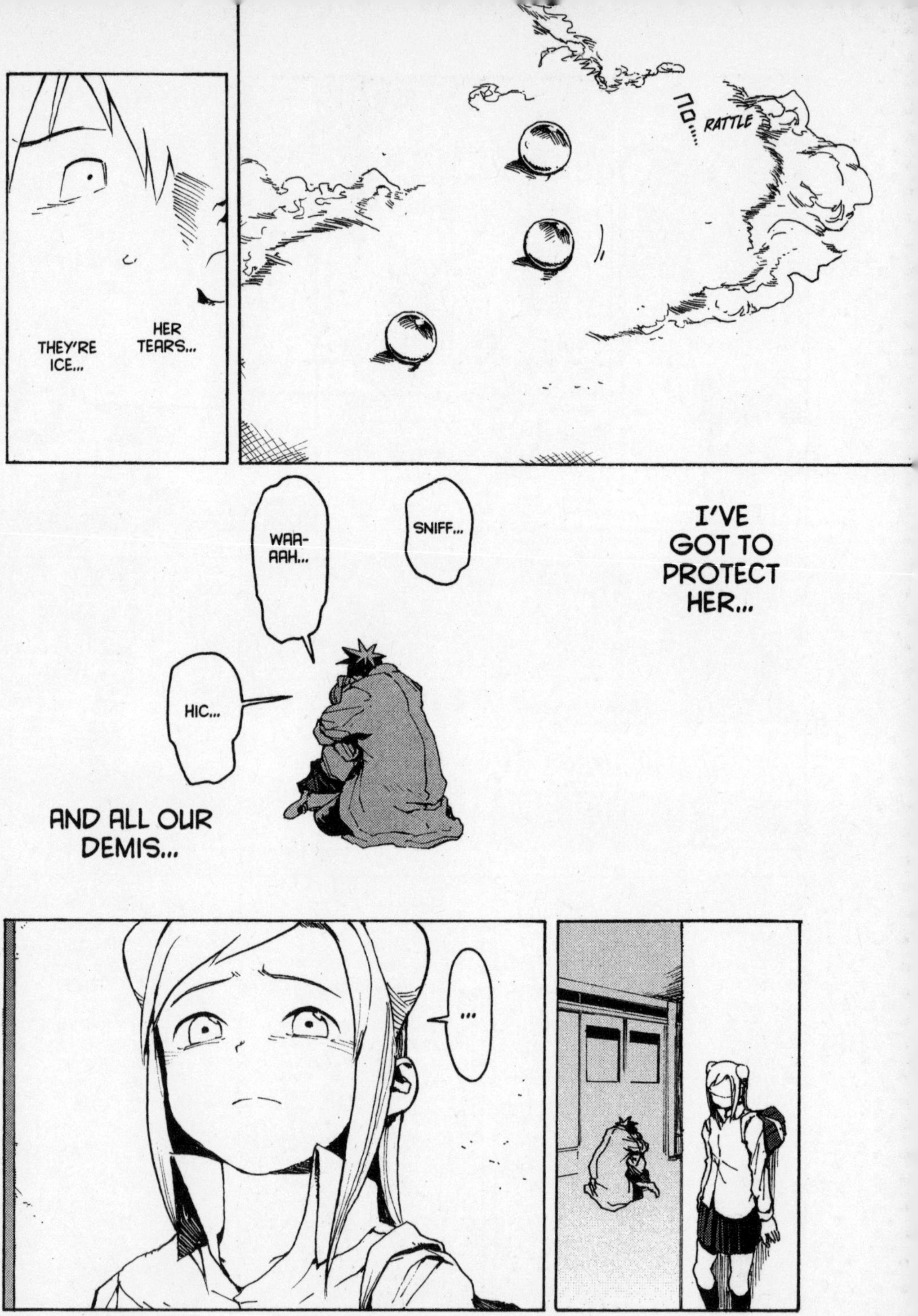

RATTLE
HER TEARS...
THEY'RE ICE...
I'VE GOT TO PROTECT HER...
SNIFF...
WAA-AAH...
HIC...
AND ALL OUR DEMIS...
...

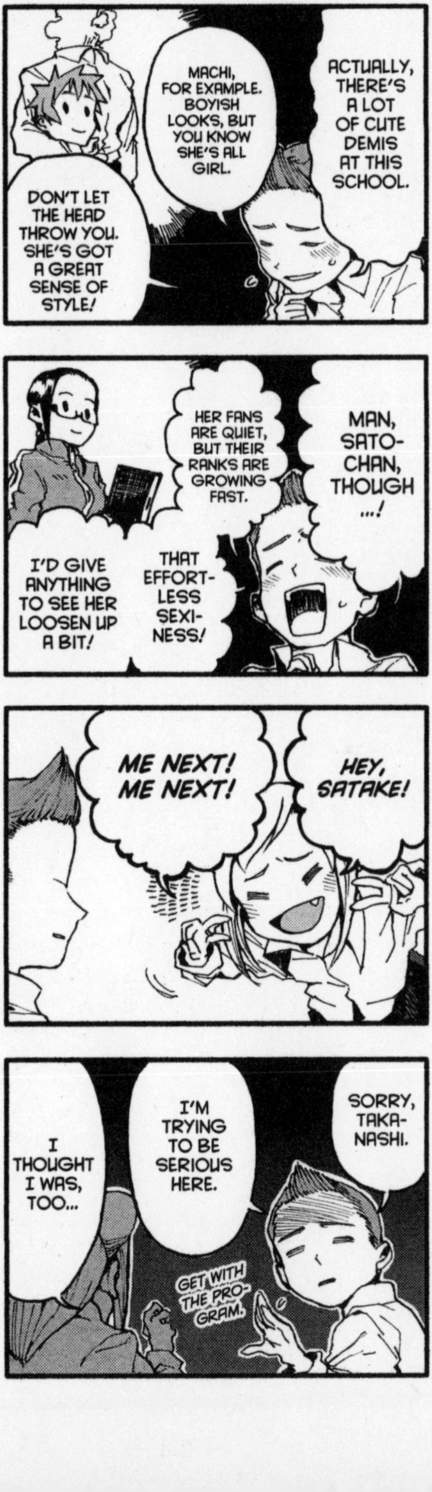
ACTUALLY, THERE'S A LOT OF CUTE DEMIS AT THIS SCHOOL.
MACHI, FOR EXAMPLE. BOYISH LOOKS, BUT YOU KNOW SHE'S ALL GIRL.
DON'T LET THE HEAD THROW YOU. SHE'S GOT A GREAT SENSE OF STYLE!
MAN, SATO-CHAN, THOUGH ...!
HER FANS ARE QUIET, BUT THEIR RANKS ARE GROWING FAST.
THAT EFFORT-LESS SEXI-NESS!
I'D GIVE ANYTHING TO SEE HER LOOSEN UP A BIT!
HEY, SATAKE!
ME NEXT! ME NEXT!
SORRY, TAKA-NASHI.
I'M TRYING TO BE SERIOUS HERE.
I THOUGHT I WAS, TOO...
GET WITH THE PRO-GRAM.

INTERVIEWS WITH MONSTER GIRLS

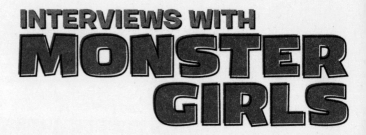

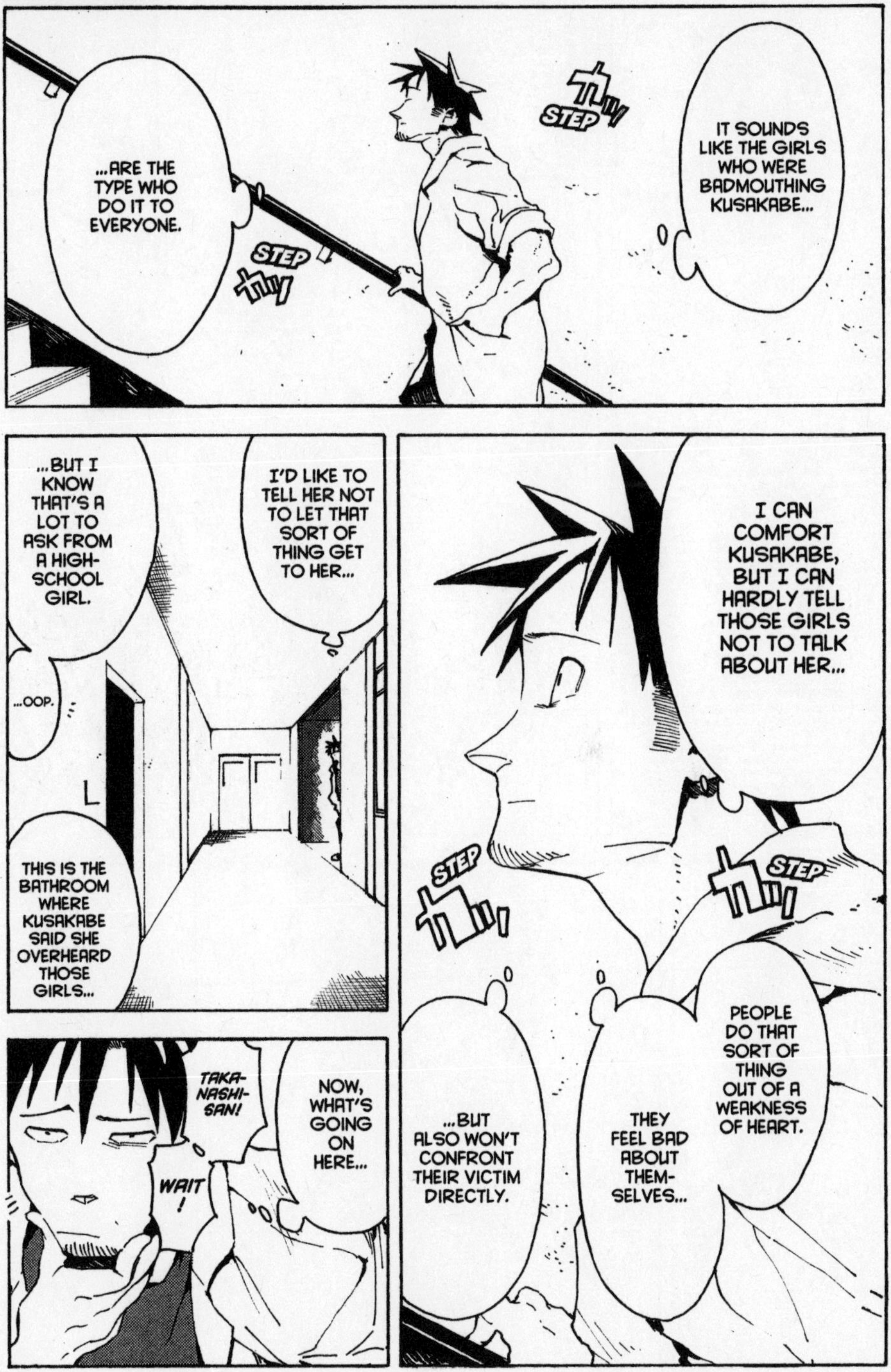
IT SOUNDS LIKE THE GIRLS WHO WERE BADMOUTHING KUSAKABE...
STEP
STEP
...ARE THE TYPE WHO DO IT TO EVERYONE.
I CAN COMFORT KUSAKABE, BUT I CAN HARDLY TELL THOSE GIRLS NOT TO TALK ABOUT HER...
STEP
STEP
PEOPLE DO THAT SORT OF THING OUT OF A WEAKNESS OF HEART.
THEY FEEL BAD ABOUT THEMSELVES...
...BUT ALSO WON'T CONFRONT THEIR VICTIM DIRECTLY.
I'D LIKE TO TELL HER NOT TO LET THAT SORT OF THING GET TO HER...
...BUT I KNOW THAT'S A LOT TO ASK FROM A HIGH-SCHOOL GIRL.
...OOP.
THIS IS THE BATHROOM WHERE KUSAKABE SAID SHE OVERHEARD THOSE GIRLS...
NOW, WHAT'S GOING ON HERE...
TAKA-NASHI-SAN!
WAIT!

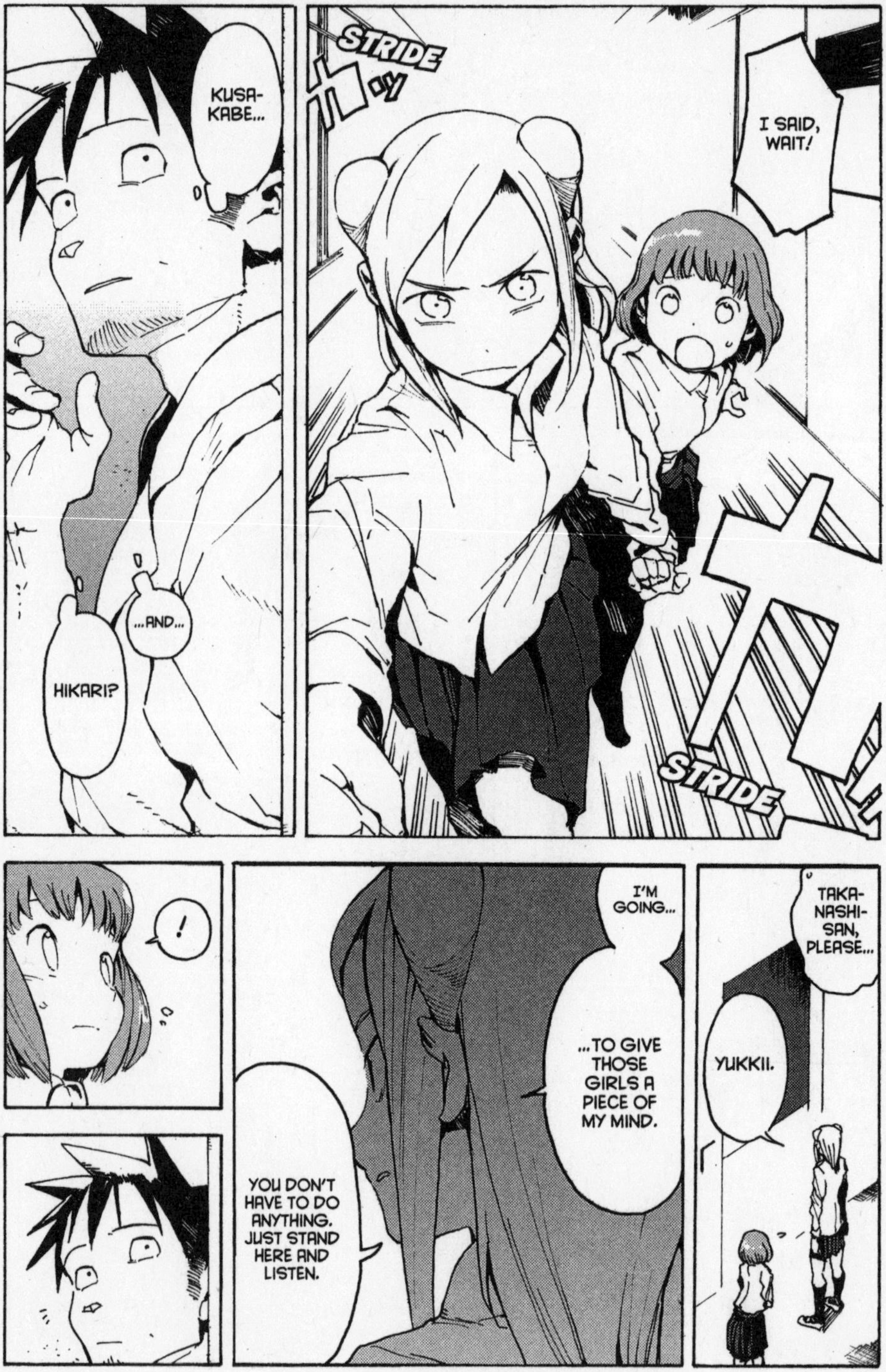
I SAID, WAIT!
STRIDE
STRIDE
KUSA-KABE...
...AND...
HIKARI?
TAKA-NASHI-SAN, PLEASE...
YUKKII.
I'M GOING...
...TO GIVE THOSE GIRLS A PIECE OF MY MIND.
YOU DON'T HAVE TO DO ANYTHING. JUST STAND HERE AND LISTEN.
!

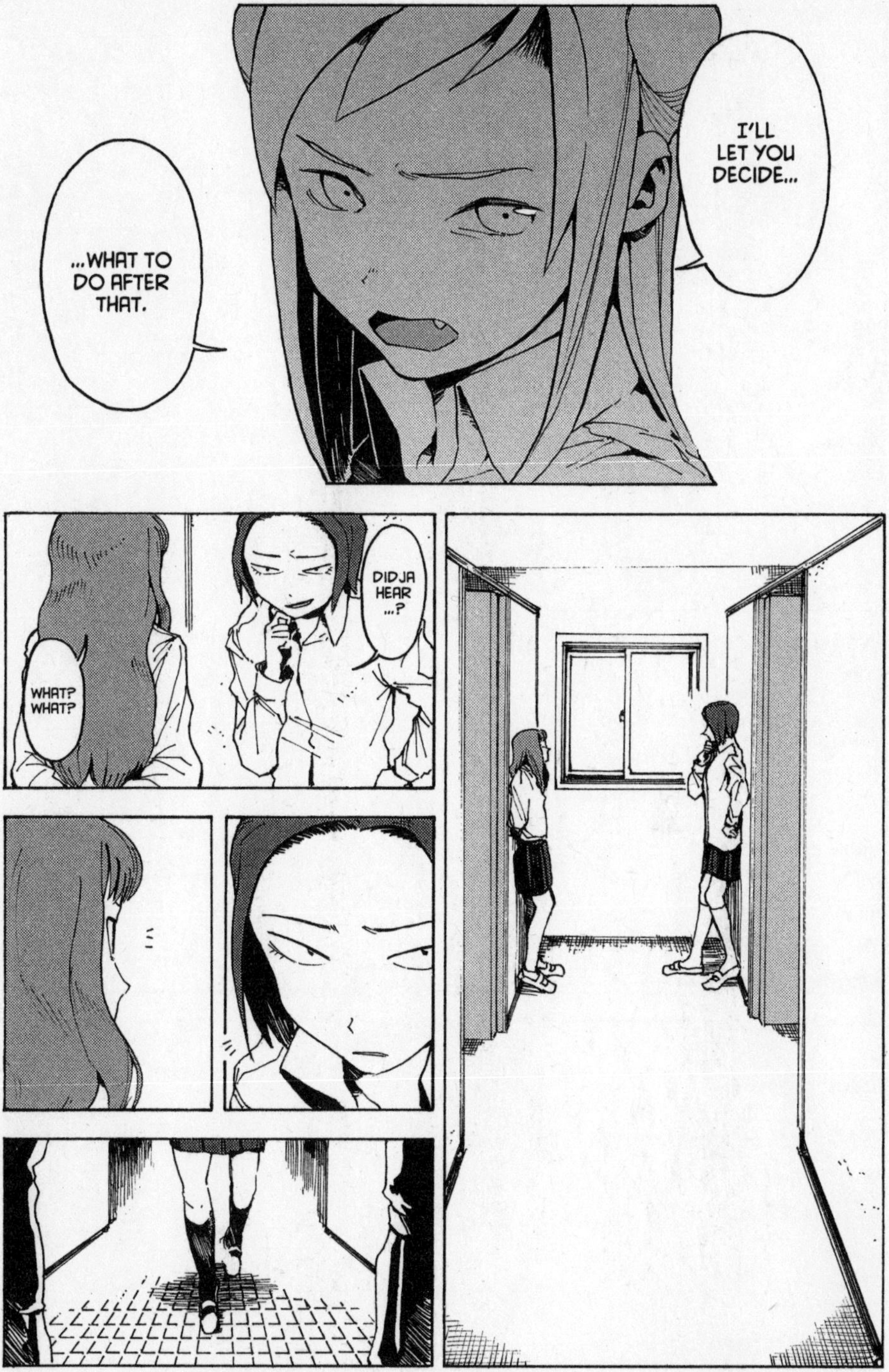
I'LL LET YOU DECIDE...
...WHAT TO DO AFTER THAT.
DIDJA HEAR ...?
WHAT? WHAT?

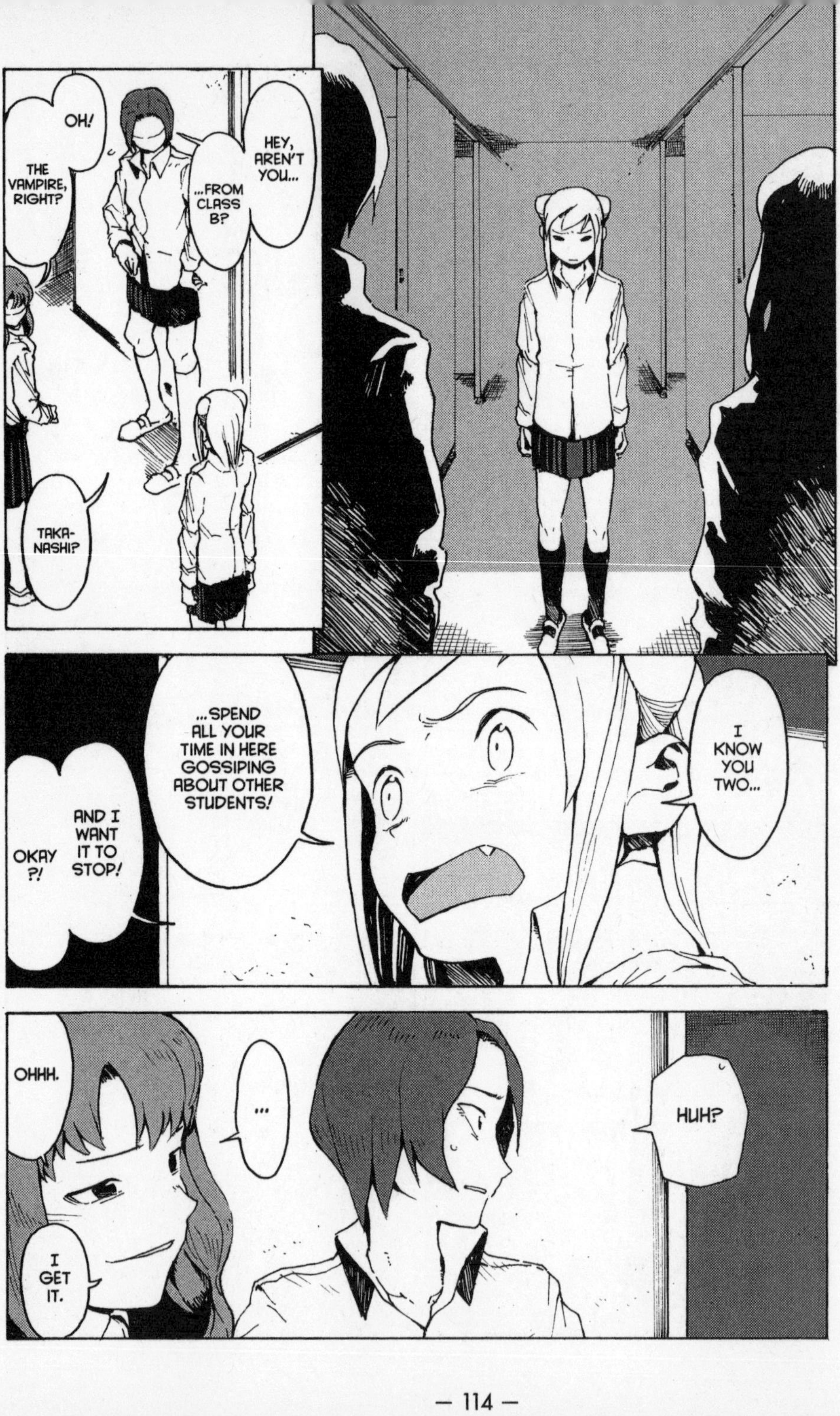
HEY, AREN'T YOU...
...FROM CLASS B?
OH!
THE VAMPIRE, RIGHT?
TAKA-NASHI?
I KNOW YOU TWO...
...SPEND ALL YOUR TIME IN HERE GOSSIPING ABOUT OTHER STUDENTS!
AND I WANT IT TO STOP!
OKAY?!
HUH?
...
OHHH.
I GET IT.

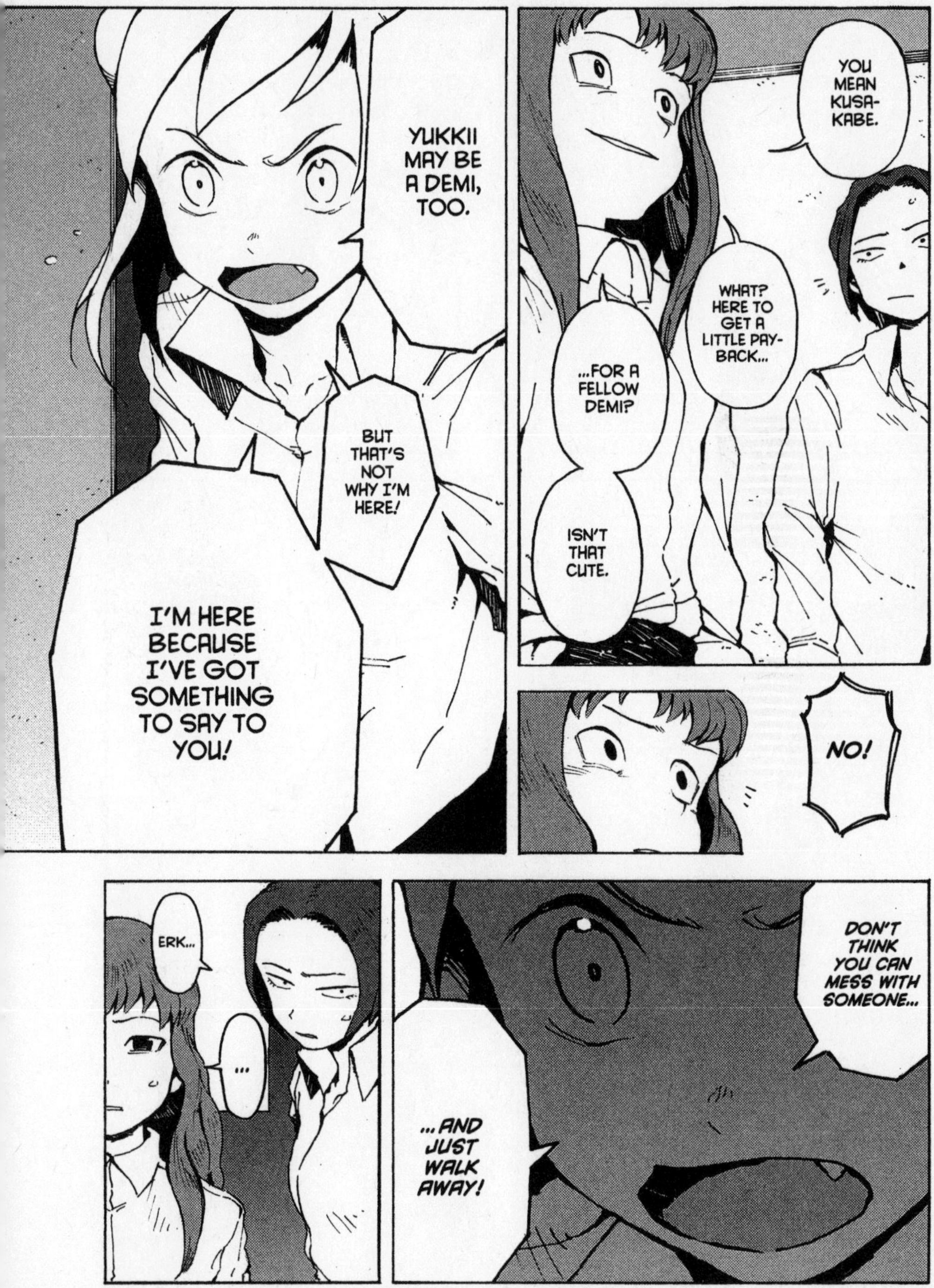
YOU MEAN KUSA-KABE.
WHAT? HERE TO GET A LITTLE PAY-BACK...
...FOR A FELLOW DEMI?
ISN'T THAT CUTE.
NO!
YUKKII MAY BE A DEMI, TOO.
BUT THAT'S NOT WHY I'M HERE!
I'M HERE BECAUSE I'VE GOT SOMETHING TO SAY TO YOU!
DON'T THINK YOU CAN MESS WITH SOMEONE...
...AND JUST WALK AWAY!
ERK...
...

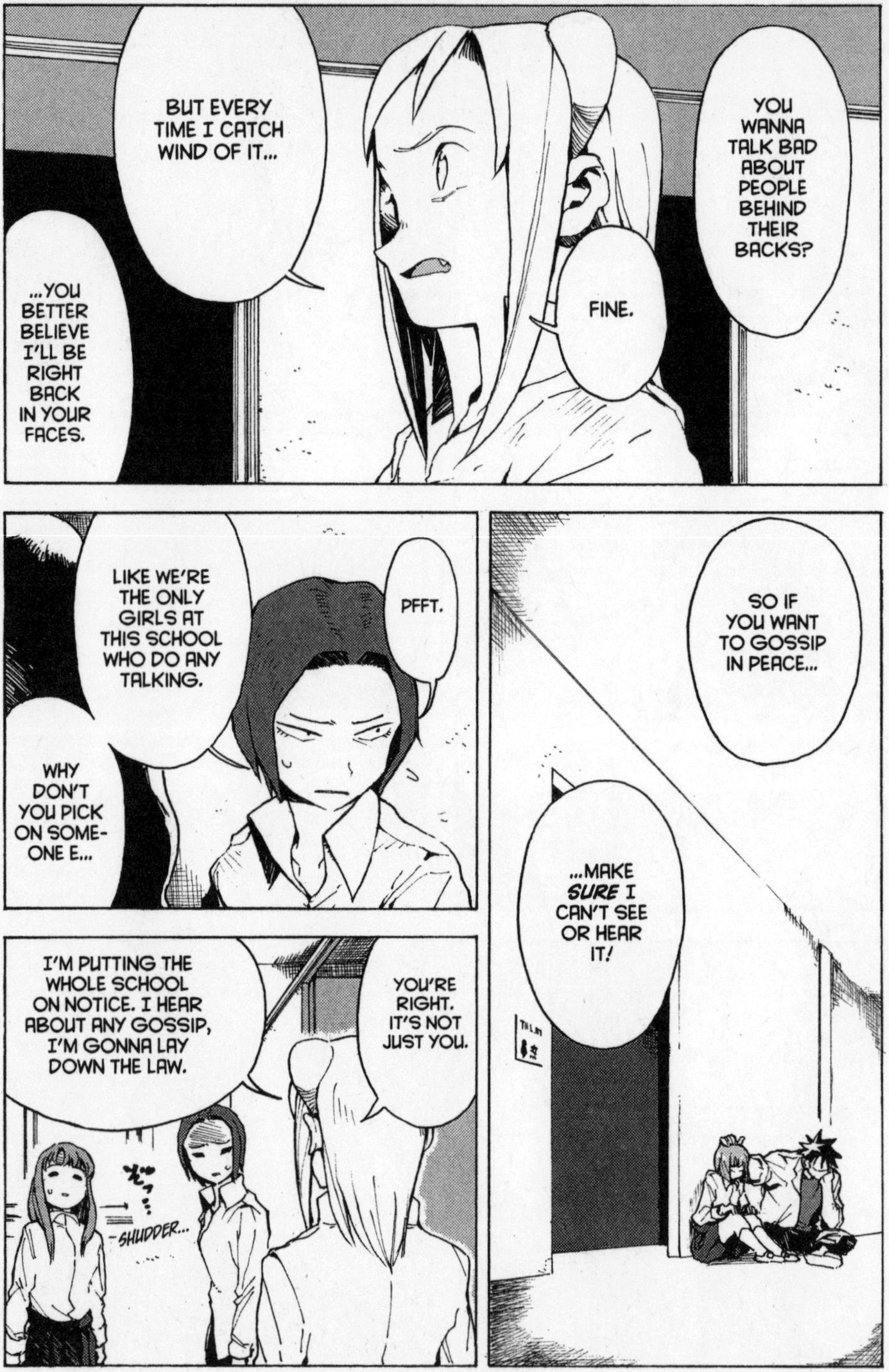
YOU WANNA TALK BAD ABOUT PEOPLE BEHIND THEIR BACKS?
FINE.
BUT EVERY TIME I CATCH WIND OF IT...
...YOU BETTER BELIEVE I'LL BE RIGHT BACK IN YOUR FACES.
SO IF YOU WANT TO GOSSIP IN PEACE...
...MAKE *SURE* I CAN'T SEE OR HEAR IT!
PFFT.
LIKE WE'RE THE ONLY GIRLS AT THIS SCHOOL WHO DO ANY TALKING.
WHY DON'T YOU PICK ON SOME-ONE E...
YOU'RE RIGHT. IT'S NOT JUST YOU.
I'M PUTTING THE WHOLE SCHOOL ON NOTICE. I HEAR ABOUT ANY GOSSIP, I'M GONNA LAY DOWN THE LAW.
SHUDDER...

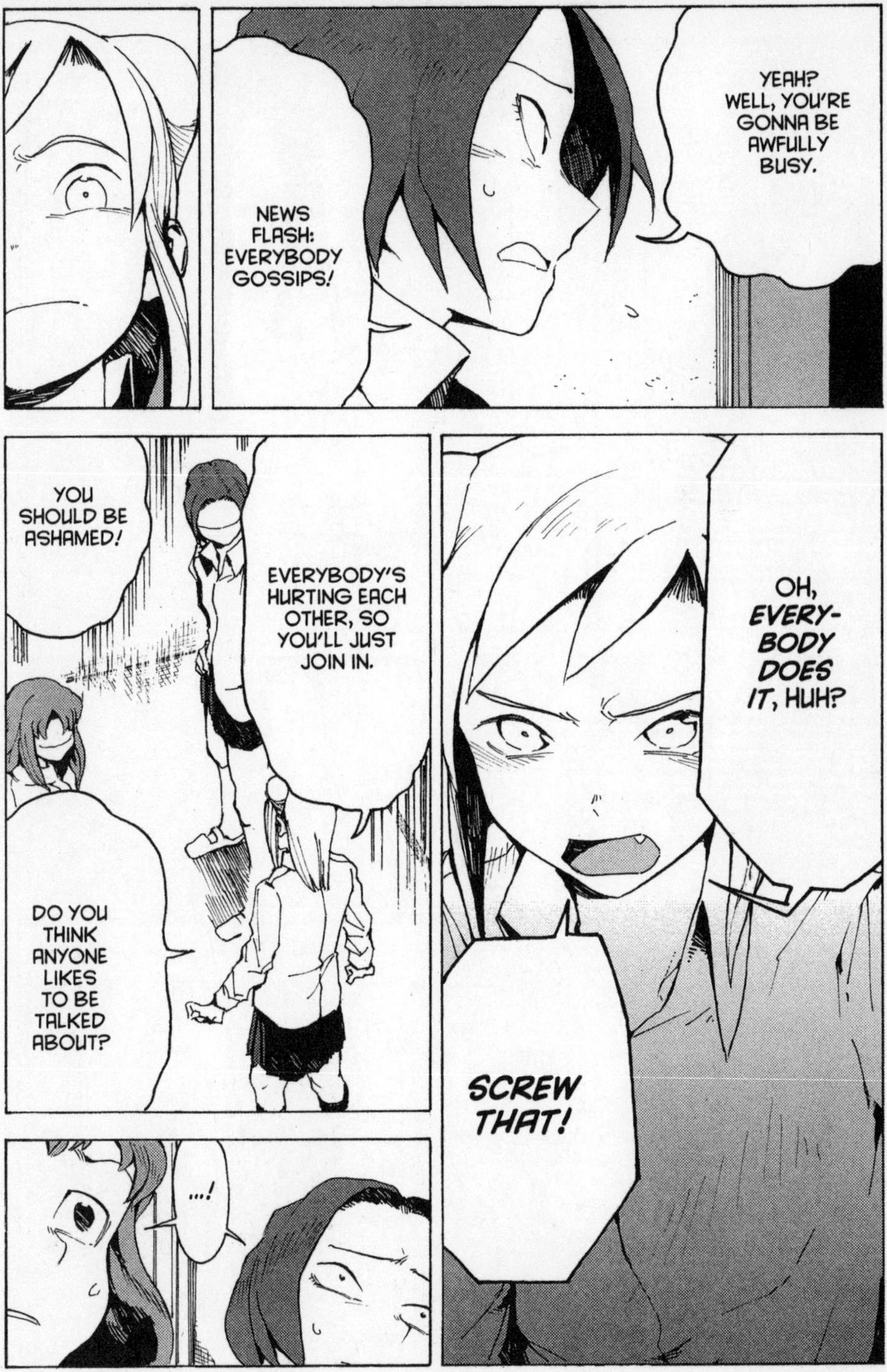
YEAH? WELL, YOU'RE GONNA BE AWFULLY BUSY.
NEWS FLASH: EVERYBODY GOSSIPS!
OH, *EVERYBODY DOES IT*, HUH?
SCREW THAT!
EVERYBODY'S HURTING EACH OTHER, SO YOU'LL JUST JOIN IN.
YOU SHOULD BE ASHAMED!
DO YOU THINK ANYONE LIKES TO BE TALKED ABOUT?
...!

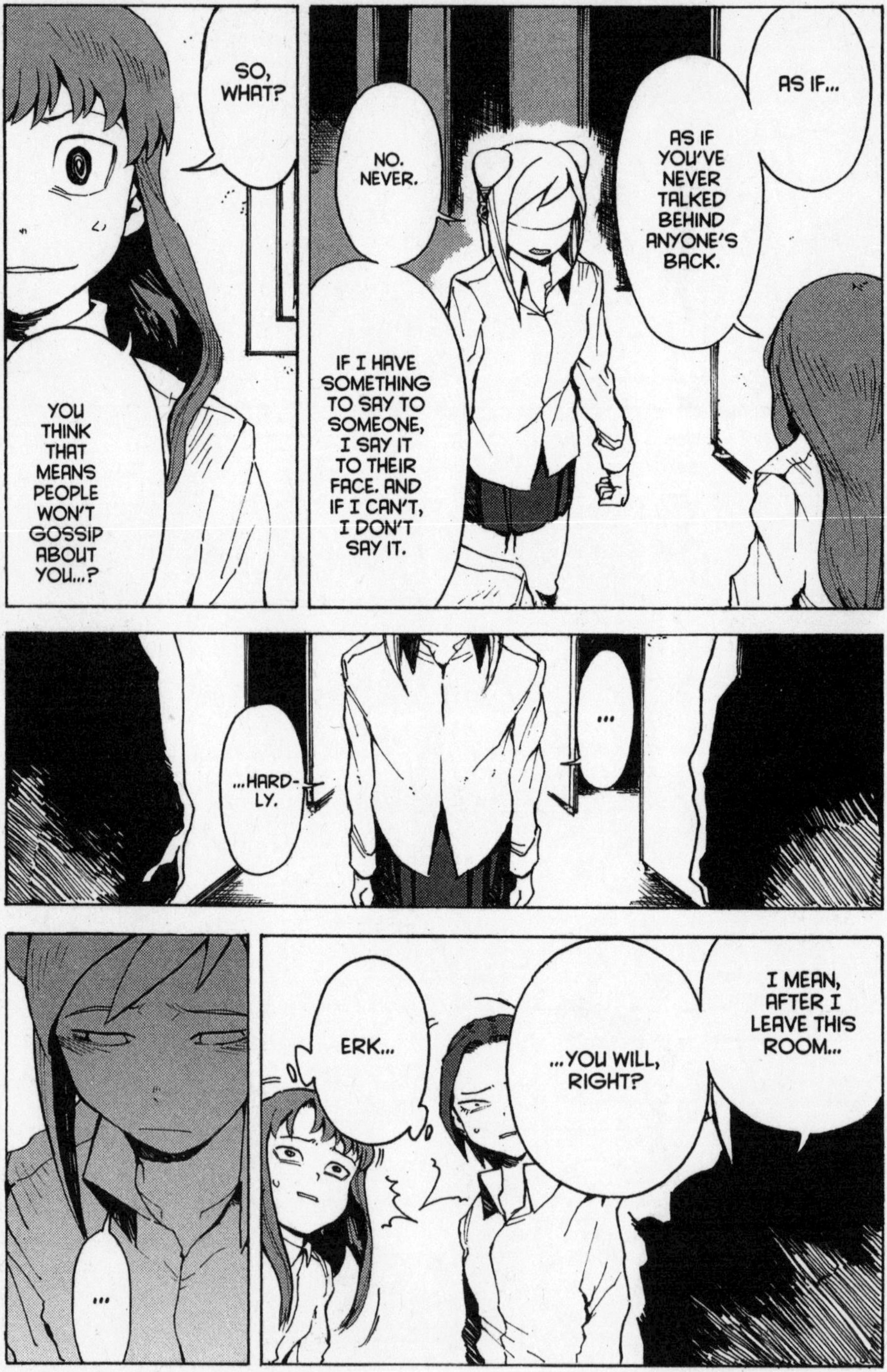
AS IF...
AS IF YOU'VE NEVER TALKED BEHIND ANYONE'S BACK.
NO. NEVER.
IF I HAVE SOMETHING TO SAY TO SOMEONE, I SAY IT TO THEIR FACE. AND IF I CAN'T, I DON'T SAY IT.
SO, WHAT?
YOU THINK THAT MEANS PEOPLE WON'T GOSSIP ABOUT YOU...?
...
...HARD-LY.
I MEAN, AFTER I LEAVE THIS ROOM...
...YOU WILL, RIGHT?
ERK...
...

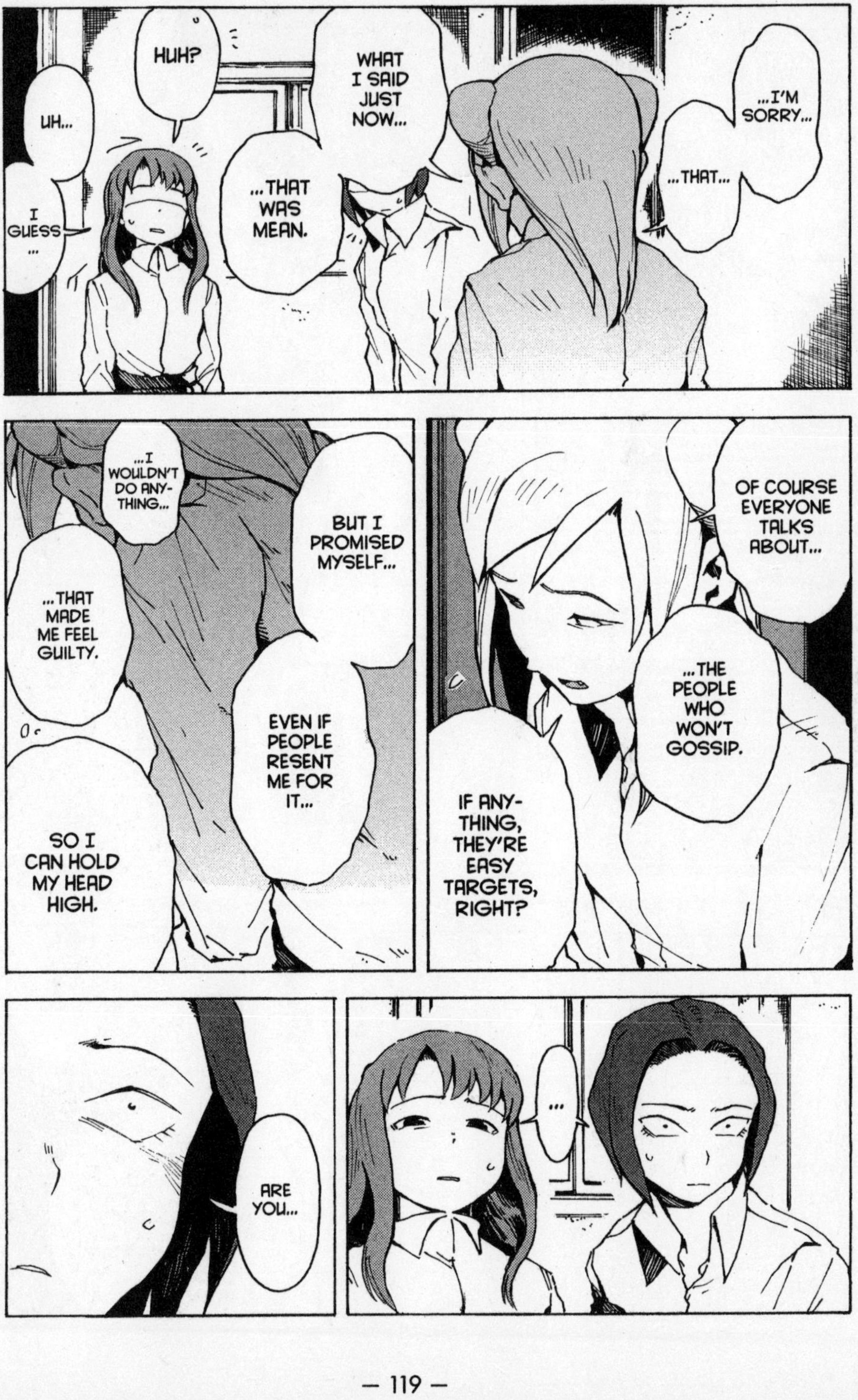
...I'M SORRY...
...THAT...
WHAT I SAID JUST NOW...
...THAT WAS MEAN.
HUH?
UH...
I GUESS ...
OF COURSE EVERYONE TALKS ABOUT...
...THE PEOPLE WHO WON'T GOSSIP.
IF ANYTHING, THEY'RE EASY TARGETS, RIGHT?
BUT I PROMISED MYSELF...
...I WOULDN'T DO ANYTHING...
...THAT MADE ME FEEL GUILTY.
EVEN IF PEOPLE RESENT ME FOR IT...
SO I CAN HOLD MY HEAD HIGH.
...
ARE YOU...

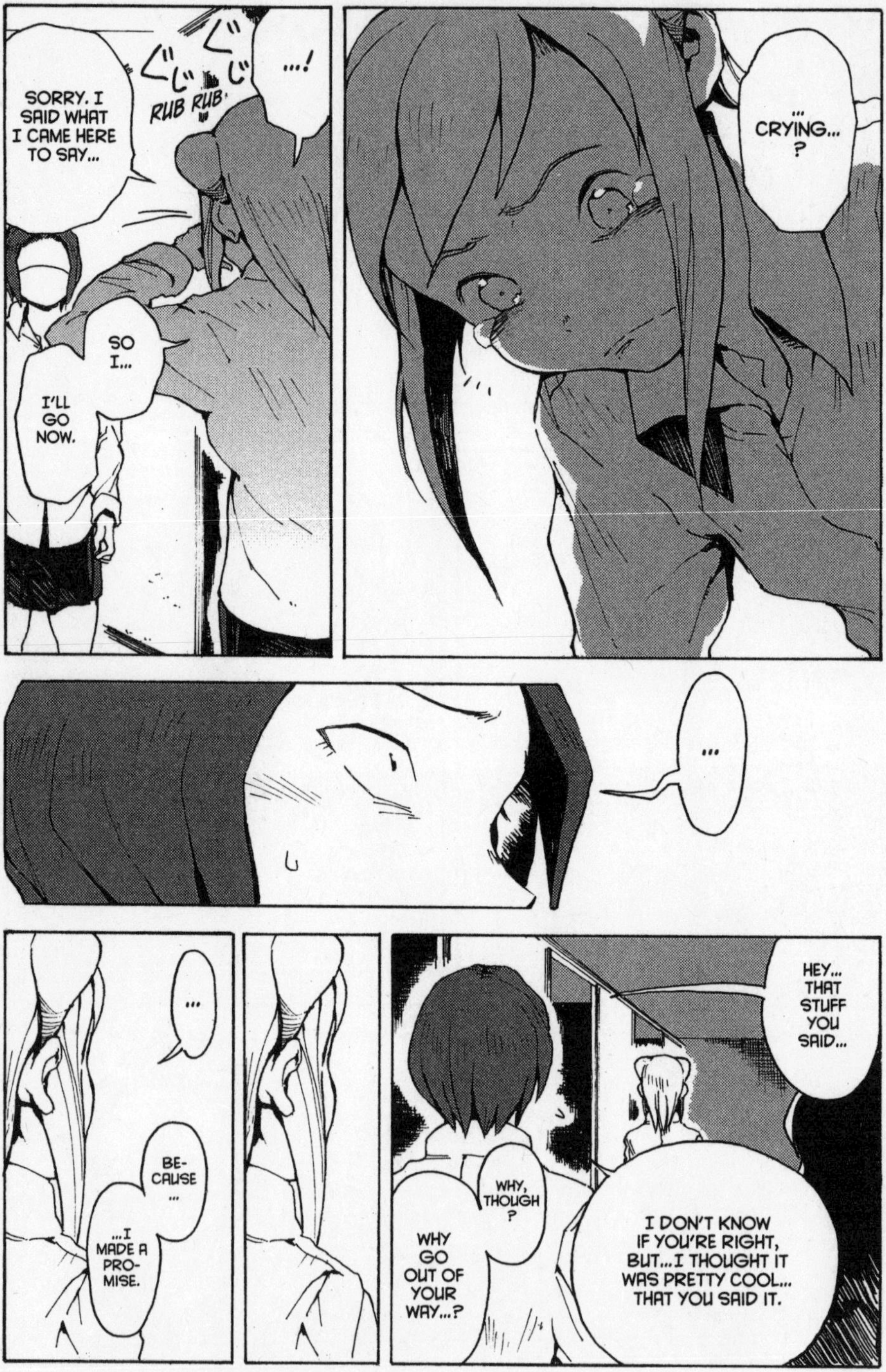
... CRYING... ?
...!
RUB RUB
SORRY. I SAID WHAT I CAME HERE TO SAY...
SO I...
I'LL GO NOW.
...
HEY... THAT STUFF YOU SAID...
I DON'T KNOW IF YOU'RE RIGHT, BUT... I THOUGHT IT WAS PRETTY COOL... THAT YOU SAID IT.
WHY, THOUGH?
WHY GO OUT OF YOUR WAY...?
...
BE-CAUSE...
...I MADE A PRO-MISE.

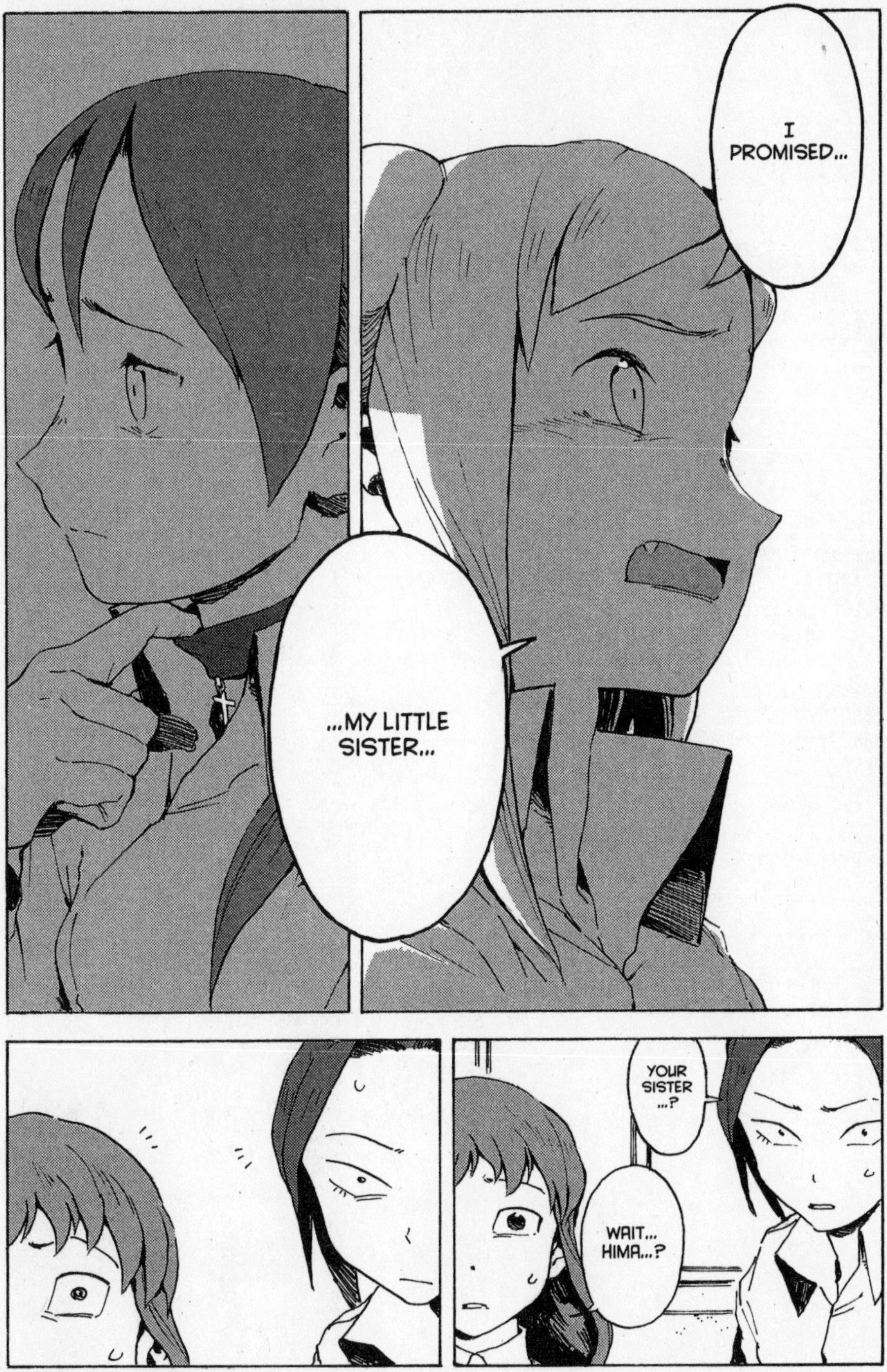

I PROMISED...
...MY LITTLE SISTER...
YOUR SISTER ...?
WAIT... HIMA...?

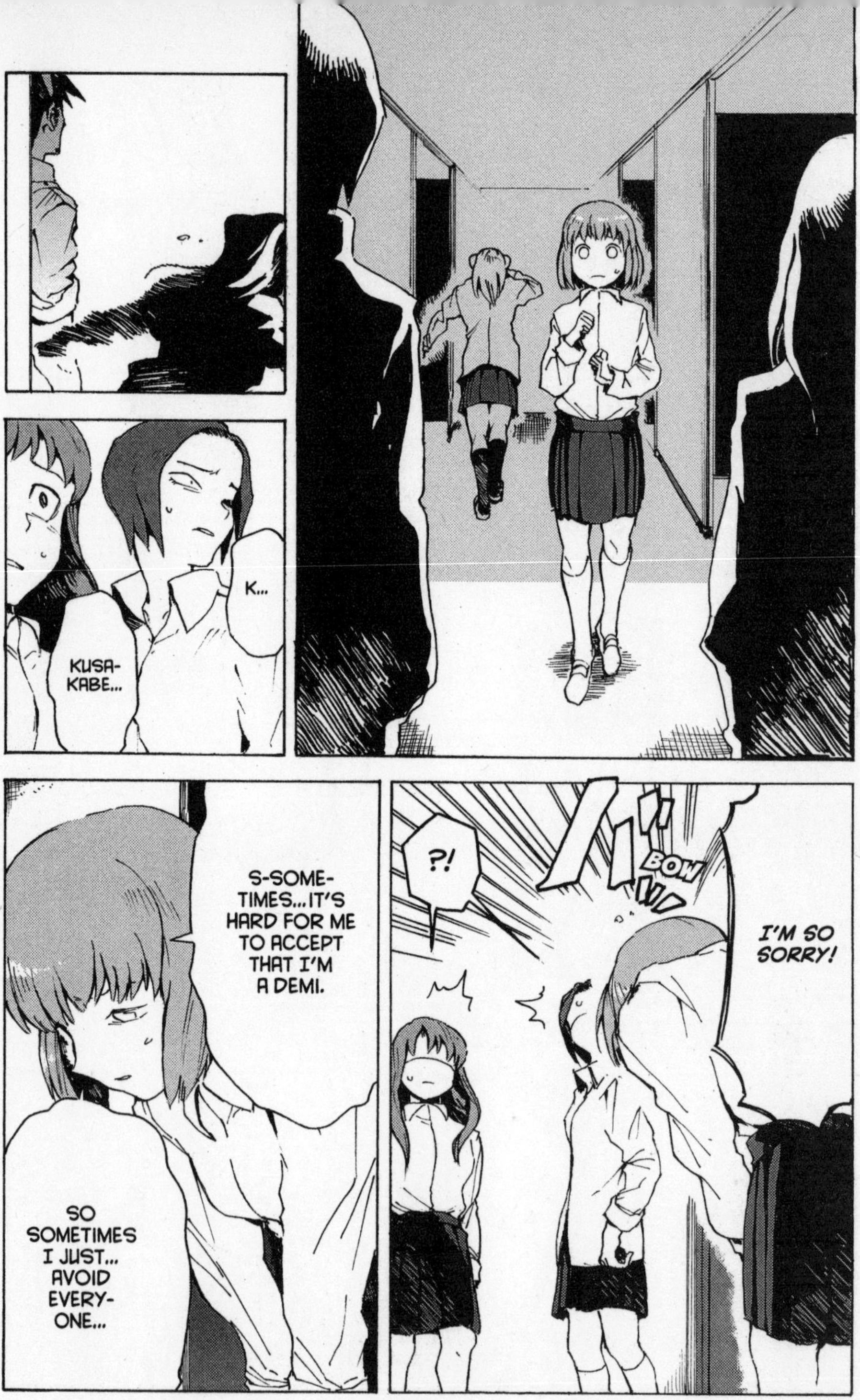
K...
KUSA-KABE...
?!
BOW
I'M SO SORRY!
S-SOME-TIMES...IT'S HARD FOR ME TO ACCEPT THAT I'M A DEMI.
SO SOMETIMES I JUST... AVOID EVERY-ONE...

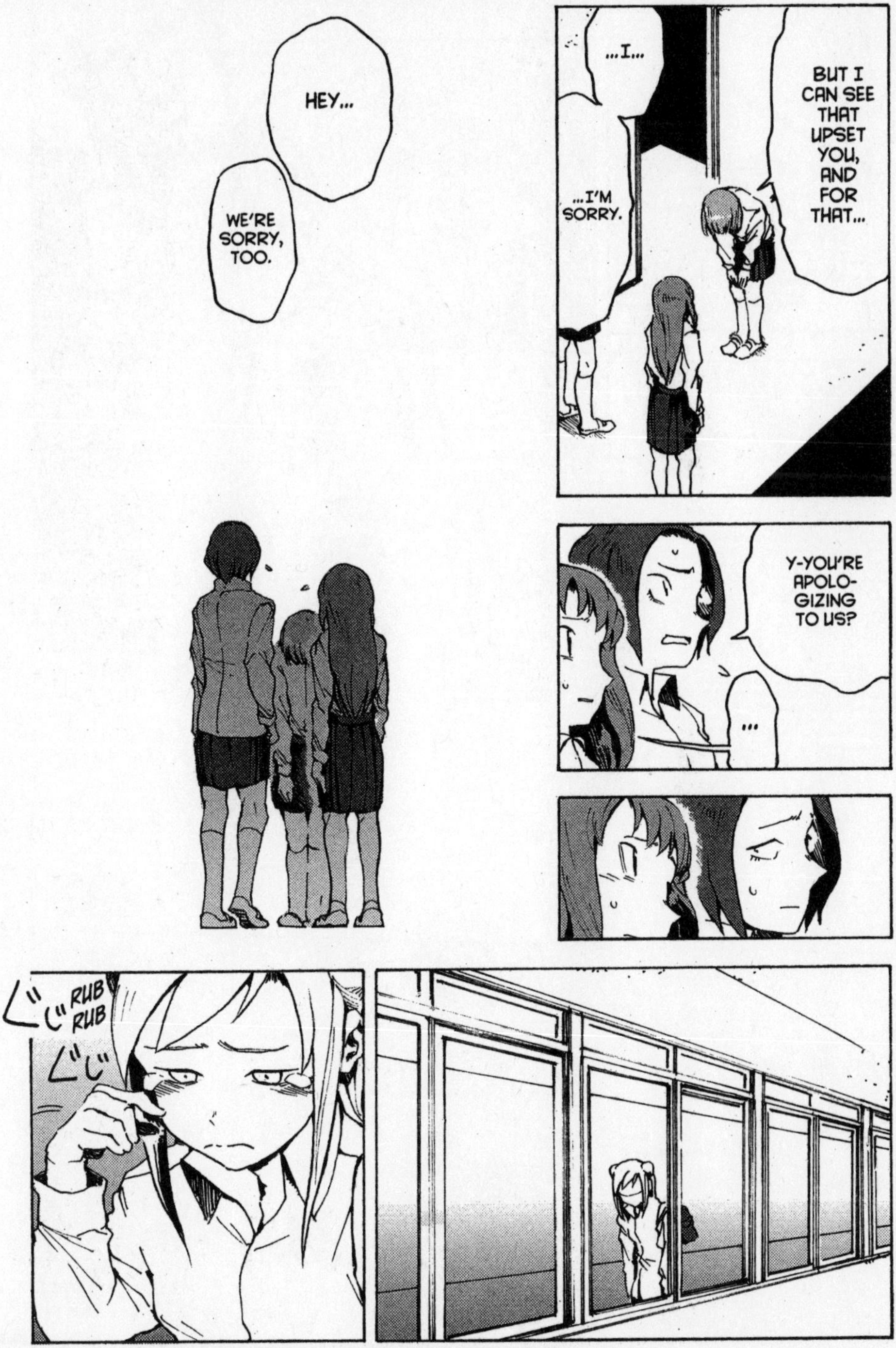
BUT I CAN SEE THAT UPSET YOU, AND FOR THAT...
...I...
...I'M SORRY.
Y-YOU'RE APOLOGIZING TO US?
...
HEY...
WE'RE SORRY, TOO.
じじ
RUB RUB
じじ

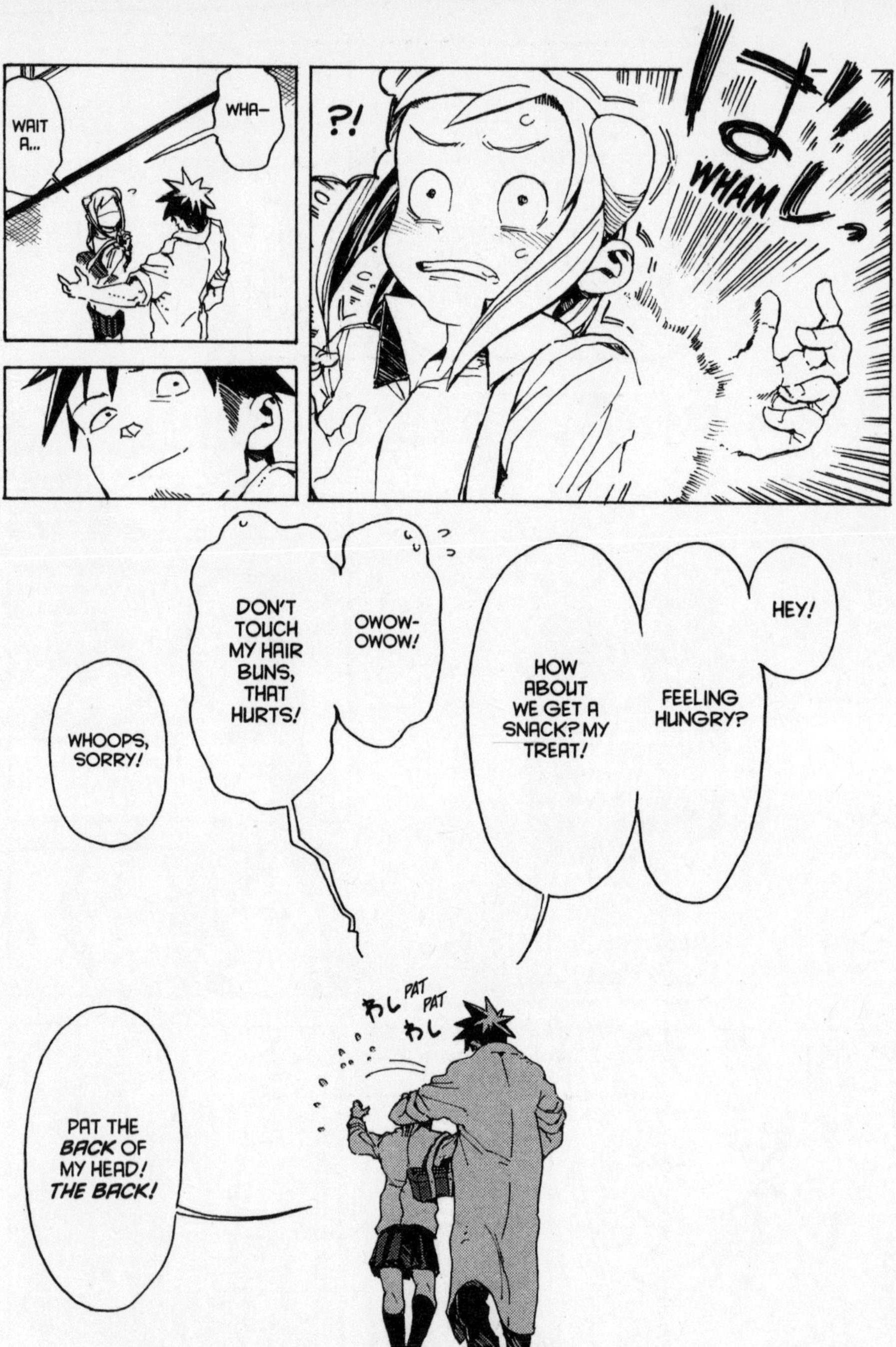

ばしっ
WHAM
?!
WHA–
WAIT A...
HEY!
FEELING HUNGRY?
HOW ABOUT WE GET A SNACK? MY TREAT!
OWOW-OWOW!
DON'T TOUCH MY HAIR BUNS, THAT HURTS!
WHOOPS, SORRY!
わし PAT PAT わし
PAT THE *BACK* OF MY HEAD! ***THE BACK!***

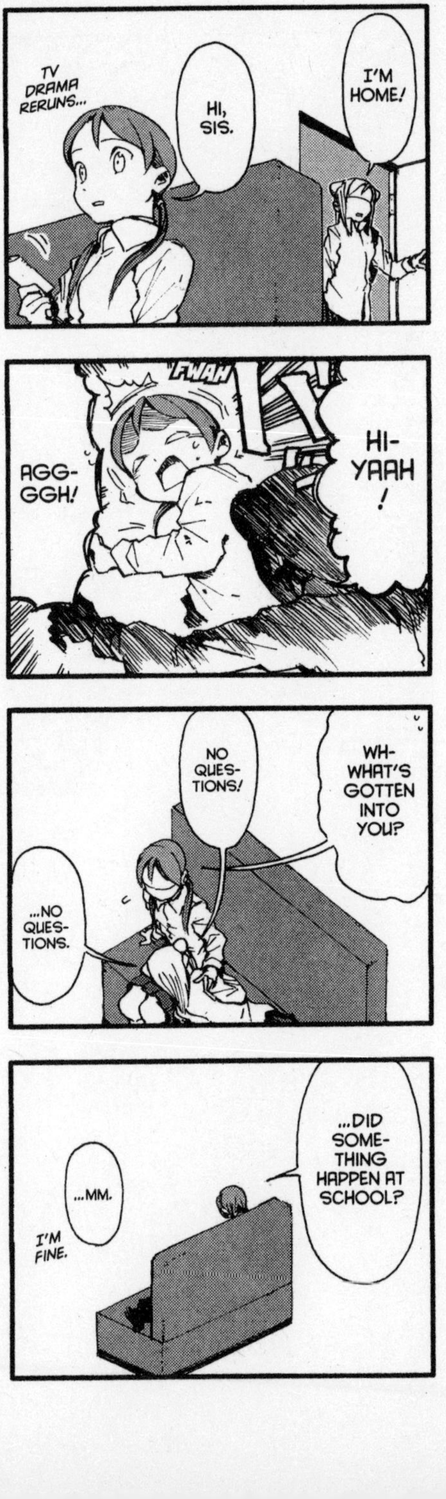
I'M HOME!
HI, SIS.
TV DRAMA RERUNS...
FWAH
HI-YAAH!
AGG-GGH!
WH-WHAT'S GOTTEN INTO YOU?
NO QUESTIONS!
...NO QUESTIONS.
...DID SOMETHING HAPPEN AT SCHOOL?
...MM.
I'M FINE.

INTERVIEWS WITH MONSTER GIRLS

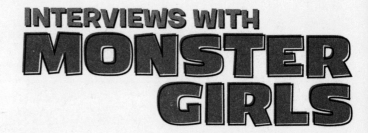

Chapter 9: Demis Just Wanna Have Hugs

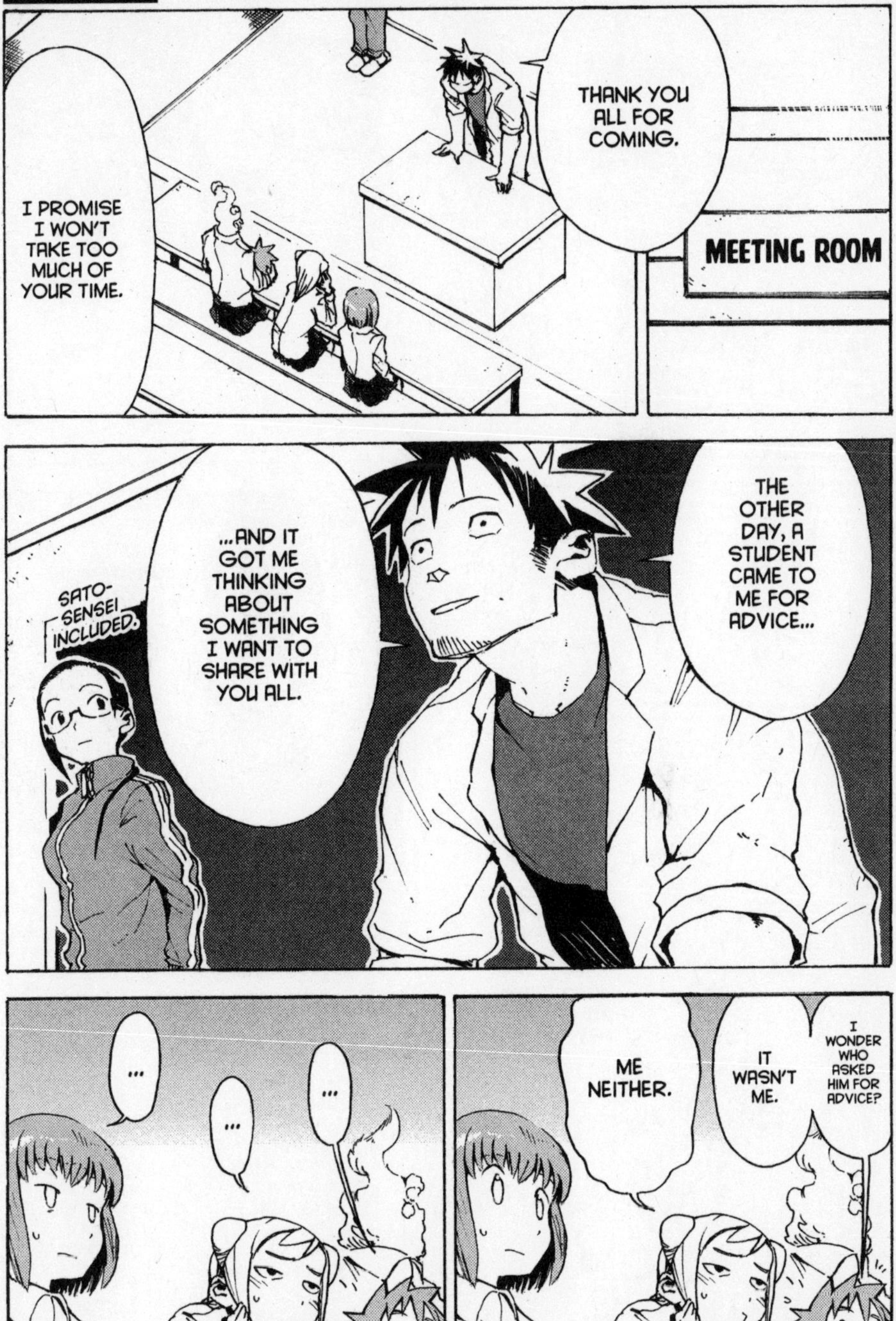
MEETING ROOM
THANK YOU ALL FOR COMING.
I PROMISE I WON'T TAKE TOO MUCH OF YOUR TIME.
THE OTHER DAY, A STUDENT CAME TO ME FOR ADVICE...
...AND IT GOT ME THINKING ABOUT SOMETHING I WANT TO SHARE WITH YOU ALL.
SATO-SENSEI INCLUDED.
I WONDER WHO ASKED HIM FOR ADVICE?
IT WASN'T ME.
ME NEITHER.
...
...
...

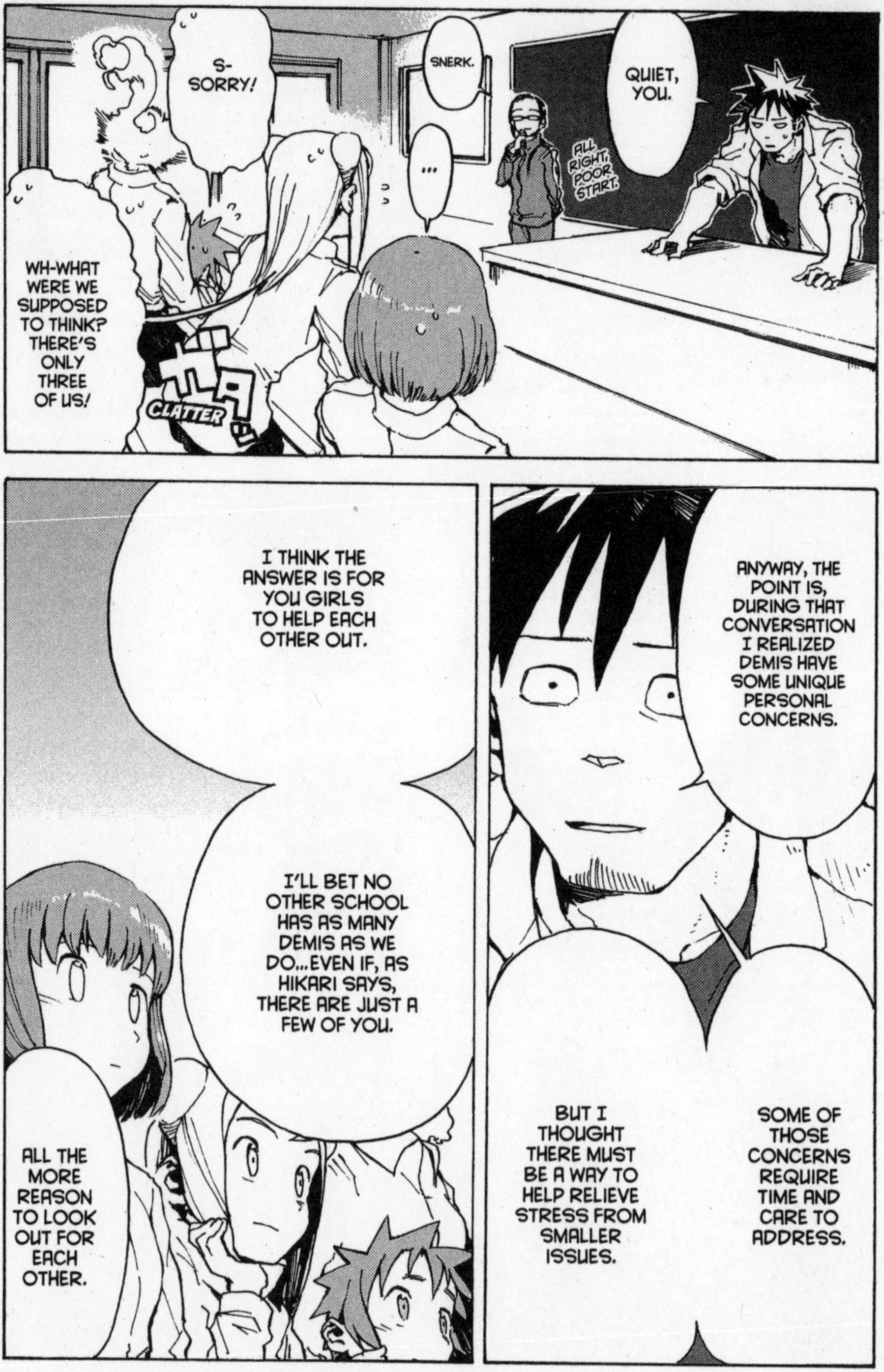
QUIET, YOU.
ALL RIGHT, POOR START.
SNERK.
...
S- SORRY!
WH-WHAT WERE WE SUPPOSED TO THINK? THERE'S ONLY THREE OF US!
CLATTER
ANYWAY, THE POINT IS, DURING THAT CONVERSATION I REALIZED DEMIS HAVE SOME UNIQUE PERSONAL CONCERNS.
SOME OF THOSE CONCERNS REQUIRE TIME AND CARE TO ADDRESS.
BUT I THOUGHT THERE MUST BE A WAY TO HELP RELIEVE STRESS FROM SMALLER ISSUES.
I THINK THE ANSWER IS FOR YOU GIRLS TO HELP EACH OTHER OUT.
I'LL BET NO OTHER SCHOOL HAS AS MANY DEMIS AS WE DO...EVEN IF, AS HIKARI SAYS, THERE ARE JUST A FEW OF YOU.
ALL THE MORE REASON TO LOOK OUT FOR EACH OTHER.

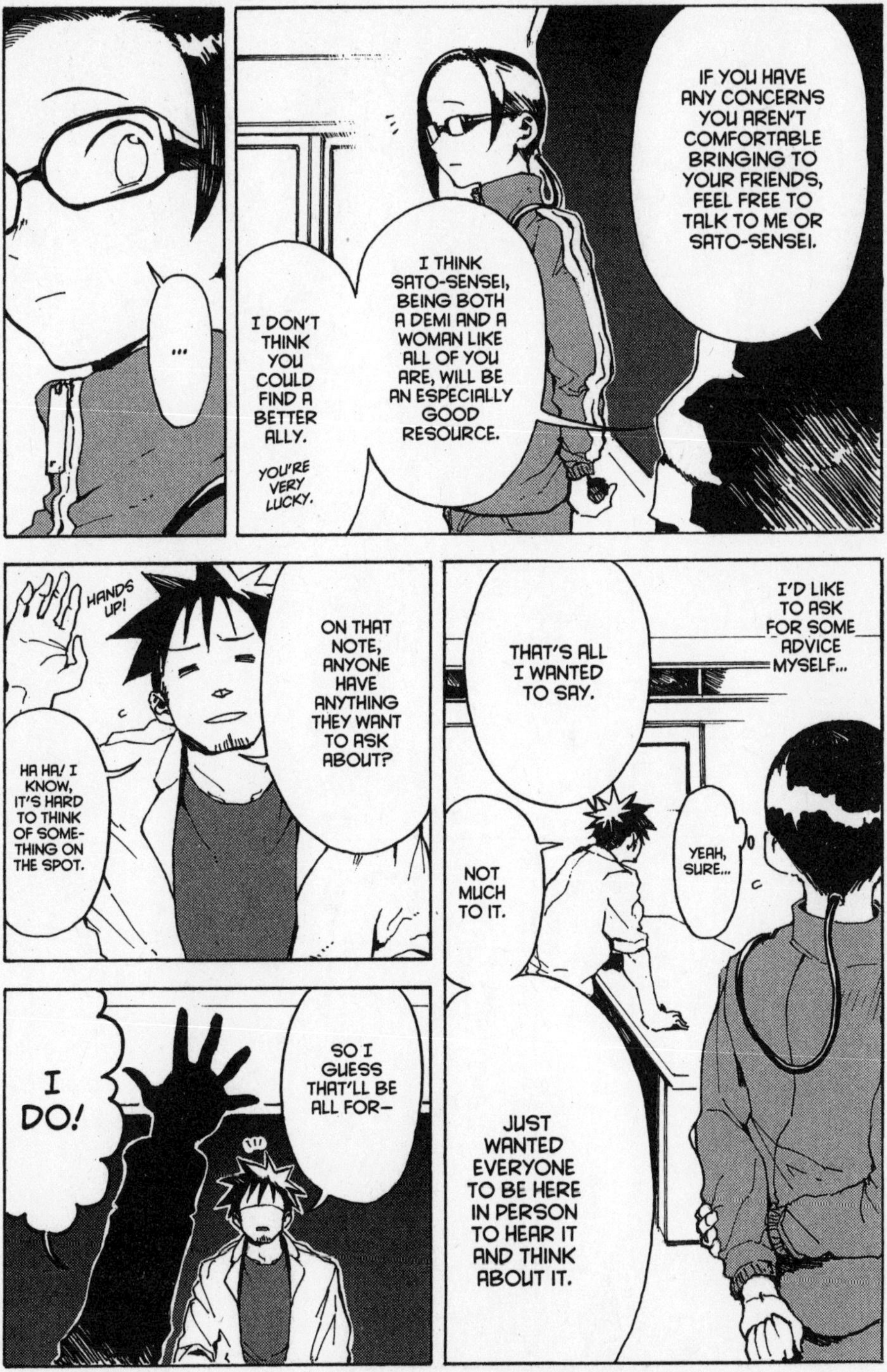
IF YOU HAVE ANY CONCERNS YOU AREN'T COMFORTABLE BRINGING TO YOUR FRIENDS, FEEL FREE TO TALK TO ME OR SATO-SENSEI.
I THINK SATO-SENSEI, BEING BOTH A DEMI AND A WOMAN LIKE ALL OF YOU ARE, WILL BE AN ESPECIALLY GOOD RESOURCE.
I DON'T THINK YOU COULD FIND A BETTER ALLY.
YOU'RE VERY LUCKY.
...
I'D LIKE TO ASK FOR SOME ADVICE MYSELF...
THAT'S ALL I WANTED TO SAY.
YEAH, SURE...
NOT MUCH TO IT.
JUST WANTED EVERYONE TO BE HERE IN PERSON TO HEAR IT AND THINK ABOUT IT.
ON THAT NOTE, ANYONE HAVE ANYTHING THEY WANT TO ASK ABOUT?
HANDS UP!
HA HA! I KNOW, IT'S HARD TO THINK OF SOME-THING ON THE SPOT.
SO I GUESS THAT'LL BE ALL FOR—
I DO!

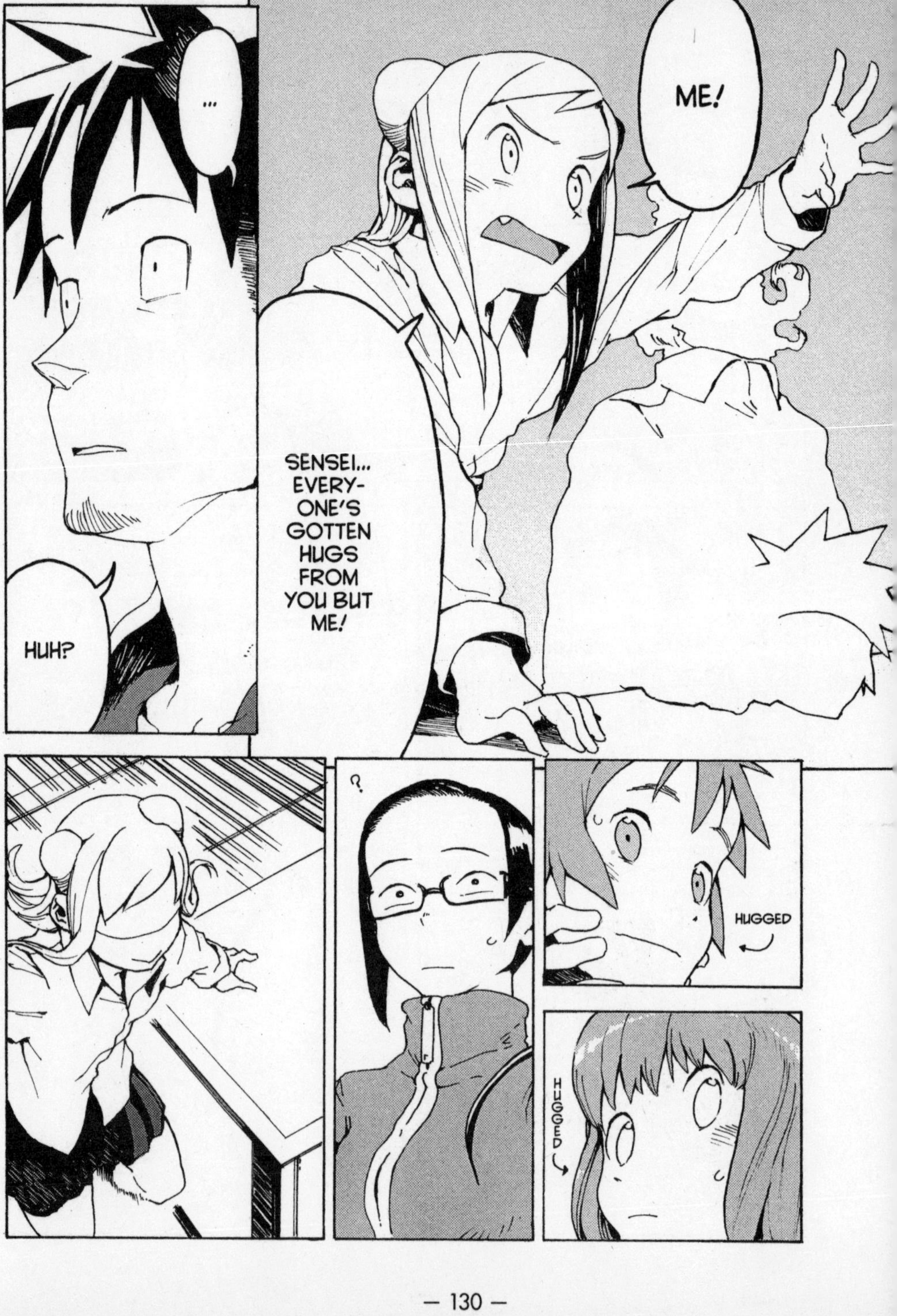
ME!
SENSEI... EVERY-ONE'S GOTTEN HUGS FROM YOU BUT ME!
...
HUH?
HUGGED
HUGGED
?

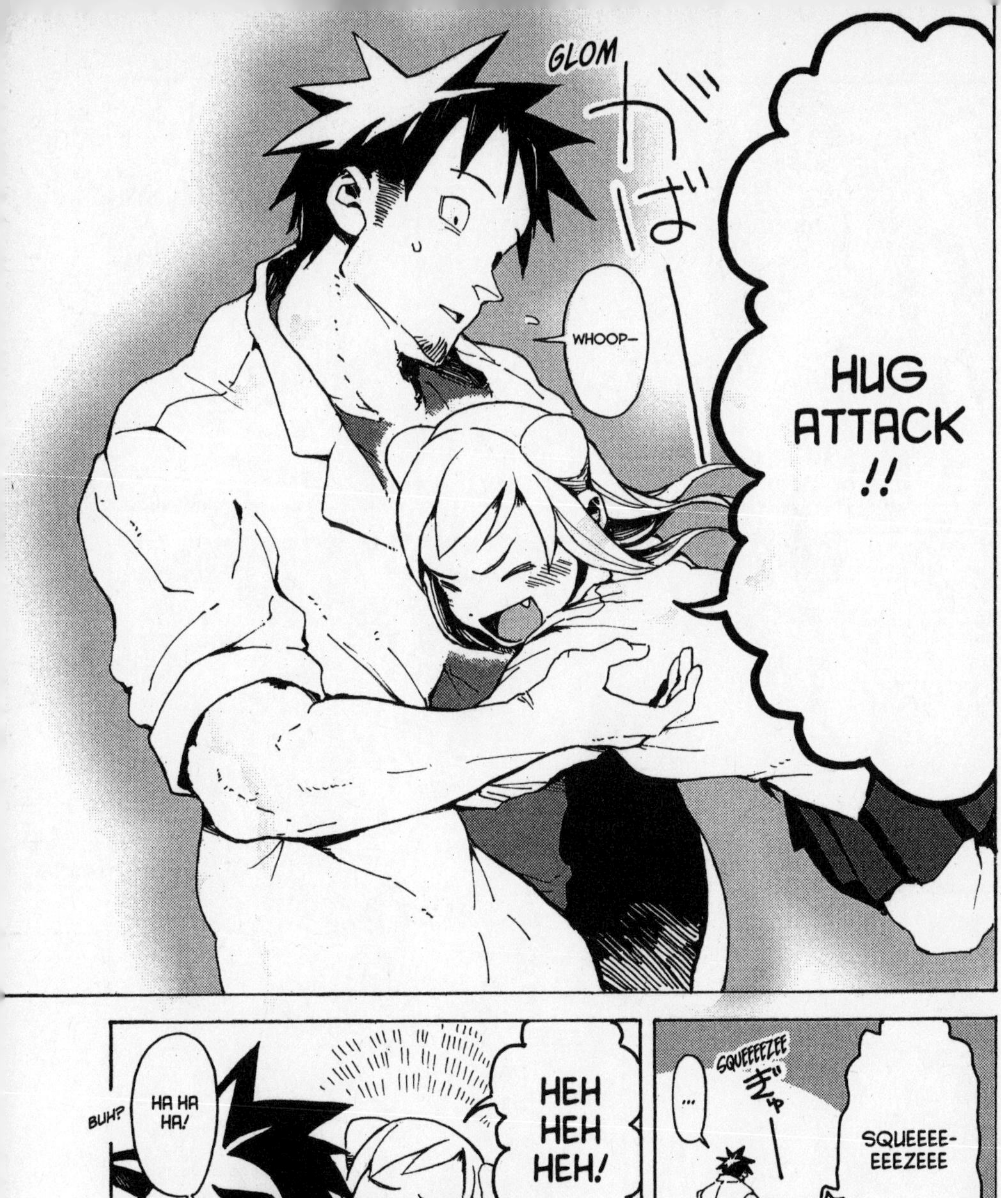
HUG ATTACK !!
GLOM
がば
WHOOP–

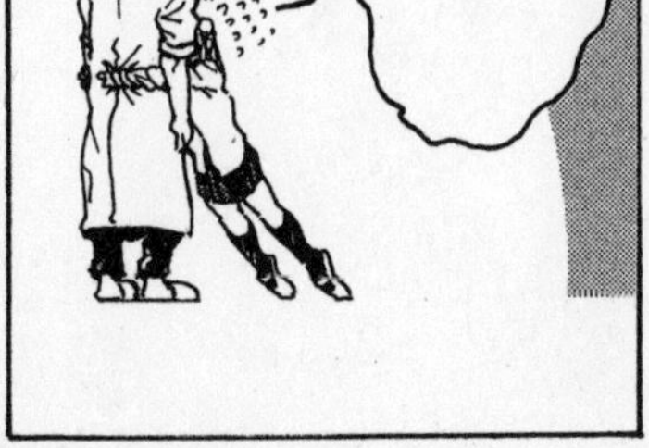
SQUEEEE-
EEEZEEE
SQUEEEEZEE
ぎゅ
...

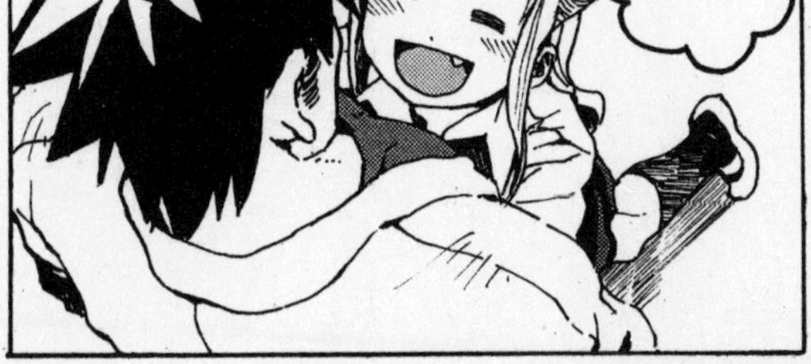
HEH
HEH
HEH!
HA HA
HA!
BUH?

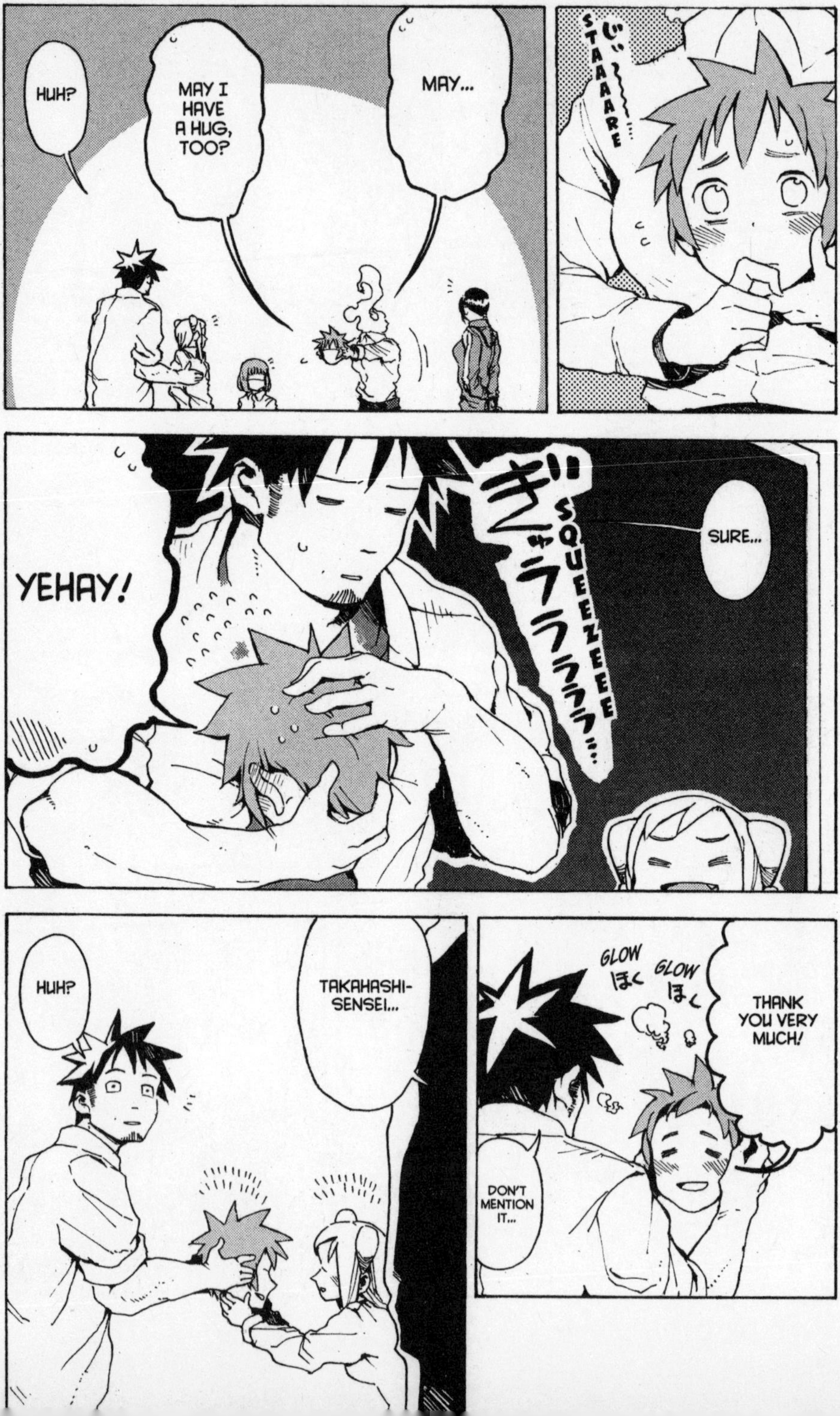
じぃ～～
STAAAARE
MAY...
MAY I HAVE A HUG, TOO?
HUH?
SURE...
ぎゅうううう…
SQUEEZEEEE
YEHAY!
THANK YOU VERY MUCH!
GLOW ほく GLOW ほく
DON'T MENTION IT...
TAKAHASHI-SENSEI...
HUH?

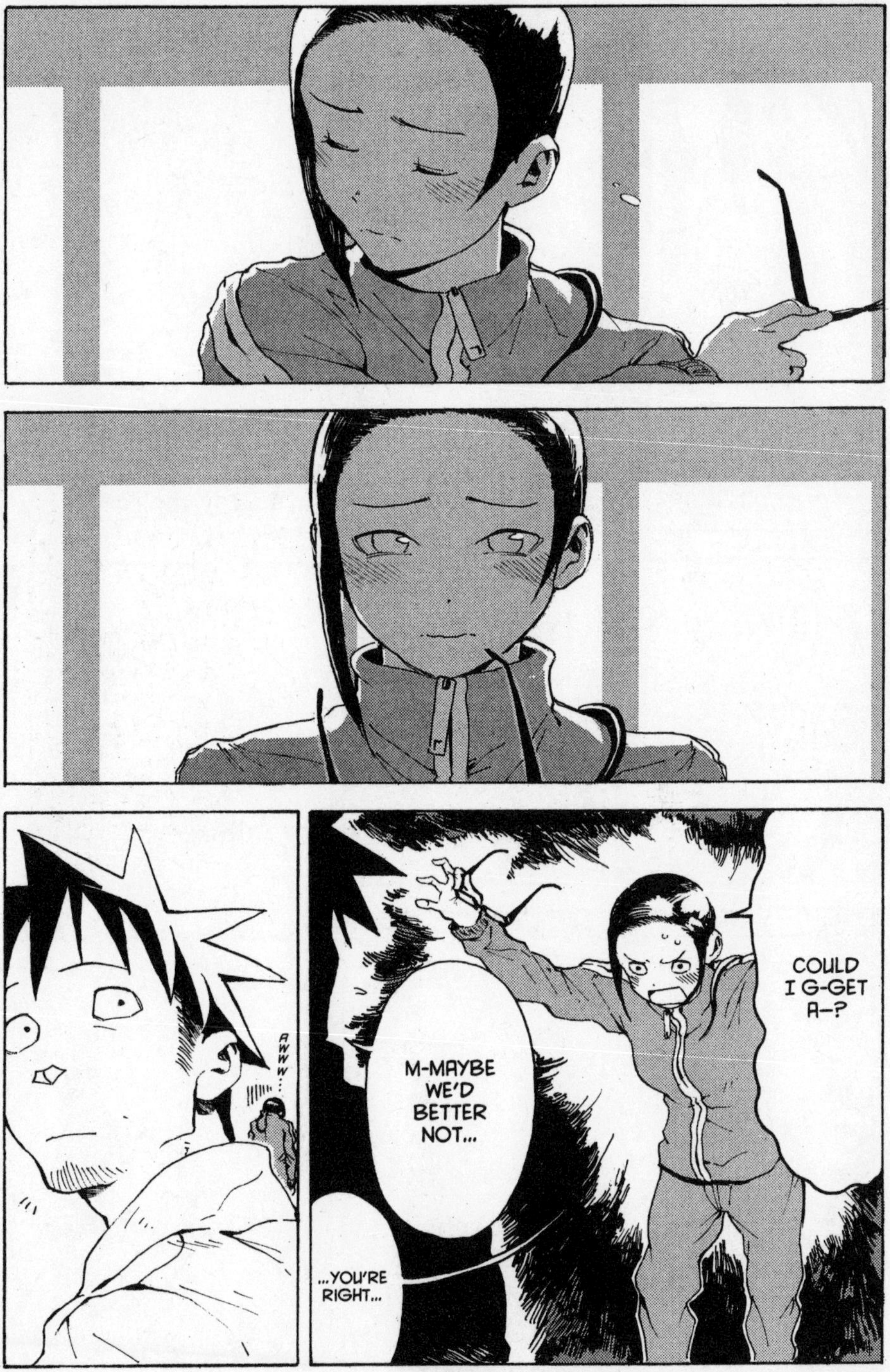
COULD I G-GET A–?
M-MAYBE WE'D BETTER NOT...
...YOU'RE RIGHT...
AWWW...

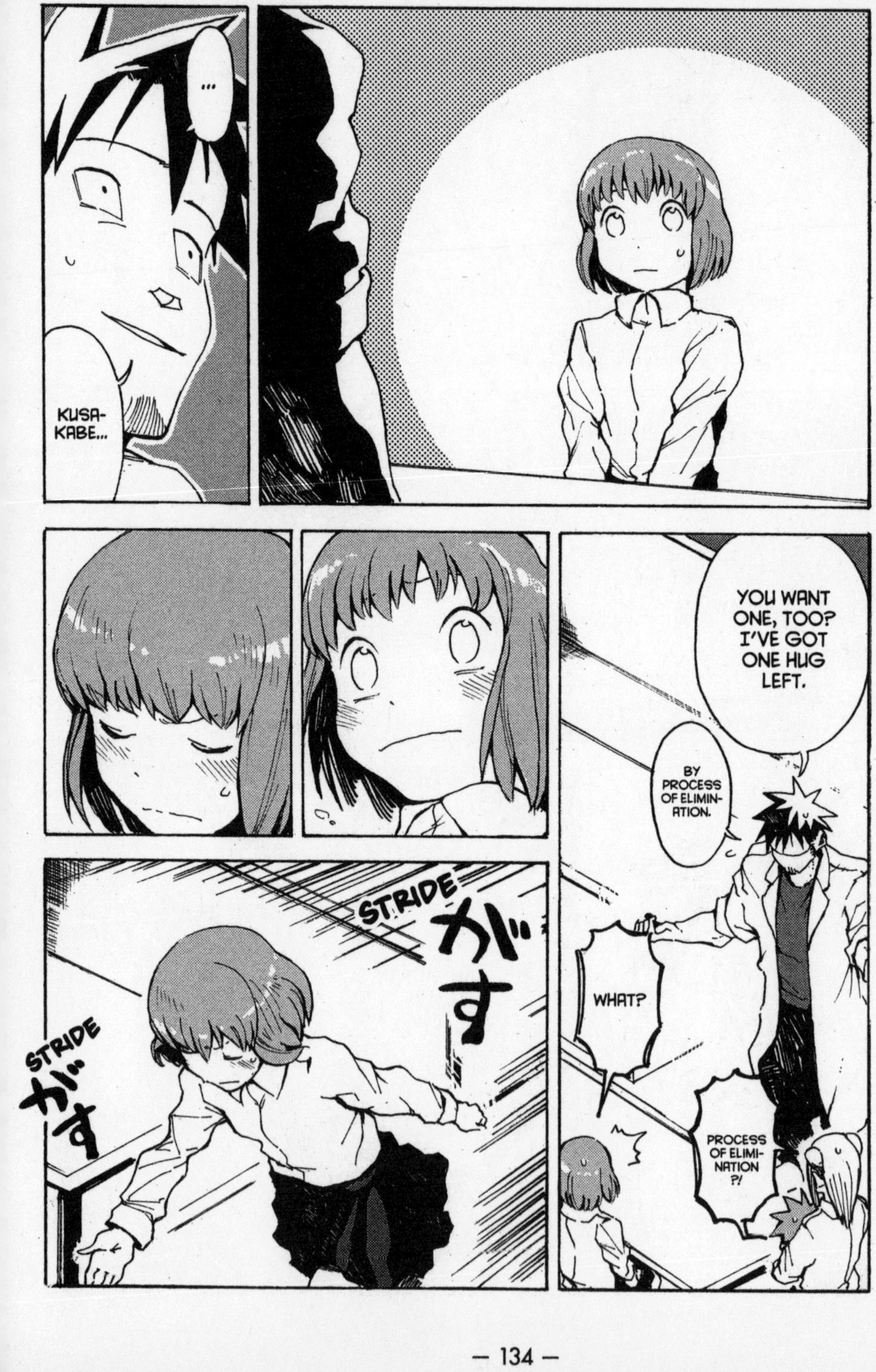
...
KUSA-KABE...
YOU WANT ONE, TOO? I'VE GOT ONE HUG LEFT.
BY PROCESS OF ELIMINATION.
WHAT?
PROCESS OF ELIMINATION?!
STRIDE
がす
STRIDE
がす

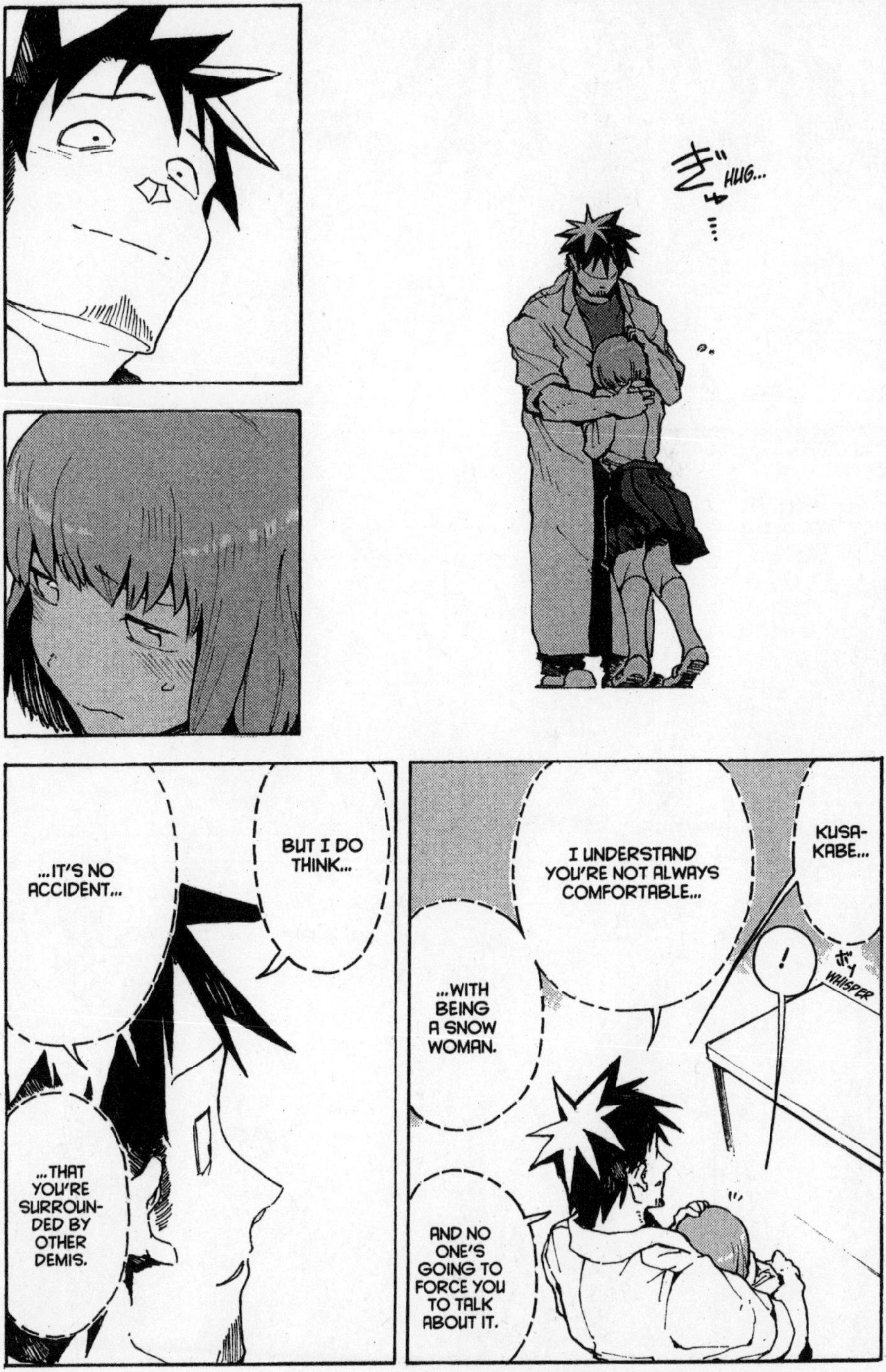
ぎゅ HUG...
KUSA-KABE...
ボソ WHISPER
!
I UNDERSTAND YOU'RE NOT ALWAYS COMFORTABLE...
...WITH BEING A SNOW WOMAN.
AND NO ONE'S GOING TO FORCE YOU TO TALK ABOUT IT.
BUT I DO THINK...
...IT'S NO ACCIDENT...
...THAT YOU'RE SURROUNDED BY OTHER DEMIS.

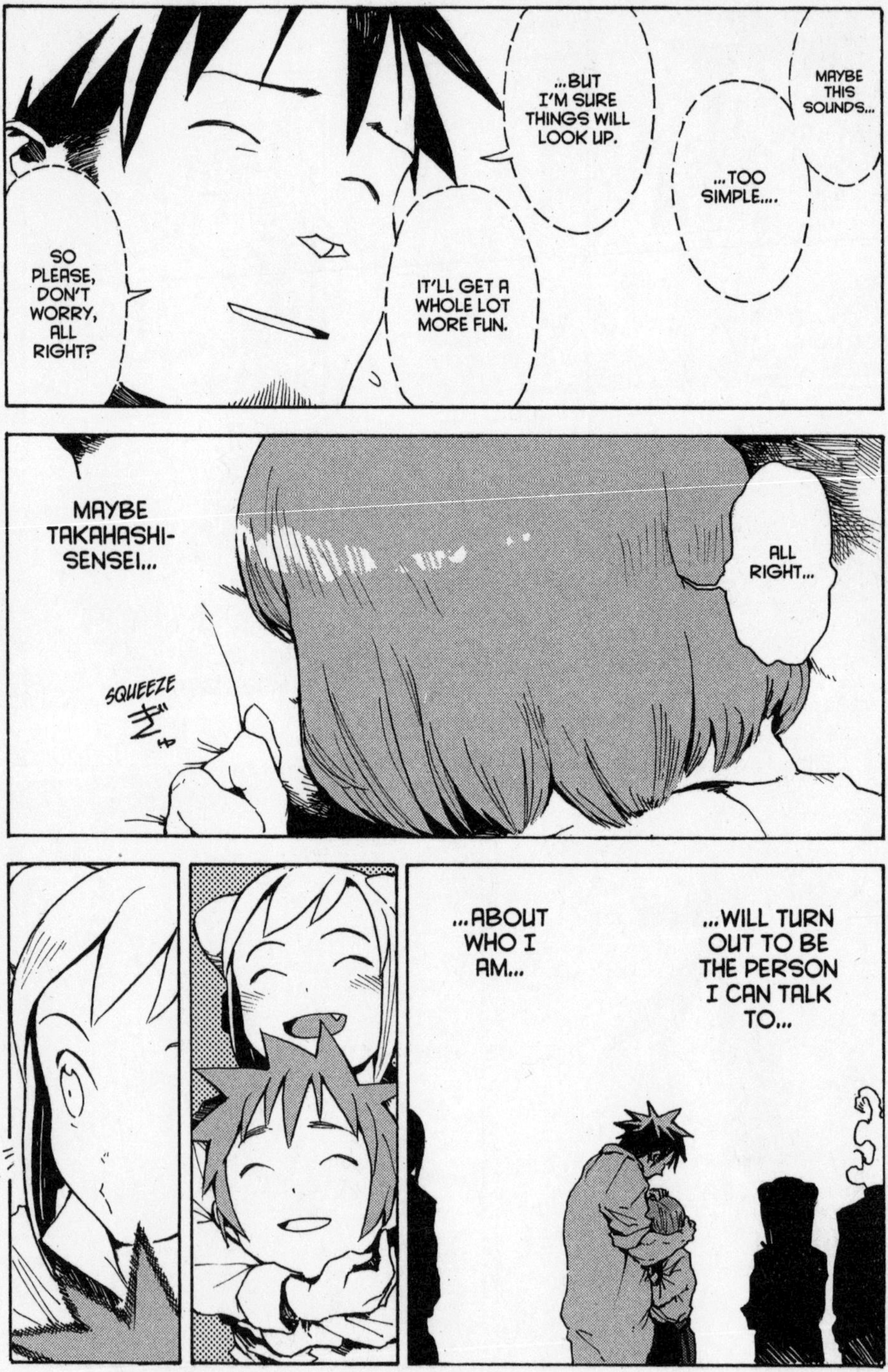
MAYBE THIS SOUNDS...
...TOO SIMPLE....
...BUT I'M SURE THINGS WILL LOOK UP.
IT'LL GET A WHOLE LOT MORE FUN.
SO PLEASE, DON'T WORRY, ALL RIGHT?
ALL RIGHT...
MAYBE TAKAHASHI-SENSEI...
SQUEEZE
...WILL TURN OUT TO BE THE PERSON I CAN TALK TO...
...ABOUT WHO I AM...

SENSEI! SENSEI!
SHE NEEDS A HUG, TOO!
ボボボ
"SHE"?
ボボ
FOOOOO
THAT'S MACHI AGAIN.
HER BODY.
YOU KNOW!
PROCESS OF ELIMINATION!
GOSH.
YOU'RE ALL RIGHT WITH THIS, MACHI?
Y-YES...
OKAY, HUG TIME.
THERE WE GO.
SMOOSH
むにゅ

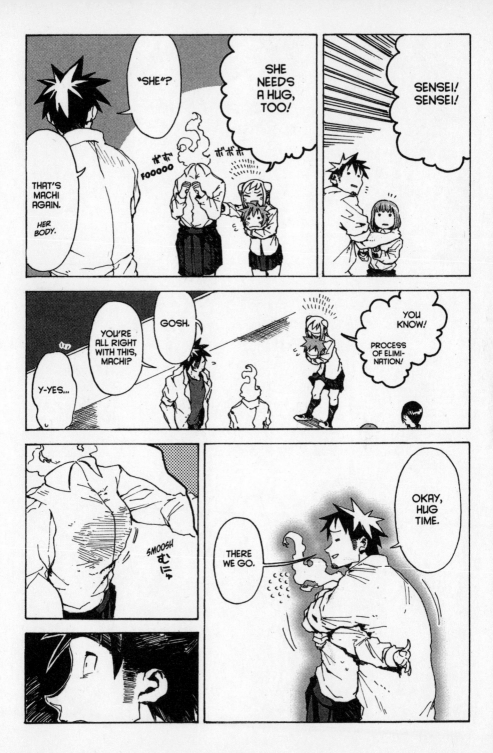

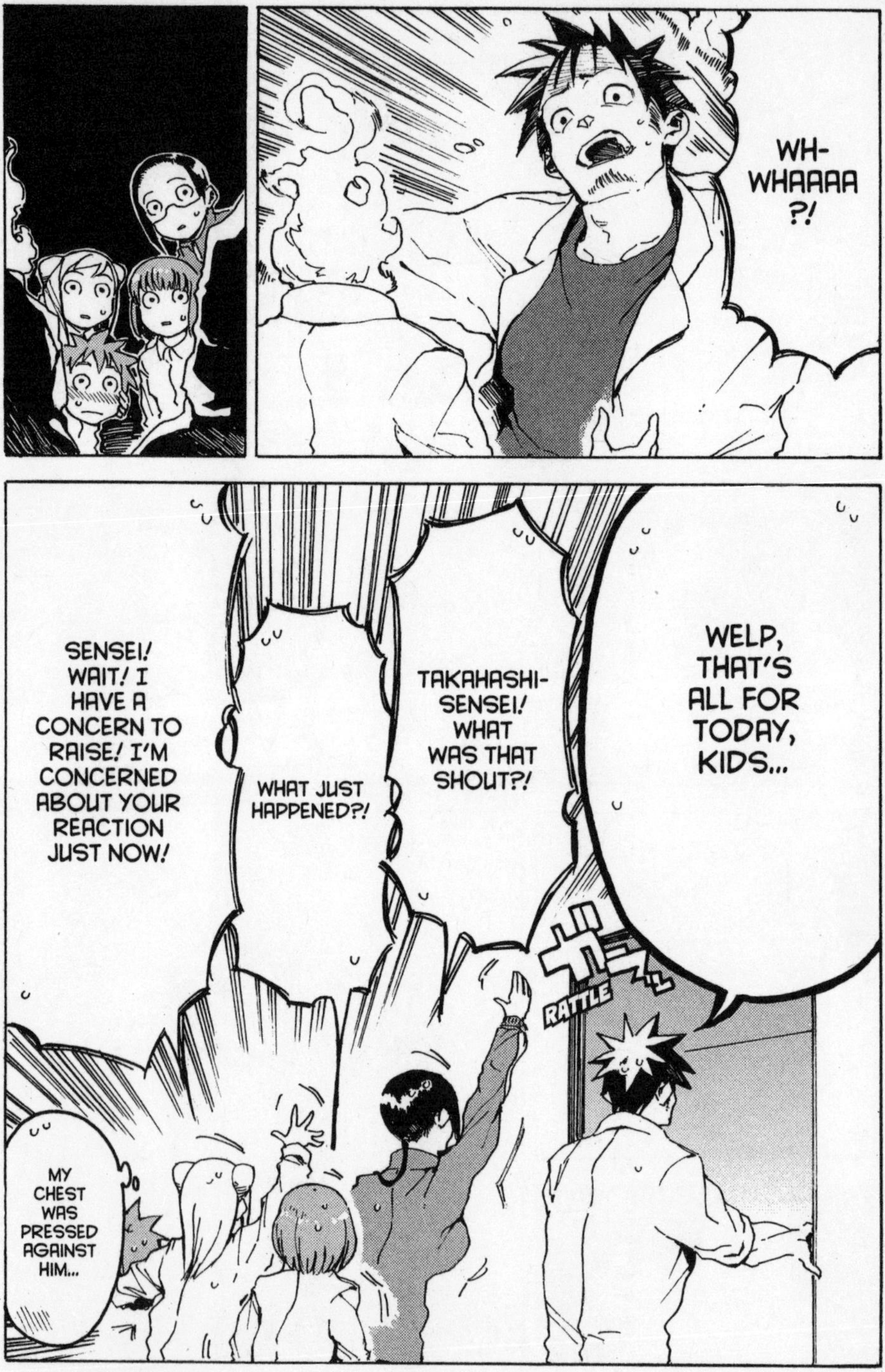
WH- WHAAAA ?!
WELP, THAT'S ALL FOR TODAY, KIDS...
RATTLE
TAKAHASHI-SENSEI! WHAT WAS THAT SHOUT?!
WHAT JUST HAPPENED?!
SENSEI! WAIT! I HAVE A CONCERN TO RAISE! I'M CONCERNED ABOUT YOUR REACTION JUST NOW!
MY CHEST WAS PRESSED AGAINST HIM...

VOLUME 1/END

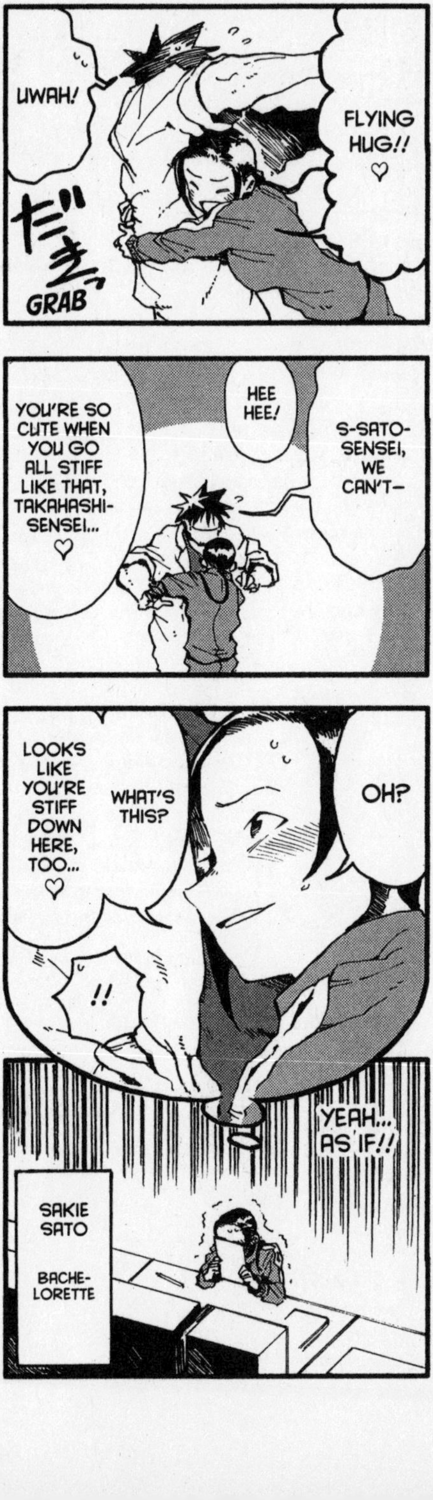
FLYING HUG!! ♡
UWAH!
だきっ
GRAB
S-SATO-SENSEI, WE CAN'T—
HEE HEE!
YOU'RE SO CUTE WHEN YOU GO ALL STIFF LIKE THAT, TAKAHASHI-SENSEI... ♡
OH?
WHAT'S THIS?
LOOKS LIKE YOU'RE STIFF DOWN HERE, TOO... ♡
!!
YEAH... AS IF!!
SAKIE SATO
BACHELORETTE

TRANSLATION NOTES

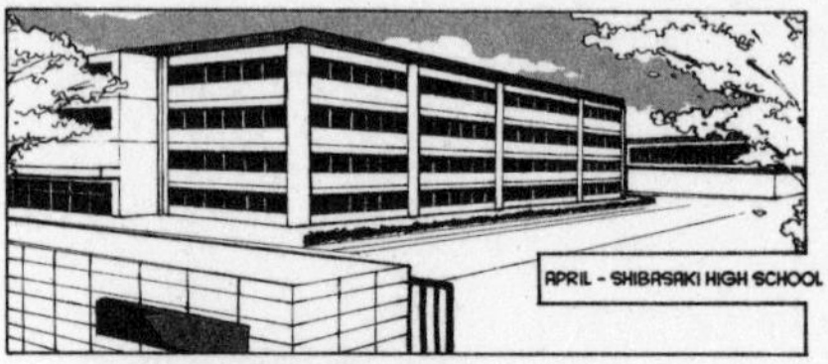
APRIL - SHIBASAKI HIGH SCHOOL

April, page 4

The Japanese school year begins in April. In principle, this coincides with the blooming of the cherry trees, which are a common symbol of youth and school life.

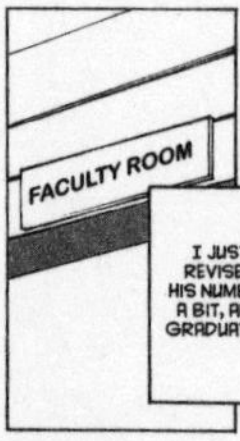
FACULTY ROOM
I JUST REVISED HIS NUMBER A BIT, AND GRADUATED.

Faculty Room, page 5

In Japanese high schools, teachers typically do not have their own offices, but share a single large room where they do their work and prepare for classes. The Faculty Room is open to students who need to talk to a specific teacher.

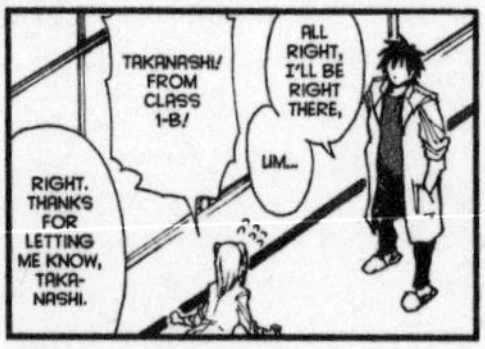
TAKANASHI! FROM CLASS 1-B!
ALL RIGHT, I'LL BE RIGHT THERE,
UM...
RIGHT. THANKS FOR LETTING ME KNOW, TAKA-NASHI.

Class 1-B, page 9

That is, year 1, class B. Students in Japanese high schools are assigned to a single home room (A, B, etc.) where they stay during the day for all classes except gym. It is the teachers, not the students, who go from room to room for each class.

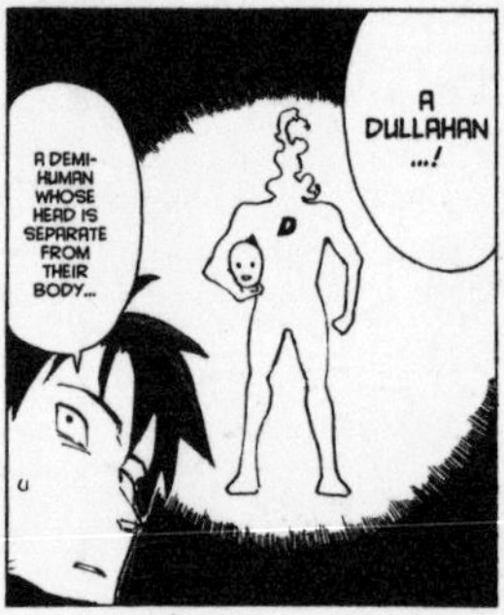
A DULLAHAN ...!
A DEMI-HUMAN WHOSE HEAD IS SEPARATE FROM THEIR BODY...

Dullahan, page 11

The dullahan is a headless horseman out of Irish mythology. They can be harbingers of death.

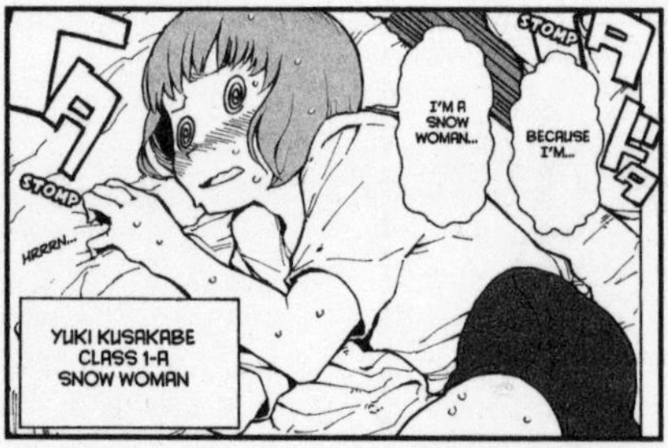
STOMP
BECAUSE I'M...
I'M A SNOW WOMAN...
STOMP
HRRRN...
YUKI KUSAKABE CLASS 1-A SNOW WOMAN

Snow Woman, page 12

The snow woman, or yuki-onna, has been a part of Japanese legend from antiquity. Often appearing in a blizzard, this woman with snow-white skin sometimes kills those who encounter her. The snow woman also features in one of the stories in Lafcadio Hearn's *Kwaidan*, where she spares a young man on the promise that he will never tell anyone of their meeting. The name Yuki means "snow."

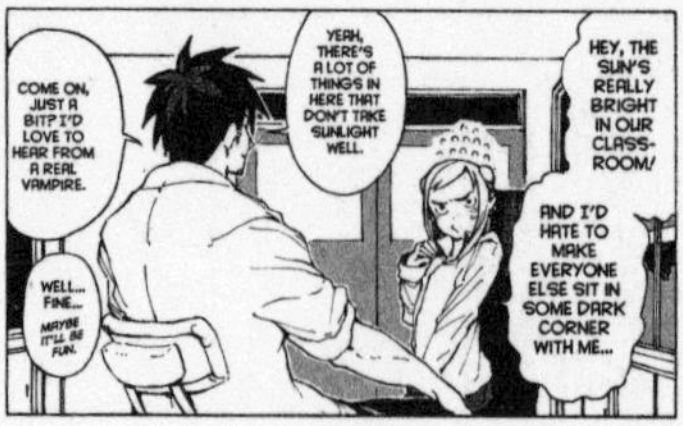
HEY, THE SUN'S REALLY BRIGHT IN OUR CLASS-ROOM!
YEAH, THERE'S A LOT OF THINGS IN HERE THAT DON'T TAKE SUNLIGHT WELL.
AND I'D HATE TO MAKE EVERYONE ELSE SIT IN SOME DARK CORNER WITH ME...
COME ON, JUST A BIT? I'D LOVE TO HEAR FROM A REAL VAMPIRE.
WELL... FINE...
MAYBE IT'LL BE FUN.

Sunlight, page 23

Ironically, the meaning of the word and name *hikari* is "light."

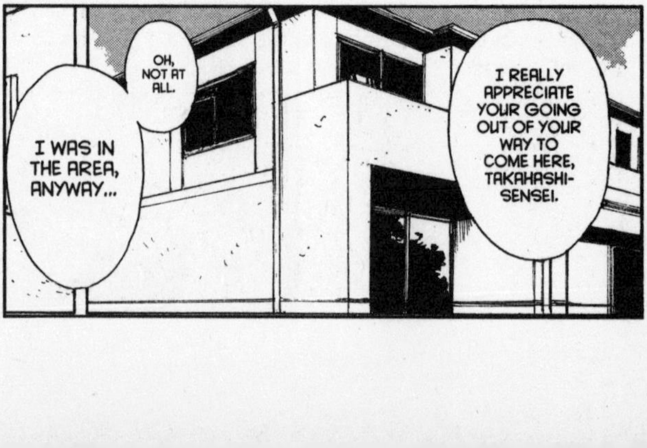
I REALLY APPRECIATE YOUR GOING OUT OF YOUR WAY TO COME HERE, TAKAHASHI-SENSEI.
OH, NOT AT ALL.
I WAS IN THE AREA, ANYWAY...

Home Visits, page 37

It's not unusual in Japan for a teacher to visit a student's home, especially if that student is having trouble at school.

My Wife is the Breadwinner, page 37
It is still uncommon in Japan for a wife to be the main earner in a household.

I KNOW OUR HIKARI IS...A LITTLE UNUSUAL.
BUT SHE'S NOT THE ONLY WAY OUR HOME IS DIFFERENT. MY WIFE IS THE BREADWINNER IN THIS FAMILY, YOU SEE.
I THINK IT'S WONDERFUL THAT HIKARI HAS A TEACHER WHO RESPECTS DEMIS.
KOJI TAKANASHI STAY-AT-HOME DAD

Okayama, page 53
A city on the coast of Honshu across from the island of Shikoku, far south of Tokyo.

YEAH, IT'S FINE.
ONE TIME, MY BODY WAS IN TOKYO AND MY HEAD WAS IN OKAYAMA!
OKA-YAMA?!
THAT'S FAR!
WHY ON EARTH...?

DON'T WORRY! THEY'LL THINK YOU'RE GOR-GEOUS, MACCHII!
YOU'VE GOT A GOOD SENSE OF STYLE, AND THAT GREAT RACK OF YOURS IS ONLY GONNA SWEETEN THE DEAL!
REALLY ...?

Macchii, page 65
Nicknames or pet names are as common in Japan as anywhere else. Hikari has coined a simple nickname for Kyoko by doubling two of the sounds in her name. Yukkii (page 112) follows the same pattern.

I TAKE THE FIRST TRAIN OUT AND THE LAST TRAIN BACK...
I CAN ONLY EVER SLEEP AT MY OWN HOUSE...
I KNEW IT WOULD BE HARD, A SUCCUBUS LIVING IN THE HUMAN WORLD, BUT MAYBE I DIDN'T REALIZE JUST HOW HARD...

First Train, Last Train, page 87
Times vary by day and location, but in general, the first train runs at around 5:00 in the morning, while the last may run at midnight or 1:00 a.m.

GLUG
GLUG
KAKI-PEANUTS

Kaki-peanuts, page 93
A common bar snack in Japan. Contains peanuts and small, crescent-shaped bits of rice cracker (often a little spicy).

Idol, page 100
Idols, now ubiquitous in the Japanese music scene, are pop stars who are recruited at a young age for their looks and public image, and developed by a talent agency into a group with mass-market appeal. Many idols start out in high school, so though these girls are just being mean, Yuki is at the right age for it.

WHAT DOES SHE THINK SHE IS, AN IDOL?

Takoyaki, page 141
Takoyaki are balls of octopus meat, fried up in a special mold and served piping hot.

Next time in *Monster Girls*...

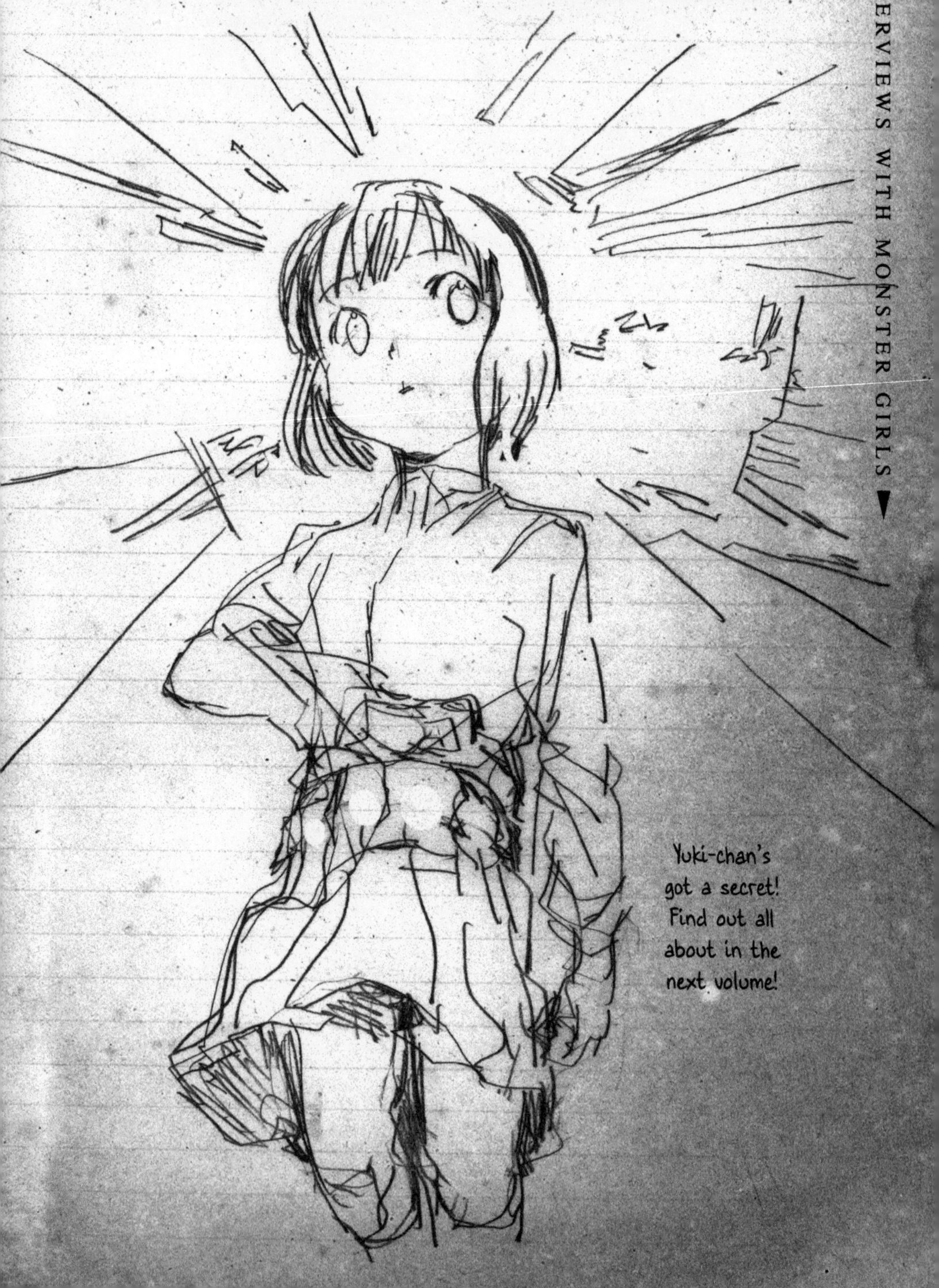
Yuki-chan's got a secret! Find out all about in the next volume!

A Kodansha Comics Trade Paperback Original.

Interviews with Monster Girls volume 1 copyright © 2015 Petos
English translation copyright © 2016 Petos

Published in the United States by Kodansha Comics, an imprint of Kodansha USA Publishing, LLC, New York.

Publication rights for this English edition arranged through Kodansha Ltd., Tokyo.

First published in Japan in 2015 by Kodansha Ltd., Tokyo, as *Demi-chan wa Kataritai*, volume 1.

ISBN 978-1-63236-358-9

Printed in the United States of America.

www.kodanshacomics.com

9 8 7 6 5 4 3 2 1

Translation: Kevin Steinbach
Lettering: Paige Pumphrey
Editing: Lauren Scanlan
Kodansha Comics edition cover design: Phil Balsman

A mysterious transfer student!

Takoyaki

Kung-Fu Master Hikari & Alien

Space Berserker Takahashi

Garrrrr!

Screee!

GET IT?
GOT IT?
MAYBE?

INTERVIEWS WITH
MONSTER
GIRLS
by Petos

Volume 2—
featuring a
Kyoko cover—
coming soon!